THE FREEDOM OF VIRTUE

Navigating excellence in the art of living amongst a world of instant gratification

TOM EDWARDS PhD
COSIMO CHIERA PhD

First published 2019 by:
Australian Academic Press Group Pty. Ltd.
Samford Valley QLD Australia
www.australianacademicpress.com.au

Copyright © 2019 Tom Edwards and Cosimo Chiera.

Copying for educational purposes
The *Australian Copyright Act 1968* (Cwlth) allows a maximum of one chapter or 10% of this book, whichever is the greater, to be reproduced and/or communicated by any educational institution for its educational purposes provided that the educational institution (or the body that administers it) has given a remuneration notice to Copyright Agency Limited (CAL) under the Act.
For details of the CAL licence for educational institutions contact:
Copyright Agency Limited, 19/157 Liverpool Street, Sydney, NSW 2000.
E-mail info@copyright.com.au

Production and communication for other purposes
Except as permitted under the Act, for example a fair dealing for the purposes
of study, research, criticism or review, no part of this book may be reproduced,
stored in a retrieval system, or transmitted in any form or by any means electronic,
mechanical, photocopying, recording or otherwise without prior written permission
of the copyright holder.

 A catalogue record for this book is available from the National Library of Australia

ISBN 9781925644142   (paperback)
ISBN 9781925644159   (ebook)

Disclaimer
This book represents an introduction to the use of specific virtues to bring about a life well lived. It is written for educational purposes only. If aspects of the text are to be applied then please do so in accordance with your: (1) scope of practice, (2) your organisation's policies/procedures, and (3) relevant codes of ethical conduct. If you wish to use aspects of this text for therapeutic outcomes then please seek guidance or training from Dr Edwards and Dr Chiera before doing so. They can be contacted at www.naturalintelligence.com.au.

Every effort has been made in preparing this work to provide information based on accepted standards and practice at the time of publication. The publisher and authors, however, make no warranties of any kind of psychological outcome relating to use of this work and disclaim all responsibility or liability for direct or consequential damages resulting from any use of the material contained in this work.

Publisher: Stephen May
Copy Editor: Rhonda McPherson
Cover design: Luke Harris, Working Type Studio
Typesetting: Australian Academic Press
Printing: Lightning Source

Dedication

To those I know who, in spite of darkness, shine.
—Tom Edwards

To my wife, Lisa, who inspires, challenges and even vexes me; but without whom my life would lack the depth, breadth and colour of the virtues about which we write.
— Cos Chiera

Contents

Acknowledgements ix
Authors' Note xi
Authors' Preface xiii

Chapter 1 — The foundational virtues 1
   What makes for excellence in the art of life? 1
   Character, morality and virtue: Similar but different 3
   If you look, you'll see virtues everywhere 6
      What virtues do we have today? 8
      Virtues in the ancient world 11
      The virtues of the three Abrahamic faiths: Judaism, Christianity and Islam 15
      Western virtues 24
      Asian virtues 27
   So which virtues are the most important? 34

Chapter 2 — Courage 37
   Courage: Are we sure we know what it is? 37
   Studying Courage 38
      Hazel Findlay and Emily Harrington: Rock climbing superstars 38
      Mawson: A man on the edge 40
      What have we learnt about Courage? 42
   Philosophical enquiries into Courage 43
   The psychology of Courage 46
      Heroism, bravery and Courage 46
      Fear 48
      Perseverance 50
   Moral courage is different 51
   Can Courage ever be a bad thing? 55
   Building Courage 56
      Finding courageous people 56
      Developing Courage 58
   In closing 63

Chapter 3 — Diligence 65

The unseen virtue 65
The benefits of Diligence: School success,
career achievement and longevity 66
If the psychological trait of Conscientiousness is
so valuable what holds us back? 69
   Two factors which hamper Conscientiousness:
   Family of origin and childhood bullying 70
   One big problem that thwarts Conscientiousness: Procrastination 72
The dark side of Diligence 75
   Burn-out 75
   Perfectionism 78
Growing Diligence in healthy ways 81
A parting thought 84

Chapter 4 — Wisdom 85

Moving from smart to wise 85
But first, what not to do in life … 86
   Misadventure 86
   Folly 87
   Foolishness 88
So what then is Wisdom? 89
   Wisdom as a philosophical enquiry 90
   The psychology of wise decision-making 91
So how do we learn to be wise? 96
   Living wisely 96
   Thinking wisely 97
   Reflecting wisely 104
   Acting wisely 106
   Bringing the three domains of Wisdom together 109
Moving to the next level 111

Chapter 5 — Honour 113

From me to us … 113
Why don't we talk of Honour anymore? 114
Opening the door to Honour 117
   Bedouin honour culture 117
   Calabrian-Australian honour culture 119

    How the professionals look at Honour 123
    The dynamics of Honour 126
        Glory comes before Honour 126
        The snakes and ladders of living in an honour culture 129
        Dishonour 134
    Growing in Honour 136
        Personal honour 136
        Group honour 138
    As we move on 143

Chapter 6 — Justice 145

    Justice holds back chaos 145
    But what is just? 146
        A just society 147
        Justice for people 148
        What if merit defined Justice? 151
    The psychology of Justice 153
    A specialised topic: Forgiveness 158
    How to grow in Justice 164
    A final word 169

Chapter 7 — Kindness 171

    Kindness is life at its best 171
    What does it mean to be kind? 172
    Ordinary Kindness: Good deeds and altruism 174
    Extraordinary Kindness: Compassion is the key 178
        Compassion eclipses empathy 179
        The purpose of compassion 181
    How do we grow in Kindness? 183
        Developing generous people 183
        Developing compassionate people 186
    Finally, be a blessing to others 191

Chapter 8 — In the pursuit of excellence: Using multiple virtues 193

    A brief recap 193
    When virtues come together we find excellence 195
        Career success: Maximising just two foundational virtues 196
        Achieving excellence in the art of living:
        Maximising three or more foundational virtues 198

    The foundational virtues as an integrated system 205
    Future dreaming 209
    Five stepping-stones to virtue 210
        Know what you value 211
        Avoid black and white thinking 211
        Live beyond yourself 212
        Be not afraid 212
        Act with integrity 212
    Final thoughts 213

Endnotes 215

Indexs 243

Acknowledgements

We wish to gratefully acknowledge the help of the following people in the preparation of this book: Mr Tim Cutrona, Ms Diana Blackburn, Ms Nicolette Gan (PhD candidate), Ms Jui Gui, Dr Abey Gunasekarage PhD, Dr Chandana Hewege PhD, Dr Sharon Hoch MBBS, Dr Jayanthi Kumarasiri PhD, Ms Barbara Matheson, Mr Craig Oakley, Rev Dr Jeff Pugh PhD, Dr Katie Richardson PhD, Dr Michelle Sanders DMin, Ms Yim-Fong Voon, Ms Jennifer Saunders and Mr Michael Walker.

We also want to acknowledge the graciousness of our wives, Laura and Lisa, in allowing us to undertake such a large project.

The Freedom of Virtue: Navigating excellence in the art of living amongst a world of instant gratification

Authors' Note

In recognition of our broad readership we have used a diversity of reference material of which most is easily accessible. These sources have been placed under Endnotes at the end of the book. Further, some material is quoted for the benefit of the reader. Normal conventions apply except when an extended quote also forms the basis of a story. In this instance the text is blocked but the font size is not reduced.

In addition, italics have been used in three ways throughout the text. Consistent with APA style italics are used for: (1) the titles of books/movies, (2) when words are taken from other languages but not in common English usage, and (3) to indicate emphasis.

Some readers may be concerned by the fact that we have used the outmoded BC/AD dating system in a book that seeks to be culturally aware. We recognise this. Nevertheless the international standard for dating years commenced at what was believed to be the birth of Christ. In addition, nonacademic readers will be most familiar with the BC/AD abbreviations.

And a disclaimer: *The Freedom of Virtue* represents an introduction to the use of specific virtues to bring about a life well lived. It is written for educational purposes only. If aspects of the text are to be applied then please do so in accordance with your: (1) scope of practice, (2) your organisation's policies/procedures, and (3) relevant codes of ethical conduct. If you wish to use aspects of this text for therapeutic outcomes then please seek guidance or training from Dr Edwards and Dr Chiera before doing so. They can be contacted at www.naturalintelligence.com.au.

T.E. & C.C.

Authors' Preface

This book was born out of curiosity and frustration. The idea emerged, as so many do, over coffee at a little bayside café we know well. Three interlinked questions occupied our thinking that summer morning about two years ago:

- From our experience in Higher Education: 'Why are Millennials so delightful, but often struggle to cope with the demands of a degree?'.

- From Cos' experience in the corporate world: 'Why do some highly skilled people stay at relatively low positions in the workforce but others, who are less talented, rise to become senior managers?'.

- And from my (i.e., Tom) work in mental health: 'Why do some clients, who present with significant issues, improve while others do not? '.

Ultimately, our conversation came around to Cos asking the personal question, 'What ingredients do my teenage daughters need to become capable women who are able to contribute to society?'.

In discussing this we came to realise that what we'd been asking about were those personal factors which made an individual stand out from the crowd, or which conferred excellence in the art of living. As we thought about the problem a little more we realised that the standard answers were not adequate to explain what we were grasping at. For example, our society places great emphasis on intelligence whether it is in school or in the workforce. But smart people are not immune from failure, nor even stupidity, from time to time. We also thought about 'family of origin' as the classic psychological cause of so many personal struggles. But stand-out people seem to overcome their background, however deprived or traumatic. Even if we look at structural inequality within society (e.g., the 'haves' vs. the 'have-nots') some people rise above their class to achieve great things. While we do not deny the benefit of a good set of genes, a stable family life, or a few brains in giving people a headstart in life this could not be the whole story. Even when we thought about psychological attributes such as resilience these too failed to explain stand-out people in any substantive way.

In frustration we turned to the life stories of people who embodied excellence to see if we could extract some key ingredient not yet seen. But as we read these stories we came to realise how difficult this task would be. For instance, gender seemed to play no part in excellence. Demographically, some who achieved great things did so off the back of a solid upbringing, yet excellence was often found as a consequence of overcoming a rough start in life. Nor was age an obvious factor in conferring excellence. While we like to attribute wisdom and mastery to older age there are plenty of stories of people who stood out amongst their peers quite young. In the end the only defining feature we could identify was not what these people had, but how they applied their talents.

At an existential level we also realised something else … Stand-out people were marked by having a purpose to their lives. For some this was a noble cause, but for many more it was a visceral need to prove a point, or to prove others wrong. Paired with this was also a strong notion of respect which took several forms. These excellent people had the respect of colleagues and friends, but also self-respect. In addition, they often had the respect of those with whom they clashed. Be it on the sports field, or across a parliamentary chamber, people of excellence are respected for who they are even if what they are doing is opposed by many.

With this in mind we felt able to pursue excellence in the art of living as a topic of study. To do so required us to lean on the psychological literature, and especially Positive Psychology, but also go much further. Over the intervening months Cos and I read biographies, engaged some of the world's great literature, thought about Anthropology as the study of people, touched on religious ideas and came to terms with aspects of Philosophy. That people are also flesh and blood meant that we could not deny a debt to Biology either. In the end we discovered that human excellence is a rich dish. It is only by combining many ingredients that we can avoid the thin taste of morality, the bitterness of character development or the honey sweetness of the happiness gurus. What we present to you, instead, is a dish called virtue.

Virtue sits in the background of daily life, but influences everything we say and do. It is about a person's style and substance in spite of their physical strength or intellect. In this way virtue is for us all, not only for the strong and the smart. While it would be easy to write a book dedicated to extolling the virtues this is not our aim. We want to identify those virtues which are foundational to our humanity. In doing so our hope is that you, and those whom you care about, will learn to use virtue and thus live to the better angels of your nature.

While some readers familiar with Positive Psychology may consider this a retelling of what Martin Seligman already espouses we would argue otherwise. While there will, inevitably, be some overlap we'd differentiate our approach in the following ways.

Ours' is not a search for happiness, but for purpose, for respect and for excellence in the art of living. In fact we would argue that finding virtue will not often bring happiness. Indeed the virtuous person often stands alone and risks much in life to achieve great things or to live authentically.

Nor is virtue about good character. As we will explain in the opening sections of Chapter 1 good character is a slippery fish. So much so that some people with an apparently bad character are most virtuous.

In addition, common virtues can be identified by undertaking a cross-cultural comparison which we too have done in Chapter 1. However, common virtues do not necessarily mean core, or foundational, virtues. We argue that foundational virtues must be common and impart a survival advantage. In this way only by performing a cross-cultural comparison of virtues with an evolutionary perspective can a small set of foundational virtues be identified. Recognising this we propose a somewhat different set of core virtues than those put forward in the early days of Positive Psychology. In fact we think some inclusions and exclusions will surprise you.

Finally, we have taken time to clearly delineate each foundational virtue so as to give them useful definitions and a limited scope. In this way we avoid any perceived confusion between strengths, values and virtues. In turn, this has the benefit of allowing us to provide specific advice to readers on how to grow each foundational virtue.

As to the structure of our book we begin by sifting a multitude of virtues and from this derive six which may be considered foundational. This is the purpose of Chapter 1. Without wanting to spoil the surprise the six foundational virtues we will uncover are: (1) Courage, (2) Diligence, (3) Wisdom, (4) Honour, (5) Justice, and (6) Kindness. For those readers already familiar with the virtues you will recognise that our list has some similarities, but important differences, with lists that have gone before. For instance where is temperance? And how is Honour a virtue? Moreover, we have removed any mystical notions of transcendence from our list placing each foundational virtue within a practical context. These are all important issues to be discussed.

Across Chapters 2 to 7 each of the six foundational virtues will be explored in depth. These chapters are ordered in a specific way. The first three, Courage, Diligence and Wisdom relate to the individual and to goal attainment. Use these three virtues and you will succeed at school, university, on the sports field and often in the workplace. However, the three remaining foundational virtues of Honour, Justice and Kindness recognise that we live and work together in families, teams and as part of a wider community. Without these additional foundational virtues life becomes lonely at best and mean-spirited at worst. Ultimately, all six foundational virtues work together as an integrated system to produce a life lived excellently.

The structure of Chapters 2 through 7 is particular. Each chapter is divided into thirds and commences with an illustration from life so as to immediately ground our discussion. We then begin to pick apart the chapter's foundational virtue using a range of academic sources. However we are not writing an academic tome and so our sources are both varied and, more often than not, easily accessible to the average reader. Technicians in each discipline will also hopefully forgive us any small oversights which are inevitable when trying to convey complex ideas to a wide audience. Finally, each chapter is brought to a close by discussing best practice when wanting to grow the foundational virtue of interest. To do so we use common contexts such as how parents and teachers can contribute to the growth of children in their care; we also consider both the workplace and community; as well as giving due weight to therapeutic interventions for those who struggle with life. Finally, throughout each chapter are a range of questions and activities designed to stimulate your thinking. We hope you enjoy them.

Chapter 8 brings all the foundational virtues together. It begins by demonstrating the extraordinary outcomes possible when multiple foundational virtues are harnessed. While several brief examples are given of people who used just two foundational virtues to great effect we have also provided a more lengthy treatment of what happens when three or more foundational virtues are maximised. Winston Churchill and Nelson Mandela will be our guides in this matter. Ultimately, the book concludes with a teaser of future work. An integrated brain-based model of the foundational virtues is briefly considered as well as some rather nifty implications. I (i.e., Tom) won't spoil the surprise but each implication has significant relevance across a diversity of professions from counselling and teaching right through to politics, advertising and even to artificial intelligence.

So, come on this journey with us. Although we will guide you we are also fellow travellers; not virtuous, just trying to be. This will be a big mountain to climb and is not for the feint hearted. Some will turn back, and we wish them well. We understand that virtue is not for everyone and that many people find their happiness in the green valleys of life. But for those of us with a little *chutzpah* summit snows loom high above and time is of the essence …

T.E. & C.C.

The Freedom of Virtue: Navigating excellence in the art of living amongst a world of instant gratification

Chapter 1

The Foundational Virtues

> **Virtue is excellence**
> — Adam Smith

What makes for excellence in the art of life?

In travelling south from Florence by train it does not take too long to come to the city of Siena. Like all medieval Italian towns it is perched atop a hill and still has heavy ramparts with which to greet the traveller. For its small size Siena feels large given that you have to walk the length of the *Via Camollia*, the *Via dei Montanini* and the *Banchi di Sopra* before finding yourself looking out onto the wide open space of the *Piazza del Campo*. Emerging into bright sunlight it's the colour that strikes you first. All the buildings lining the piazza are terracotta red and at the far end is the strong fortress of the *Palazzo Pubblico* with its high bell tower capped in white marble. Crossing the piazza and going inside the palazzo one is immediately struck by the wealth of the city given that all the public chambers are adorned with magnificent frescos and paintings. While we could get distracted looking at any number of them our interest is particular. Next to the Map Room is the enigmatically named Room of the Nine. Around this austere chamber are the frescos we have come to see. What makes them of special importance is that they are not merely decorative. Their purpose was to present an allegory of good and bad government to Siena's rulers as they pondered matters of state. In some way the painter saw his work as an antidote to the daily politicking that went on.

Although the fresco depicting bad government is damaged the artist's intentions are nevertheless clear. It warns onlookers that tyranny will replace justice at the heart of government when vices such as avarice, cruelty and vainglory are let loose. By contrast, the frescos depicting good government cover the remaining walls and are bathed in warm sunlight. Again, the artist's message could not be clearer. With good government comes peace and prosperity for all. And to ensure this general happiness, the rulers of Siena are to look to the virtues of justice, temperance, fortitude (i.e., courage) and prudence (i.e., wisdom) amongst others.

Given the fractious nature of medieval Italian politics we doubt that Siena's rulers always embodied these virtues. Perhaps it was enough to aspire to them. Yet, for us, what is important is that these frescos tapped into a singular truth about human nature. Talent, money, power, prestige etc. are all empty vessels — it is what we do with them that matters. In recognising this we first glimpse the value of virtue and open the door to human excellence in general. As such, our thesis is a simple one ... Intelligence is useful, and skills are needed, but excellence in life comes down to mastering a set of personal qualities.

To demonstrate this point let's move forward to our own time and read the following true story:

> Take a young kid from America's Midwest. Yes, he was born with a solid intellect and had the advantage of coming from a well-off family, but he nevertheless understood the value of a strong work ethic from an early age. First he sold newspapers for pocket money and then worked in a grocery store to earn a little more cash. All the while he completed school with good enough marks to gain entry into a respected university. Growing into manhood our friend completed his Bachelor's degree before turning his sights on postgraduate study in business. However, Harvard knocked him back. With trademark grit this young man was not deterred and simply applied to Columbia instead. But this was not a second-best choice for Columbia's business programme had excellent teachers and he knew it. Not surprisingly our friend graduated with a master's degree soon enough.
>
> For years the young man worked his way up in the world, such that by his early 30s he was a millionaire. Nevertheless this was only the beginning. Through various partnerships, and by possessing an ability to see opportunities that others could not, this

fellow developed a formidable business reputation. So much so that by 60 he was a billionaire.

Yet that was only the background story to a much more interesting person. As his biographer wrote:

> 'Warren Buffett is not easy to describe. Physically, he is unremarkable, with looks often described as grandfatherly. Intellectually, he is considered a genius, yet his down-to-earth relationship with people is truly uncomplicated. He is simple, straightforward, forthright, and honest. He displays an engaging combination of sophisticated dry wit and cornball humour. He has a profound reverence for all things logical and a foul distaste for imbecility. He embraces the simple and avoids the complicated.'[1]

Warren Buffett is, by any measure, a person who embodies business excellence. But his business acumen is matched by his personal qualities: '… simple, straightforward, forthright, and honest'. To these we could also add a diligent work ethic, a temperate lifestyle and a good deal of wisdom. In fact we would argue that it is Buffett's personal qualities, his virtues, which underscore his business success.

Nor is Warren Buffett unique in this regard for we could have chosen any number of successful people from disciplines as diverse as Science and Music, right the way to people who have founded NGOs and done other remarkable things. Talent is the first step towards excellence and education is necessary, but without the personal qualities to match then one simply suffers a 'failure to fly'.

Character, morality and virtue: Similar but different

All people who embody excellence have personal qualities which account for their success in life. Virtues if you will. But before we can show you what these are it is necessary to separate virtue from similar sounding words such as morality, values and character. This is not to be pedantic, but to show you how much richer the study of virtue is when compared to these other terms.

Take, for example, morality. At its best morality carves out a space for each of us to live our lives relatively free from harm by labelling some actions as 'good' or 'bad'. But it is also a most abused term. Often morality is simply a means to restrict behaviour based on the fears or desires of a community and its leaders. Because of this morality tends to shift with each generation landing on this issue or that without any clear underlying principle. Nor does morality seek to uplift or enliven us, but only to condemn. For these reasons, amongst others, morality can be so unvirtuous. Nevertheless morality does, at times, point to what is good and thereby virtuous so cannot be entirely ignored.

We might hope that values fair better than morality when looked at from the perspective of virtues. But we're not that lucky. Scratch below the surface of a business' value statement or a school's attempt at values education and a number of problems arise. For example, whose values are we talking about? Values tend to be compartmentalised according to family, class, religion etc. For this reason schools are often places of contested values with children stuck between their family's expectations and those of their teachers. To make matters worse, values are often imposed by the powerful on the powerless. Sometimes governments even do this by *fiat* through school curricula, welfare agencies and other means of State control. So, to the extent that values are contested and fought over shows them to be relatively virtueless. They are, in effect, only a surface-level response to deeper issues.

As for character this gets closer to virtue. A person of good character is both moral and virtuous. But … this assumes we are looking from the perspective of polite society. They are the ones who award the honour of 'good character' and do so in accordance with their own particular values. Indeed the most excellent of people are often irascible, if not downright disagreeable. In some ways we could even say that Oscar Wilde and Ghandi both went to jail, in part, for their bad character. To use the modern phrase: 'They just wouldn't get with the program'. So, excluding some extremes in behaviour, a bad character is not necessarily a bad thing. It may even point to a person of excellence.[2]

Ultimately virtue *is* the word we're after when looking to describe those personal qualities which imbue excellence. Furthermore, virtue has a long and honoured history going back millennia which prevents it from blowing about on the breeze. Diverse cultures also consider many of the same virtues to be important which speaks to virtue as the basis of our shared humanity. In this way virtue uplifts and unites us all. So, in the broadest terms, to talk of virtue is to talk of that which is both tangible and of the greatest good.

But to come to terms with virtue is not an easy task. For example, there is no one accepted definition of virtue. In fact cultures around the world have tended to settle on definitions which grasp at only a part of the whole. For, '… [in ancient Greece virtue was about] practical reason … [in India it came to mean] mindfulness and … [in China virtue led to] doing 'what is appropriate' (*yi*)'.[3] By contrast, when we try to get at virtue in its entirety we often dissolve into vague aphorisms that make little sense to anyone but philosophers or religious devotees. For instance, what are we to make of virtue when it is described in the following ways according to the Chinese notion of *Tao*,

> In his every movement a man of great virtue
> Follows the way and the way only.
> As a thing the way is
> Shadowy, indistinct.
> Indistinct and shadowy,
> Yet within it is an image;
> Shadowy and indistinct,
> Yet within it is a substance.
> Dim and dark,
> Yet within it is an essence.[4]

Or alternatively,

> A man of the highest virtue does not keep to virtue and that is why he has virtue. A man of the lowest virtue never strays from virtue and that is why he is without virtue. The former never acts yet leaves nothing undone. The latter acts but there are things left undone.[5]

Although both statements sum up the nature of virtue according to *Tao* neither is much help to you and me.

Yet there is a middle road between selective definitions and vague generalities. For instance, Plato and his mentor Socrates recognised that whatever virtue is, it brings happiness in the form of contentment to the community and to each person.[6] A generation later Aristotle also recognised that becoming virtuous required a ' … disposition [or habit] of the mind … [involving] choice of actions and emotions …'.[7] In other words, virtue was not something mystical but involved practice in making good life choices. In taking a more cerebral approach St Thomas Aquinas (13th century) picked up on virtue as being '… a good quality of the mind, by which we live righteously [i.e., well], [and] of which no one can make bad use …'.[8,9] And in the 19th century Nietzsche considered another important aspect of virtue in his book *Beyond Good & Evil*.[10] In it he came to see virtue not based in reason, but as a visceral quality of being human and expressed in the struggle against overwhelming existential realities.

So what then is virtue? In the simplest terms virtue can pertain to a number of admirable qualities which allow you to live to excellence and fully play your part in community life. Yet while we can quickly recognise virtuous qualities virtue itself must be practiced, if not struggled for. Nor is this struggle a simple one for virtue brings together the will, cognition and action. In fact, virtue is only seen in action. And as for the outcome of a virtuous action? It may bring a happy life but there are dangers in saying this. For instance, virtue is squandered if happiness is equated to frivolity which typically lacks virtue. Or, more significantly, people who aspire to virtue often suffer. We need only consider Ghandi and Dr Martin Luther King Jr to know what virtue cost them. But in saying this, virtue, although a stony path, is an excellent one. For at the end of the path one usually finds both purpose in life and respect. Its true outcome therefore is a life well lived.

 Activity 1.1

> List those personal resources which have helped you succeed in life. Once done sort them into two lists. On one side put those aspects related to education, skills and intelligence. On the other side place your personal qualities. Look at your personal qualities. What specific virtues are you strong in?

If you look, you'll see virtues everywhere

Not all virtues are created equal. Rightly enough different virtues seem to apply when charting one's career, pondering on the nature of the 'good society', or even when trying to achieve some sort of spiritual enlightenment. This being so the singular purpose of our first chapter is to identify a small set of 'foundational virtues' from many other 'situational virtues'. Or to put it another way … To identify those virtues which hold true *all of the time* from those which hold true *only in specific circumstances*. In this way we will have separated the gold from the dross and found something truly useful in living to excellence.

 Activity 1.2

> Think about all the parts of your life including relationships, home-life and work. Now list all the good qualities (i.e., virtues) needed for each to go well. Are some virtues more common than others? What does this say about which virtues you should cultivate to live an excellent life?

The method we will use to sift virtues is known as a cross-cultural survey. What we'll do is dip into a range of societies, past and present, and look to see what each held to be important. Ultimately we will assert that those qualities held consistently across cultures represent foundational virtues.

Although we have done the spade-work for you it is worth pausing for a moment to understand the immensity of the task and some of the difficulties therein. First of all every one of us has a worldview. This is the lens through which we see the world and judge right from wrong. For many of us our worldview is Western and influenced by the liberal democracies in which we live. To not recognise our worldview and/or to expect others to hold the same worldview is a beginner's mistake that could quickly lead to a number of erroneous value-judgements. For example, fully fledged Western liberal democracies account for only 19 countries out of 167 recently surveyed.[11] To expect much of the rest of the world to hold our opinions about civil society would be wrong. A Western worldview appears even more 'boutique' when we divide the world by economics and by population. Two of the world's three largest economies are Asian and the 10 most populous countries span four continents.[12, 13] Therefore any fair cross-cultural survey needs to let go of a Western bias as much as possible.

Even so, pragmatism clips our wings. While we recognise the virtue traditions of Africa, the Americas and First Nations people globally we are forced to focus our attention on the Eurasian landmass given that these cultures have both a strong written record of virtue as well as well-developed virtue ethics. Politically this makes sense too for our world see-saws between the influence of Europe and China, often pivoting at the Middle East.

Finally, any cross-cultural survey of the type we have undertaken will be flawed to some extent simply because of the range of texts which have to be covered, each in its own language. Neither Cos nor I are linguists and so we admit our reliance on the work of others. Beyond this we have to accept that any text chosen for study comes with its own context. That is, who wrote it and why? In the simplest terms written histories and other forms of communication are often the works of powerful men. As such they represent the ideas of cultural elites, rarely ever a low-born person or a woman. However, we have addressed this problem when we can in Chapter 1 and deliberately counteracted it in the later chapters of our book for virtue is everybody's business. In this way we hope we have minimised any bias.

So how do we handle these limitations of our cross-cultural survey? It simply means that as we proceed we don't take things for granted. The evidence is incomplete, so be it. It's what we've got to work with. But there is still enough intersecting evidence to clearly demonstrate that all people hold only a few virtues in the highest regard. These will become our foundational virtues and the subject of later chapters.

To help us identify foundational virtues we will also use the following three pointers as a guide:

1. Each of us inhabits a body which we use to interact with the world about us. This means that the foundational virtues play out in the real world.

They are practical, not mystical. Put another way, foundational virtues confer survival advantage and so are subject to evolutionary pressures. While some may argue that vices may also be the result of evolution, and we don't disagree, virtue is different by providing a long-term survival advantage extending to kith and kin alike. Vice, on the other hand, often has one absent themselves from the gene pool all too quickly.

2. That foundational virtues are shared across societies means that we should see them time and time again as we take a peek into our past. But what do smelly Mongol warriors on the Asian Steppe have in common with the effete French aristocracy of the 18th century? The answer is that they have a lot in common if we put dress and manners aside. *The trick in identifying foundational virtues is to see what lies beneath morality, values and character so as to exclude what is specific to time and place.* To help with this we have clustered related concepts around a single named virtue.

3. Finally, we have also assumed something akin to Occam's Razor when searching for foundational virtues. *In particular, there will likely only be a small set of them.* Pragmatically, this is a good check on our reasoning for if the list of foundational virtues becomes too long then it is likely that we have confused some with situational virtues, personal strengths or character traits.

So there you have it, the remainder of Chapter 1 is all about sifting virtues. What's nice is that much of the spade work has been done for you. So just sit back and enjoy the ride. Nevertheless, for those who love to read the end of a mystery first you can always jump to page 34 and find out 'who dun it' before moving directly into Chapter 2.

What virtues do we have today?

Contemporary virtues are a good place to begin; partly because we live them every day and so they sound familiar; partly because many of them are so new that they can be dispensed with rather quickly as being either novel or fashionable.

Western culture is hard to define in a rapidly changing and globalised world. In one direction largescale migration is shifting notions of culture in places such as Europe and Australia. In another direction China is hyperventilating on Western consumerism and all that comes with it. But, in the context of Anglo-American culture, we may suggest that attributes including wealth and fame are revered by many as something akin to hedonistic virtues.

More substantially, today's virtues are often agenda-based being either political or personal. By political virtues we do not mean the grand civic virtues of '... Life, Liberty and the pursuit of Happiness.' or, as the French would have it, *liberté, egalité* and *fraternité*. Today's political virtues are expressed in terms of rights-based campaigns. They are virtues in action. To name these virtues we could use 'weasel words' such as political correctness but this would be unfair as many times these new virtues take an optimistic tone. For example embracing diversity is, perhaps, the greatest political virtue of our time. But surprisingly diversity, or even tolerance, is not foundational to who we are as humans even if it is a genuine expression of a generation.[14] Not only is the virtue of diversity recent, but even the virtue of toleration is only a few hundred years old. More important still is that beneath both virtues lies something far older and more substantial — the virtue of justice. Therefore while diversity and tolerance may be situational virtues, expressed in a time and place, justice is the superior virtue and a contender to be considered foundational.

Moving swiftly from political virtues to personal virtues, morning TV is awash with well-meaning lifestyle gurus inviting us to be better, think bolder, and live happier. A hard ask first thing in the morning as we swill-down coffee, battle to get kids ready for school and submit to the inevitable traffic chaos. Nevertheless the jolly invocations of these people represent, in a broad way, the second — and more substantive — type of virtues common today. These being virtues based in personal strengths, wellness and psychology.

In a formal way Psychology has been articulating strength-based virtues for decades, often with solid research to back most claims. Initially, Humanist Psychology elevated self-esteem to the position of a virtue some decades ago. Since then self-esteem has become a mainstay in education right the way through to HR management practices. But the impetus for strengths-based virtues really took-off following the publication of Martin Seligman's book *Authentic Happiness* in 2002.[15] In fact strengths-based virtues are a pillar of his Positive Psychology movement.

Primarily interested in character strengths Seligman and his colleagues also began their research with a cross-cultural analysis of seminal texts. From this work they identified 24 strengths that acted as routes to six core virtues which, in turn, came to represent the beating heart of Positive Psychology and our path to authentic happiness. In a nod to the ancient Greeks four of these core virtues were either the cardinal virtues, or adaptations thereof, while two seemed a bit 'New Age-ish'. In particular Seligman and his colleagues posited core virtues of wisdom (and knowledge); courage; justice; temperance; humanity; and transcendence.

In spite of the benefits Positive Psychology has rendered to multitudes of people a number of criticisms have been levelled at Seligman's virtue work. At a broad level some authors dislike its focus on the creation of personal happiness. For instance, Seligman draws upon ancient Greek notions of 'the good life' in understanding happiness. However, somewhere between Athens and America the ideas get a little muddled. For what the Greeks saw as the good life was not about positive emotion so much as fleeing from the anxieties of a world in tumult (i.e., *ataraxia*). As such the good life, although having practical outworkings which does make life pleasant, was primarily an existential concern.[16]

While colleagues within psychology have expressed similar concerns in the following way,

> The question arises of whether there are better things in life than the pursuit of happiness, for example, living a significant, valuable life, which is not necessarily happy. Meanwhile, a happy life may not be meaningful or valuable. Indeed, there are people and cultures in which happiness is feared.[17]

While another author was quite cheeky when he wrote that, 'Seligman says nothing about the possibility that some people find happiness, gratifications, and feelings of fulfilment by exercising vices [not virtues].'[18]

As to the core virtues themselves Seligman does not always help his case. At times compound terms have been used to describe single virtues (e.g., wisdom and knowledge) while at other times multiple definitions have been put forward. For example, the rather mystically named virtue of transcendence has been described as both 'connections to the larger universe' and that which 'provide[s] meaning'.[19] Of greater concern, however, has been when Seligman discards a level of rigour stating things like, '... what courage means for a samurai differs from what it means to Plato ....'[20] No, one virtue one concept. More formally, this important point was taken up by Kristjánsson when he wondered how the different character strengths that lead to core virtues may relate, overlap, or even collide.[20] So, in summary, while the general thrust of Positive Psychology has been a gift to many important conceptual work remains to be done. Put as a question, this ongoing work can be stated by simply asking whether happiness as a goal, and its attendant core virtues, simply reflects the needs of contemporary America or is universally true?[18, 22]

Taken together, contemporary virtues are an interesting mix of the personal, the political and the psychological. They hold some truth but we suspect that this can only be seen by reflecting on them from across millennia and so it is to the ancient world that we now turn.

Question 1.1

a. In thinking about your community what virtues are you aware of?

b. If you are a psychologist, counsellor or teacher what experience have you had with:

(1) Positive Psychology in general; and

(2) its core virtues in particular? Did those for whom you care achieve a sense of happiness?

Virtues in the ancient world

Having realised that the value of contemporary virtues are difficult to adjudicate we might be best to return to our roots and look for virtues which have stood the test of time. These, if anything, will surely be foundational.

While we have probably carried virtue with us since we first walked on the Africa savannah evidence of virtue goes back a mere 5000 years and corresponds to a time when people came together across the Ancient Near East to farm and trade. In doing so our ancestors developed systems of writing to record daily transactions and, as luck would have it, also discovered that this new invention could communicate a story, preserve a history or even disseminate law. It is these records that have passed down to us today and which speak of virtue.

The Ancient Near East is a mighty big place and within it a number of societies developed at various times between the 2nd and 3rd millennia BC. Some of the earliest societies were the city-states of Mesopotamia which sat within the borders of modern-day Iraq. Following the Fertile Crescent north along the Euphrates River and diverting west we come to another cluster of societies which sprang up on the shores of the Mediterranean Sea. The Phoenicians and the peoples of the Bible being prominent amongst them. While to the south ancient Egypt arose to become a mighty civilisation whose monuments inspire awe to this day.

Beyond the Ancient Near East a number of other significant societies also sprang up — albeit over a long time span. These too we cannot ignore. Far to the east in modern day Pakistan the Indus River people had built cities by the 3rd millennium BC. In the 2nd millennium BC, and far to the west, the Phoenicians had struck out on the Mediterranean Sea trading as far away as the Atlantic coast. By the 1st millennium BC, the Greek city-states had already come to blows with Troy and were soon to see off the Persians. And last, but by no means least, there was — of course — Rome.

To deal effectively with so many different cultures from long ago we need a plan. In the first instance we're not going to discuss the Indus River people, Troy or Phoenician Carthage given that their influence was extinguished in antiquity. We're also going to carve off ancient Judea to a later section of this chapter pertaining to the three Abrahamic faiths. We'll also leave Rome for our discussion on Western European virtues given that it bridges the ancient and medieval worlds. That being said, what we are left with are two very old societies, Mesopotamia and Egypt, and an anomaly called Athens which matured as a consequence of Persian aggression.

In addition to their great narratives of courage and perseverance (e.g., hero stories and flood epics) the societies of the Ancient Near East were centred around community much like the Middle East of today. Be it Sumer, Babylon or Egypt a prime concern was the maintenance of right relationships. At a grand level an example of this is the ancient Egyptian notion of *Ma'at*.[23, 24] This guiding principle ordered the universe as much as the relationships between the Pharaoh and his people, between an employer and employee and between a parent and their child. *Ma'at* was relational. More practically, the Babylonian king Hammurabi (1810 BC to 1750 BC) also imposed a concept of right relationship, and of justice, on his people when he promulgated his Code of Laws. These 282 very sensible laws regulated everything from wages and contracts right through to managing issues of slander and negligence.[25]

Additional to the virtues of right relationship and of justice the ancient world was fascinated by wisdom. Although we will consider Jewish wisdom literature a little later on let's now dip into the Egyptian *Sebayt*. In doing so we do not find high-minded arguments but delightfully a wisdom born of hearth and home. Take, for example, Ptah-hotep who was a senior official in the Egyptian bureaucracy and loved both his wife and son. In passing on a little advice to the boy Ptah-hotep extolled virtues of truthfulness, self-control, wisdom and humility. He spoke also of the value of hard work. But, in a more charming way he also confided to his son about happiness in marriage when he said, 'Fill [your wife's] stomach, clothe her back; oil is the remedy of her limbs. Gladden her heart ... Be not harsh ...'.[26] Good advice from well over 3000 years ago.

So while people love to think about heroic narratives from the past which highlight the importance of virtues such as courage and perseverance these are only part of a much bigger story. The Ancient Near East valued relationships before all else, upheld justice and sought to be wise amongst many other things.

With some licence let's now jump a 1000+ years and conclude our discussion of ancient virtues by looking at that anomaly called Athens. Why is it an anomaly? Because no other society of the ancient world would have thought to elevate reason beyond relationship. Indeed Athens is an anomaly twice over for this odd little city-state has come to influence all of Western thinking.

Coming ashore at the Athenian harbour of Piraeus in the 4th century BC we would have found some of the most notable scholars of all time jostling and competing to see whose ideas were most worthy. Not that it was all high-minded rhetoric, for these were real men who laughed and drank and squabbled as we do now. As one story goes, Plato had recently defined for his students what it meant to be human. Rather pleased with himself he considered us all to be 'featherless bipeds' (i.e., two legged). To show how stupid this definition was Diogenes, known as The Dog, caught a chicken, plucked it and threw it over the wall at Plato. As students scattered Diogenes called out to Plato, 'Here's your man …!'.[27] So don't think of these philosophers as remote even if their ideas appear so.

As to virtue we will have to limit our discussion to two ideas only or we will get lost. The first of these is to name and describe what many, not all, Greeks scholars called the cardinal virtues. This was a core list and which, even today, forms the backbone of much scholarly work into the virtues. The second idea we will contend with is how Aristotle considered virtues to operate. Together these two ideas will give us a reasonably good structure-function view of how many Greeks understood virtue.

The cardinal virtues comprised: prudence (i.e., practical wisdom); temperance; justice; and courage. At first, Plato discussed these seminal virtues in the context of how to develop a workable city-state out of an almost tribal culture. They were therefore an answer to a question rooted in political philosophy, not human potential.[28] Nevertheless in so much as a person has arms and legs and a beating heart all controlled by a brain we are each a polity of sorts. Therefore these four cardinal virtues have come to embody the essential qualities of an ideal person. They were, and often remain, the measure of personal excellence.

Let's now turn to each cardinal virtue in turn. Prudence, unlike our risk-based definitions of today, was originally about notions of insight and discernment. It was a form of wisdom and from it sprung free will.[29] As for the cardinal virtue of temperance this is easy to explain for it has always been about self-control. Next comes justice. However, our courtroom view of justice was not exactly what classical scholars had in mind. For them, living in a world of great inequality often meant the 'haves' holding onto their wealth while the 'have-nots' tried to take it. As such, justice to the Athenians was more like something Marx would have recognised for it ordered economic relationships, but did so in the context of reciprocity and even a little generosity.[30] Finally courage (i.e., fortitude) was a hotly debated topic in ancient Greece. Not only were Athens and Sparta always at loggerheads but only recently had the Persian Empire threatened annihilation. For these reasons the Athenians typically spoke of courage within a military context.

Turning now to how the virtues functioned, only a generation after Plato along came Aristotle. While Aristotle added to the list of virtues by writing about magnanimity, liberality, gentleness and other good qualities he also took a scientist's eye to how they worked.[16, 31] What made this specific contribution to virtues scholarship even more remarkable is that can be explained relatively easily. At its simplest, virtues function along a line between two extremes of behaviour. Take, for example, courage. This cardinal virtue exists on a line somewhere between rashness and timidity. To be rash in ancient Greece meant that life would be exciting, but probably short and bloody. Alternatively, at the other end of the line exists timidity. Here life becomes safe, but very mundane. Yet, between the two is a point where we find the gusto to handle all sorts of difficult situations but not the need to rampage through life. In effect we have located the virtue courage.[30] But Aristotle was also a nuanced thinker. He therefore considered virtue to lie at the mean point between two extremes of behaviour but also remarked that one should consider, '… the right time, … the right occasion, [acting] towards the right people, for the right purpose and in the right manner …'.[32] In this way the mean point was never set but could move about as circumstances dictated.

In now bringing our brief survey of ancient virtues to a close what can we say? While we must hold prudence, temperance, justice and courage highly we also have to add to them an ability to do relationships well, a homely wisdom and also not forget Ptah-hotep's injunction to be kind.

Question 1.2

a. If you are a pastor, senior manager or community leader what is your perspective on the importance of good relationships as a virtue?

b. If you work in mental health you'll be aware of a variety of presenting issues which involve frayed and fractured relationships. What place might the virtues have in helping clients to mend relationships and do life better?

The virtues of the three Abrahamic faiths: Judaism, Christianity and Islam

Voltaire once quipped, 'If God did not exist then we'd have to invent Him.'. Although rather scurrilous there is an important edge to what he was trying to get across. Religion has many functions in people's lives. At its best it provides a relationship with the Divine but, more pragmatically, religion extols people to live better. It can even be a school for virtue. Given that the three Abrahamic faiths claim over 3.9 billion adherents worldwide we now turn to examine their contribution to virtue.[33]

Judaism ranks as one of the world's oldest continually practiced religions and at its core is *Torah*. *Torah* was given by God to Moses and encapsulates all of Jewish life. In this way it is a virtues-rich document. To expedite matters there is, within *Torah*, an excellent summary of Jewish virtues found in the *Book of Exodus*. While Christians know this list as the Ten Commandments we will refer to it below by its Jewish name — the Ten Statements (i.e., *Aseret ha-Dibrot*) and order them accordingly.[34] Let's read,

1. I am the L-rd your G-d, Who brought you out of the land of Egypt, out of the house of bondage.
2. You shall have no other gods before Me. You shall not make for yourself a graven image, nor any manner of likeness of any thing that is in heaven above, that is in the earth beneath, or that is in the water under the earth. You shall not bow down to them, nor serve them. For I the L-rd your G-d am a jealous G-d, visiting the iniquity of the fathers upon the children of the third and fourth generation of them that hate Me; and showing mercy unto the thousandth generation of them that love Me and keep My commandments.
3. You shall not take the name of the L-rd your G-d in vain; for the L-rd will not hold him guiltless that takes His name in vain.
4. Remember the Sabbath Day, to keep it holy. Six days you shall labor and do all your work; but the seventh day is a Sabbath unto the L-rd your G-d. On it you shall not do any manner of work — you, your son, your daughter, your man servant, your maid servant, your cattle, and your stranger that is within your gates. For in six days the L-rd made heaven and earth, the sea and all that in them is, and rested on the seventh day; wherefore the L-rd blessed the Sabbath Day, and hallowed it.
5. Honor your father and mother, so that your days may be long upon the land which the L-rd your G-d gives you.
6. You shall not murder.
7. You shall not commit adultery.
8. You shall not steal.
9. You shall not bear false witness against your neighbor.

> 10. You shall not covet your neighbor's house; you shall not covet your neighbor's wife, his manservant, his maid servant, his ox, his ass, nor anything that is your neighbor's.[35]

Most importantly, the Ten Statements provide Jewish scholars with a way to order relationships such as between God and His people, between a person and their family and between people generally.[36] In this way we grasp a central aspect of Jewish life and return to something that is becoming familiar — the important virtue of right relationships.

In addition, the same Ten Statements have come to be seen as categories under which all 613 *mitzvot* (or rules of The Law) can be placed. This too helps us in understanding Jewish virtues for in the first five statements we see an emphasis on respect for God and for parents/teachers who act in His place. While in the second five statements we are, at first, confronted by justice-based prohibitions. But in flipping these prohibitions to make positive statements we also learn about respect for one's self and others.[37]

But beyond *Torah* we also have a rich wisdom literature to help us understand Jewish virtues. Given that we have already touched on other forms of wisdom literature from the ancient past let's not tarry too long here but simply say that the Jewish wisdom literature is astonishing for its utter humanity. In it we identify with Job's pain, rejoice and anguish in equal measure with the psalmist and nod knowingly as an old king of *Ecclesiastes* describes how his life has come to naught. Within this wisdom literature we can also clearly identify virtues such as forbearance, courage, wisdom, temperance and justice amongst others.

Although having ancient roots Judaism remains a vibrant religion today. Therefore we should also consider Jewish virtues in their contemporary context. In doing so four stand out: courage; hope; justice; and charity.

Without explicitly saying it former Chief Rabbi Sacks highlighted the value of courage and hope when he declared,

> Against that fear [of death] we say from the beginning of *Ellul* to *Sukkot* that monumental psalm of David: 'The Lord is my light and my salvation. Whom then shall I fear? The Lord is the stronghold of my life. Of whom then shall I be afraid?' ... Let us take to heart King David's insistence that faith is stronger than fear.[38]

While courage and hope are virtues of the individual Judaism is the religion of God's chosen people. As such, the corporate virtues of justice and charity are likely to be of equal, if not greater, importance; and of them we read,

While cultivating a pious life through study and contemplation is at the heart of Jewish worship of God, *Torah* makes clear that that piety must necessarily translate in society through a striving for justice. ...
Even the righteous and those who practice other *mitzvot* can be punished by God for failure to protest against injustice. Silence or passivity in effect communicate compliance or acquiescence to what is wrong. As Holocaust survivor Rabbi Abraham Joshua Heschel wrote, 'Indifference to evil is more insidious than evil itself.'[39]

And as for charity,

> ... *gemilut hasadim*, [is] often translated as 'loving kindness'. Whereas *tzedakah* is focused on monetary assistance and the poor, *Gemilut hasadim* [sic] is performed spontaneously out of a spirit of generosity and benevolence, given to both rich and poor, living and dead ... [there is] no minimum or maximum standard [for this] ...[39]

Charity is, in the end, the very soul of community life.

Turning now to the second of the Abrahamic faiths, Christianity began as a small Jewish sect some two thousand years ago on the rocky shores of the Sea of Galilee. However it would be a mistake to consider Jesus to be simply a teacher of ethics. For believers He is no less than the Messiah! For this reason His mission was not so much to teach a better way to live but to reconcile people to God. Yet, to the extent that Jesus' ministry was helpful to people in the here-and-now it had a virtue ethic.

In understanding this aspect of Jesus' ministry we must first remember that He and his disciples did not live in a virtues neutral world. They were Roman subjects in a Greek-speaking part of the Empire and by ethnicity Jews. As such, Jesus' virtue ethics was not invented so much as grounded in *Torah* and referenced the wider culture. Then again, that a three year ministry would ultimately have global implications suggests that He also spoke to something very deep within us all.

So what was Jesus' virtue ethic? Beginning with His Sermon on the Mount Jesus gave light to the virtues of meekness, righteousness, mercy, purity of heart and being peaceable.[40] He also implied the importance of courage and steadfastness when he warned his listeners that they would be persecuted for their beliefs. But Jesus' Sermon on the Mount is not remembered for its shopping-list approach to virtue. It's power lies in its subversive implications. Without stating it directly Jesus was actually preaching against false virtues, such as arrogance and hypocrisy, which are beloved of the powerful everywhere.

Later in his ministry Jesus goes so far as to name one virtue, before all others, which sums up His approach to living well. Under the guise of a prickly question from a legal scholar Jesus extracts the following answer, "Love the Lord your God with all your heart and with all your soul and with all your strength and with all your mind'; and, 'Love your neighbour as yourself.".[41] Not to be made a fool of the scholar pushed back asking, 'And who is my neighbour?'. Jesus now checkmated him by telling the Parable of the Good Samaritan which is a story of fulsome love shown by a despised Samaritan traveller to a bashed Jew lying beside a road. So, in moving well past the legal question of '... who is my neighbour?' Jesus provided a singular virtue ethic framed by unbounded love.

But can love be a virtue? Yes it can. John the Evangelist took up this point in antiquity just like Bishop Michael Curry did so when he preached on the power of love at the wedding of Prince Harry and Meghan Markle.[42] But love can only be a virtue when wrestled from the grip of sentimentality and made practical in the lives of people. As a simple demonstration of this point it was Christians who pioneered social welfare in antiquity, large public hospitals in the Middle Ages and social justice in the 19th century (e.g., William Wilberforce).[43, 44] Christians even had a hand in writing the *Universal Declaration of Human Rights* in the 20th century. Love is therefore practical and very much a virtue.

Yet to begin and end our discussion of Christianity so quickly would be a travesty for this religion and its adherents have shaped the West and influenced the development of every continent in some way. So, to extend our discussion a little let's briefly touch on the lives of just two prominent Christians: the archetypal St Paul; and the intellectual giant — and virtue scholar — St Thomas Aquinas. While we could have just as easily delved into the lives of early Christian martyrs such as St Catherine, great teachers including St Francis of Assisi, or reformers like Martin Luther, the lives of Paul and Aquinas speak directly to our argument.

While St Peter may have been entrusted by Jesus with the care of the Church it was his counterpart Paul who framed much of the New Testament and thus what can loosely be described as a prototypic Christian worldview. Both a skilled political operator and theologian on the move Paul's own writings give us the clearest picture of the man and the virtues he espoused. Of himself we can consider the virtues of courage and diligence to be foremost. For here was a man who was tempered by harsh circumstance and who struggled in faithfulness over a long ministry that would ultimately claim his life.

Yet in spite of his personal trials Paul was not overcome with despair and gladly proclaimed a virtues-potent, or Spirit-filled, way of life to all believers. For example, as an observant Jew he would have been aware of the Gifts of the Spirit put forward in the Old Testament book of *Isaiah* which either state or imply virtues such as wisdom, fortitude and righteousness amongst others.[45] Interestingly, in putting forward his own list Paul takes a more decidedly mystical approach while also retaining core virtues such as wisdom.[46] But he doesn't stop there. In his letter to the church in Galatia (i.e., modern day Anatolia) Paul also describes something he calls the Fruit of the Spirit being '… love, joy, peace, forbearance, kindness, goodness, faithfulness, gentleness and self-control …'.[47] Not only is this an excellent list of Christian virtues but importantly each is consistent with Jesus' preaching on the overall virtue of love.

Finally, Paul also shifted people's understanding of virtue when he used it to help heal rifts in fractious churches. By considering virtue as a corporate good, rather than for individual gain, Paul created a powerful virtue ethic based around relationship. In a number of his letters Paul takes up this issue of corporate virtue and extols believers to be peaceable, humble, well-intentioned, generous and forbearing. All of which can be summed up in a brief passage from his magnum opus — *The Letter to the Romans*,

> Love must be sincere. Hate what is evil; cling to what is good. Be devoted to one another in brotherly love. Honour one another above yourselves. Never be lacking in zeal … Be joyful in hope, patient in affliction, faithful in prayer. Share with God's people who are in need. Practice hospitality.
>
> Bless those who persecute you … Live in harmony with one another. Do not be proud, but be willing to associate with people of low position. Do not be conceited.
>
> Do not repay anyone evil for evil … [L]ive at peace with everyone …
> Do not be overcome by evil, but overcome evil with good.[48]

While Christians, and the Church, have often failed to heed Paul's message what cannot be disputed is both its emphasis and importance. Utopian — yes. But an ethic which has burrowed deeply into the Western tradition over two millennia.

Moving some 12 centuries forward in time we could not conclude our discussion of Christian virtues without a brief discussion of St Thomas Aquinas for he was a virtue scholar *par excellence*. He was also the person most responsible for founding the Western tradition when he looked to both Jerusalem and Athens for inspiration. As such he bequeaths us a legacy from both St Paul and Aristotle. More importantly, however, Aquinas' lasting contribution may very well have been to place that which is good, or virtuous, near the centre of Western thought when, just as easily, we could have developed a worldview characterised by cold utility or wanton excess.

Born into a well-off family living in the town of Aquino, which is situated between Rome and Naples, the young Thomas came of age just at the time when classical Greek thought was being reintroduced back into Europe and universities such as Oxford, Cambridge and the Sorbonne were establishing their reputations. Being both bright and energetic he threw himself into this new world of learning and emerged, years later, as one of its greatest champions.[49]

Aquinas' seminal text was the augustly titled *Summa Theologica* in which he not only drew together classical scholarship and Christian thought, but demonstrated a precise method of reasoning which is wonderful to behold even today. In particular, Aquinas extended and updated Aristotle. In terms of the virtues Aquinas' greatest achievement was to argue for the addition of three theological virtues by building on the 1st century work of St Paul. For Aquinas faith, hope and love were not just 'human goods' but equally as beautiful as the cardinal virtues of prudence, courage, temperance and justice. The only difference being that unlike the cardinal virtues, which are intellectual in origin, the three theological virtues were gifts of God alone.[50]

That Aquinas' argument was right is perhaps best suggested by the fact that the three theological virtues remain areas of active research even today. For faith is linked to wellbeing; hope is vital in the treatment of depression; and love is linked to longevity. His was a rich summary of the Christian life and one which has wide appeal.

Having now discussed virtues inherent in both Judaism and Christianity let's shift our attention to the youngest of the Abrahamic faiths — Islam.[51] According to an early biographer Muhammad was born in Mecca in 570AD. By lineage he was a member of the prominent Banu Hashim clan of the Quraysh tribe, but such distinctions mean little to an orphan. In fact Muhammad never got to know his father, Abdullah, and probably had only a scattering of memories of his mother, Aminah. Luckily, the young Muhammad did find a lasting home when he came under his uncle's protection and so it was in the household of Abu Talib that he would grow into manhood.

Abu Talib taught Muhammad well, even having him take part in a tribal council aged only 12. Watching on the young adolescent got to observe the older men debate whether a person's clan status should be sufficient grounds for protection when a dispute flared up. For a society in which blood feuds were common, and justice haphazard, this was an important point to settle amongst the elders. Ultimately the old men came to the conclusion that the righteousness of a person's case, and not their status, should guide matters of law in Mecca. For Muhammad this Pact of the Virtuous, as it became known, was to have a lasting impression. So much so that a strong belief in justice was to become a guiding principle of Islam.

At 40 years of age Muhammad had his first revelation. Ultimately, these encounters would continue off-and-on for the rest of his life and eventually be compiled into what we know today as the *Qur'an*.

The *Qur'an* is an interesting, and important, book whether you are Muslim or not. Not only is Islam the majority religion in countries from North Africa all the way to Indonesia, but is the world's fastest growing religion.[52] For followers of the two other Abrahamic faiths it may be surprising to realise that the *Qur'an* honours both Moses and Jesus as prophets and thus provides points of coherence and dissonance between the faiths. While, for those people interested in world affairs, the *Qur'an* has particular value for it provides a window into Muslim cultural identity. An identity founded in Abraham's first, but abandoned, child.

As for the *Qur'an* itself, its message is encapsulated in four ideas. First, God is unique, He is one. Therefore Islam is a staunchly monotheistic religion. Second, the *Qur'an* is the word of God. Even the sayings and actions of Muhammad, as written in the *Hadith*, cannot compare with it. Third, Muslims are called to prayer and good deeds. In this way Islam is a practical religion. Fourth, and finally, there will be a Day of Judgement in which each person will be '… paid back for what [they] did …' in this life.[51, 53] Justice, therefore, is central to the divine plan.

But to read the *Qur'an* clearly, and extract virtues from it, takes a level of scholarship for Islam is not a monolithic religion so much as a loose confederation. Therefore when we want to search for virtues we need to be aware that the two main factions of Islam, the *Sunni* and the *Shi'a*, take contrasting positions on important topics while each has developed within it a diversity of schools, be they legal or theological. Even at the individual level a Muslim may describe themselves as a 'literalist, traditionalist, reformer, mystic' or even a 'rationalist.'[51]

Intellectually the *Qur'an* also needs to be read within a framework that values subtle reasoning.[51] For example, while the *Qur'an* stipulates the amputation of a hand for theft this was overlooked in times of famine as far back as the second caliph.[54] The caliph's reasoning being that to do otherwise would be to violate the overall intent of the message for the sake of a single verse. The Muslim perspective on war, to use another example, is also a clever demonstration of reasoning. For now the earlier revelations of Muhammad, which uphold peace, are held in tension with later revelations about the use of armed conflict for self-protection. In this way peace is valued, but not at any price. Islam is also an international religion and so has had to adapt to local cultural practices. According to the reasoning of scholars and jurists, assuming local practices do not conflict with the *Qur'an*, and hence *shari'ah*, they are passively accepted. And as for *shari'ah* itself while some jurists would codify it the scholars prefer to leave it as a wide open space. For after all it is a way of life — a path to be followed — which leads to water.[55]

Having said this let's now focus our attention on Islamic virtues.[56] Of prime importance to a Muslim is their relationship with God. Right belief links faith with understanding to give right conduct. The effect of which is to bring about the experience of *islam* (i.e., peace) in the life of the believer.[51, 57] But the quality of this relationship is different to that understood by both Jews and Christians. For in Islam there can be no familiarity with God as Jews had in the desert of Sinai, while it would be extraordinary for a Muslim to address God as 'Abba, Father' (i.e., Daddy) as Christian do. In this way a Muslim's relationship with God emphasises only the holy and explains why virtues such as humility, patience and gratitude are so important.[58, 59, 60]

In addition, maintaining right relationships between people also characterises virtue. In this case through the exercise of justice and kindness. Concentrating our efforts on justice the controversial scholar Tariq Ramadan writes, 'Many eminent Muslim scholars and thinkers have affirmed, from the earliest days, that the supreme Islamic virtue is justice.'[61] It is even one of the names of God. However the justice discussed in the *Qur'an* is of a particular, and subtle, kind. For example we read,

> We decreed for them a life for a life, an eye for an eye, a nose for a nose, an ear for an ear, a tooth for a tooth, and a wound for a wound. But if a man charitably forbears from retaliation, his remission shall atone for him.[62]

The same revenge sentiment is also echoed elsewhere in the *Qur'an*.[63] But ... it is only lawful to take revenge to the extent of the harm done and this presents a catch-22. For who is to judge equivalence? An 'eye for an eye ...' might sound obvious but brawls and melees are rarely ever so neat. And what if a vengeful person gets it wrong and goes overboard? They now become a sinner and open themselves to judgement. Ultimately this form of justice has everyone realise the futility of revenge, the virtue inherent in forbearance and forgiveness and that in all matters God is sovereign.

In addition, relationships flourish with kindness. In fact justice without kindness, or mercy for that matter, is cold. It has all the hallmarks of a vice without leaving the bruises. But kindness goes beyond being a corrective for justice. In daily life it is expressed in overtly positive ways. Be it in the care for others, in alms giving, or in hospitality Muslims excel.[64] Indeed, if you have ever eaten at a Muslim home you soon realise that hospitality, as a joyous form of kindness, is elevated to the level of a virtue all its own.

Finally, Muslims take human dignity very seriously. What's interesting is that dignity comes in two forms. Initially it is a gift from God and so given to all people independent of their status.[65] But there is also that form of dignity which we bestow on ourselves by acting virtuously and by displaying a nobility of character. For Muslims, Muhammad was the exemplar of this. But what sort of virtue is dignity? In fact it has been a virtue from the earliest times although typically given a different name. In so much as dignity is consistent with self-respect, speaks of integrity and of a good reputation it relates to personal honour. A form of honour that becomes embedded within a community's honour as seen by how relationships are structured and maintained.

To see how these ancient virtues play out in a contemporary context we need do no more than turn briefly to the *Cairo Declaration on Human Rights* as the Muslim-world's response to the West's *Universal Declaration of Human Rights*.[66] For instance, justice and kindness come together in Article 3(a) which states,

> ... in case of armed conflict, it is not permissible to kill non-belligerents such as old men, women and children. The wounded and the sick shall have the right to medical treatment; and prisoners of war shall have the right to be fed, sheltered and clothed.

While honour is dealt with both by declaring the family as '... the foundation of society ...' (i.e., Article 5[a]) and by highlighting the importance of an individual's reputation (i.e., '... one's good name ...', in Article 4). But perhaps the most interesting aspect of the *Cairo Declaration* for Western readers is the subjugation of all human rights to *shari'ah*. In this way honouring God is, in the end, paramount.

We have now wound our way around the three Abrahamic faiths and their perception of virtue. But whether we look to Jerusalem, Rome or Mecca we find remarkable consistency. In each of these three significant world religions positive relationships, justice and compassion all have their place. Even if violence is often committed in God's name.

Question 1.3

If you belong to one of the Abrahamic faiths what has been your experience of virtue? How have the virtues of your faith tradition influenced your life?

Western virtues

Although some would make the argument that Christian virtues are Western virtues this would be simplistic. While it is true that they represent a cluster of relevant virtues the argument fails to consider how social and environmental pressures shape a society. Moreover, when discussing the West we have to consider an immense time span and several stages of development therein. For this reason discussing Western virtues is an immensely difficult task likely to get us lost somewhere between the fall of Rome in the 5th century AD and World War I in the 20th. Moreover, there is simply no adequate way to cover a geography that extends from the bright blue waters of the Mediterranean to Nordic fjords and, in recent centuries, extends to other continents as well. To this end all we can do is provide the headlines and a little commentary hoping this will be enough to give us a flavour for Western virtues as they have been historically understood.

The way we intend to do this is to first focus on Rome as the cradle of the West. From our discussion we hope you will get an appreciation for what virtues there were at the beginning. We will then assume the Dark Ages and medieval world were little more than a continuation of a Roman mindset applied within a feudal political system. Ultimately, we hope to show that the early modern age — which gave birth to our own — was important for just one reason. It concluded by swapping one key virtue for another. The effects of which we feel even today. Together, these three vignettes should give a sense of the development of Western virtues even if our discussions are curtailed.

To talk of Roman virtues is also complex for here was a civilisation, not just a society. Geographically it spanned the Mediterranean, pushed towards the Middle East and extended as far north as Germany and Britain. It also lasted for an immense period of time. What's more, the value of Rome to our discussion is immense given that it came to shape our law, language and religion. No matter how difficult to pin-down Roman virtues cannot be ignored.

In taking a snapshot of Roman virtues we can do no better than look at Maximus' *Factorum ac Dictorum Memorabilium Libri IX* (i.e., *The Nine Books of Memorable Deeds and Sayings*).[67] This text is a treasure trove of upper-class Roman values at a time when the Republic had not yet faded from memory, nor was the Empire in its final bloated phase. As such it captures a slice of Roman life at a critical juncture in its history. Overall the text contains 1000 short stories, or snippets of gossip, that together give an unrivalled view into the lives of men and women from so long ago.

Given the scope of Maximus' work we can't hope to go into detail but we can, at least, list some of the virtues he explored. For example, hard virtues such as military discipline, courage, endurance and a determination to succeed are obviously going to be discussed by a good Roman. Yet, surprisingly enough, Maximus holds these in tension with quieter virtues such as self-control, wisdom, generosity and compassion — even love. Finally, for those acting as public servants he recognises a third category of virtue and includes within it a necessity to hold the public's trust, to act loyally towards friends and benefactors and to show gratitude. Rome, after all, was an honour culture.[68]

Let's now chew on two snippets of Roman life. In doing so you'll soon get an appreciation for Roman virtues. The first story is the gossipy tale of Tertia Aemilia and thus presents a female perspective on proper Roman behaviour. The second story relates to old one-eyed Zaleucus — and we'll leave you to discover how he lost that eye in a moment.

So,

> Tertia Aemilia, the wife of Scipio Africanus and the mother of Cornelia, was a woman of such kindness and patience that, although she knew that her husband was carrying on with a little serving girl, she looked the other way, [as she thought it unseemly for] a woman to prosecute her great husband, Africanus, a conqueror of the world, for a dalliance. So little was she interested in revenge that, after Scipio's death, she freed the girl and gave her in marriage to one of her own freedmen.[69]

Excluding Scipio Africanus' obvious vices wasn't Tertia Aemilia an understanding wife ... But more than that she displayed with great dignity the virtues of self-control, kindness, generosity and even honour by protecting both her own reputation and that of her husband's.

By comparison the story of Zaleucus brings together a different set of Roman virtues including courage, justice, wisdom and mercy. But more importantly it does so in a most unexpected way. Let's read ...

> Nothing could be braver than the following acts of justice. Zaleucus had protected the city of Locri with the most beneficial and useful laws. His son was found guilty on the charge of adultery, and in accordance with the law that Zaleucus himself established, he should have had both his eyes gouged out. All the citizens, out of respect for the father, wanted to exempt the son from the rigours of the law, but Zaleucus resisted them for a long time.

> Finally, he was won over by the pleas of the people, so he gouged out one of his own eyes first, and then one of his son's, thereby leaving each of them with the ability to see. He carried out the punishment required by his own law, but with an admirable blend of justice, he divided himself between the roles of a merciful father and a strict lawmaker.[68]

But Rome could not last, no superpower ever does. Riven by internal strife and external threats Rome fractured in the 5th century AD. While the Eastern Empire would continue in majestic fashion for another thousand years its Western neighbour fared much worse. But this was not a dark age as we were taught at school. Boethius still wrote his philosophy, far to the north great sagas were composed to honour local heroes and, in time, the most beautiful illuminated manuscripts would be painstakingly created by cloistered monks.

In terms of virtue, however, the feudal world concentrated on only three — courage, diligence and honour. To demonstrate this we need look no further than the stories of Beowulf, Arthur and Roland. Right through the Medieval Period stories of this sort were loved and speak to us of what the people of that time held as important. But even more than courage and diligence the virtue of honour was paramount.

In fact honour was the only ubiquitous virtue of Medieval Europe. Nor was honour an exclusively marshal, or male, virtue for everyone owed a debt of honour to someone else in this feudal world. Children to their parents, wives to husbands, apprentices to their master, peasant farmers to their local lord and knights to greater lords still. And all owed a debt of honour to their king, emperor and ultimately to the Pope himself. Be it in obedience, an annual rent, or service at arms Western Europe was one vast hierarchy built on mutual obligation. Yet honour was not just about how a society was structured but also how it functioned. For honour was also played out in specific ways. For example, a knight could insist on trial by combat to uphold his honour while a lady of the court would protect her honour (i.e., chastity) at all costs. Therefore, and in spite of class distinctions, honour was Medieval society's guiding principle.

Inevitably the Medieval Period had to give way to change. Into this new world first came the likes of the Medici bankers and then, on their coat-tails, all sorts of commoners with a *penchant* for business large and small. The Early Modern Period had arrived. But honour still persisted, for the *nouveau riche* gentry sought to emulate the nobility by carrying swords, bearing armorial badges and having portraits painted. They were a new social class with deep pockets and fragile egos keen to uphold the old ways for new ends.

In fact it was not until the 18th and 19th centuries that we saw the first great shift in European virtues since Roman times. Coinciding roughly with the French Revolution honour slowly gave way to justice as the pre-eminent European virtue.

While the Third Estate forced political justice on the French nobility, in London people such as William Wilberforce took up the call for emancipatory justice and in so doing ended the slave trade. In the decades which followed Marx and Engels argued and plotted economic justice for factory workers. While, by the end of the 19th century, even Pope Leo XIII had joined the fray calling for social justice.

So there you have it, a short summation of European virtues bookended between Rome and our own time. Who'd have thought. The takeaway message is this: courage; diligence; honour; and justice. On these four virtues stand all the achievements of the West.

Question 1.4

How do the virtues of honour and justice play out in your own life?

Asian virtues

To complete our cross-cultural survey of the virtues, and so discover those which may be considered foundational, we have one last feat to perform. Somehow we have to adequately deal with Asian virtues even though they can, to Western ears, be the most mysterious of all. While we could make life easier for ourselves by considering individual countries, and comment on their national characteristics, this would be a 'red herring' for countries reinvent themselves in revolution from time to time. On the whole it is better to avoid national sentiment and consider those philosophical/religious pillars which have supported Asian cultures for millennia.[70] It is in them that we will find a clear path to virtue.

Beginning with Hinduism, given its ancient roots, we can begin to grasp what may be considered virtuous practices in amongst a complex set of scriptures and cosmology by focusing our attention on the Five *Yamas* and *Niyamas* as the basis for an ethical life.[70] Bound up with the practice of yoga and its sutras we read of:[71]

- *Ahimsa*, or non-violence,
- *Satya*, or truthfulness,
- *Asteya*, or non-stealing,
- *Brahmacharya*, or sexual restraint,
- *Aparigraha*, non-avarice/greed,
- *Sauca*, purity of mind, speech and body,
- *Santosa*, contentment with your circumstances,

- *Tapas*, self-discipline,
- *Svadhyaya*, study in self-reflection,
- *Ishvarapranidhana*, contemplation of the highest reality.

Of this list the first five precepts are the *Yamas* and the second five are the *Niyamas*. Breaking them down we can see that *yamas* relate to an ethical way to live and are typically phrased according to 'Don't ….'. *Niyamas*, by contrast, are couched in terms of 'Do …' and focus on religious observance and spiritual awakening. Although the *Yamas* are often considered more virtue orientated, being about just and temperant ways of living, the *Niyamas* also consider virtues such as self-discipline, or diligence.

Nor do Hindu scholars stop there. Amongst the many texts which discuss ethics ten *yamas* are often mentioned, not five, and these extend to virtues including forgiveness, fortitude, compassion, sincerity and the avoidance of gluttony.[72] As for *niyamas* they too can be extended out to ten in number.[73] While many of these practices are religious in orientation they do include virtues such as generosity and humility.

Looking at Hindu virtues from a slightly different perspective we can bring together the idea of *yama* and *niyama* under the concept of *dharma* which speaks to '… the moral order of the universe and a code of living ….'.[74] From this perspective we learn that there are two sorts of *dharma*, one relative to a person's position in life, and one absolute. *Svadharma* is *dharma* as duty and is conditional on person's age, gender, and social standing. By contrast *sadharana* is common to all. Within this framework *ahimsa* (i.e., non-violence) and *satya* (i.e., truthfulness) are virtues of the highest standing while other virtues such as the forbearance to forgive, self-control, wisdom of different sorts and various forms of justice play a supporting role.[75]

Turning now to that other great Indian tradition, Buddhism, we glimpse something of Buddhist virtues reasonably simply when we read, 'To keep away from all evil, cultivate good, and purify one's mind is the advice of all Buddhas'.[76] Yet this statement is so precisely wrought that we may miss the point if we don't consider it within a larger context.

Three main forms of Buddhism are practiced: *Theravada*; *Māhāyna*; and *Vajrayana*. They also correspond to broad geographical areas. *Theravada* is practiced in South and South East Asia, *Māhāyna* in East Asia and *Vajrayana* in Tibet through to Northern Asia. Not surprisingly, these forms of Buddhism have points of overlap and contrast. Even within the larger *Māhāyna* tradition we read, '[t]he *Yogācārins* criticised the *Mādhyamikas* for tending towards nihilism, whilst the *Mādhyamikas* criticised the *Yogācārins* for tending to substantialism, setting up mind as an ultimate entity when all was equally 'empty" (authors' italics).[77] As such, we must be careful not to treat any statement about Buddhism as wholly correct in, and of, itself. Moreover, a Buddhist mindset can confound Western analytical thinking for reality is held provisionally and the practice of Zen is the practice of nothing in particular. So, as we move forward, recognise overlap with Western virtues but do not hold to this too tightly. A Buddhist worldview is all its own.[78]

Given this, what can we say of Buddhism and its virtues that may be considered approachable? To this end let's turn to the Four Noble Truths as the canonical statements of Buddhism. In brief, they relate to the nature of suffering; its relationship to craving; the benefits of stopping this craving; and how to achieve this release. In turn the fourth Noble Truth is itself known as the Noble Eightfold Path.

Of great help to us in discovering Buddhist virtues are the eight virtuous practices of the Noble Eightfold Path (see Table 1.1). For example, virtues such

TABLE 1.1
The Noble Eightfold Path of Buddhism[80]

Purpose	Stage	Meaning of stage
Wisdom	Right understanding (*Samma-Ditthi*)	To understand the nature of reality and the path set-out by Buddha.
	Right attitude (*Samma-Sankappa*)	To develop a conscientious and compassionate attitude.
Moral virtues	Right speech (*Samma-Vaca*)	One's speech should be direct and uplifting.
	Right action (*Samma-Kammanta*)	A person should avoid doing harm (e.g., killing, stealing and sexual immorality).
	Right livelihood (*Samma-Ajiva*)	A good livelihood is one which is meritorious but also ethical in its intent and practice.
Concentration	Right effort (*Samma-Vayama*)	To diligently focus one's efforts on that which brings wholesomeness/wellness.
	Right mindfulness (*Samma-Sati*)	To develop an awareness of things as they truly are.
	Right concentration (*Samma-Samadhi*)	To detach, gain inner stillness and achieve a state of equanimity.

as justice, temperance, diligence, truthfulness and compassion are all present, but so are others. Not only does wisdom get interpreted in a new way but what do we make of virtues related to wholesomeness, mindfulness and equanimity? In addition, that each virtuous practice is preceded by the word *Samma* what are we to make of this? In simple terms *Samma* pertains to 'Right …' as in 'Right speech', 'Right action' etc.. For a Westerner this probably invokes notions of right and wrong but such categories are not so helpful here. The intention is not a value judgement so much as to impart the idea of 'Holistic speech,' or 'Holistic action' etc.. In this way Buddhist virtues tend to sit more gently upon people even if many remain nebulous. So, while the Noble Eightfold Path is simple to describe, and is certainly virtuous, it is not always clear or adaptable.[79]

Perhaps a more practical way to appreciate Buddhist virtues is to look at the vows expected of people if they wish to enter more deeply into the spiritual life and then reduce these to the Five Precepts which represent the '… basic building blocks of a healthy society and foundation of the spiritual practice for lay people.'.[80] While vows may differ depending upon circumstance, within the Tibetan tradition they can be refined to 10 in number and be divided three ways. Therefore vows pertaining to virtuous actions of the body revolve around:

- Not taking life,
- Not taking possessions by force/deceit, and
- Avoiding sexual immorality.

Vows pertaining to virtuous speech include:

- Not deceiving others,
- Avoiding slander,
- Avoiding harsh speech coming from envy or anger, and
- Avoiding idle talk.

Finally three vows pertain to what are called virtuous actions of the mind. They are:

- To avoid thoughts of greed,
- To not be malicious, and
- To avoid false perceptions of others and the world.[80]

In turn these can be distilled into the Five Precepts:

- Abstain from killing,
- Abstain from stealing,
- Abstain from indulging in inappropriate sexual relationships,
- Abstain from lying, and
- Abstain from ingesting intoxicants.

Not surprisingly, there is resonance between these vows and precepts and the Noble Eightfold Path. More broadly, there is even overlap with Hindu virtues. And as for the virtues themselves we see a strong emphasis on temperance and justice which leads to a particular sort of wisdom founded on a deep care for one's self and for other people.[81] Finally, and almost by-the-by, the practice of Buddhism is hard work. If you are not convinced then just ask anyone who has attended a Buddhist retreat. Therefore, as a byproduct of living the Noble Eightfold Path one additional virtue must also be recognised — persistence. Without it, movement towards enlightenment as the end-point of Buddhist practice would be impossible.

Question 1.5

> If you have practiced either Hinduism or Buddhism what has been your experience of the virtues? How have these influenced your life?

Although Buddhism crossed the Himalayas into China two millennia ago the Chinese already had indigenous virtue practices of their own. Like the Greeks these practices were also born out of tumult; except, in the Chinese context, virtue largely remained a matter of politics and power. For some, this meant withdrawal from worldly affairs as virtue (i.e., *wu wei*), for others it meant cultivating a way of being that was flexible to changing events. As to specific virtues, the records and literature of the day suggest three important personal attributes amongst many others: (1) respect for ancestors; (2) the avoidance of arrogance; and (3) temperance. In this way propriety is upheld and self-cultivation furthered.[16] Consistent with this short list one philosophical system began to rise in prominence; ultimately coming to influence neighbouring countries such as Japan, Korea and Vietnam. Indeed Confucianism is even lauded in the West. For these reasons we must explore it further.

Confucius was a rough contemporary of Gautama Buddha writing at the start of the 5th century BC. Although born into a noble family this assured him of nothing given his father's polygamy and untimely death. While starting life in humble circumstances Confucius' fame grew when he opened a school for all, not just for the well off. Ultimately he fell under the notice of the Duke of Lu. Confucius was now honoured with senior government posts, rising eventually to become a Minister within the Duke's government. Whether he succumbed to court intrigue, or became bored with the administration of government, Confucius left Lu at the age of 55 to travel about China offering his services where they might be useful. However while this new enterprise began in hope it was, for the most part, an unhappy time for Confucius' intellectual skills went relatively unnoticed. So eventually, with 'tail between his legs', Confucius returned to Lu and settled down into quiet retirement.[70, 82]

To understand Confucius' teachings we have the benefit of his writings and, in particular, the *Analects*. Yet his system of thought is also unique, if not idiosyncratic at times. But if we are prepared to reflect on our own lives and our relationships, good and bad, we can capture something of what he was trying to say.

To begin with, Confucius labelled the ultimate virtue as *ren*. Sometimes translated as generosity, or benevolence, it represents our true nature which Confucius held to be essentially good. Therefore *ren* sums up the best in humanity.[16] This point is exemplified in the *Analects* when 'Fan Ch'ih asked about *ren*. The Master [simply] said, 'Love your fellow men ….'[82] Therefore while *ren* may be expressed in acts of benevolence we most often *feel it* when, from time to time, we share a deep sense of connectedness with others. By implication, *ren* also describes the wellspring from which we should act. Indeed it is said that all other virtues descend from *ren* and sum together to make *ren*.[83, 84]

Next we come across *li*. This virtue relates to notions of respect, but more properly denotes ideas of '… propriety or reverence ….'[85] Thus *li* governs how one conducts one's self for, as Confucius wrote, '… Boldness without … propriety, becomes insubordination …' and thus virtueless.[86]

At a broader level *li* also describes that invisible web of relationships which binds families together and brings us all into community as much as the relative ease with which we relate to others.[16] Confucius went on to detail his understanding of *li* by identifying five types of relationships, all of which required a deliberate way of engagement if they were to work well. So, in the case of a son relating to his father there is the expectation of filial piety, or obedience. But, to 'balance the ledger', the father is equally obligated to show kindness in return. As such *shu*, or reciprocity, now becomes central to a

Confucian understanding of relationships as much as the Golden Rule.[87] In this way *shu* imparts a sense of justice to otherwise problematic relationships.

The virtues of *yi* and *zhi* are similar, but also different. While *yi* can be translated as 'righteousness', it is perhaps better thought about as honesty or uprightness.[16] Moreover, it also contains within it the implication of having an intuition for what is right to do, rather than just knowing what is morally appropriate (i.e., *chih*); even although circumstance, morality and decision-making still remain aspects of *yi*.[88] As such, *yi* has within it the idea that there is an inherent, or absolute, form of 'right' which helps a person identify one particular action amongst the many possible in any given situation. Moreover, this right action is right irrespective of its consequences. Therefore, within a Confucian worldview 'right' is judged on motive more than outcome. This is quite at odds with a Western mindset which would have 'the ends justify the means'.[84]

While *yi* is an intuitive way to solve problems the more solution-focused approach is expressed by the virtue of *zhi*. This virtue uses assembled facts to construct knowledge before applying that knowledge in right ways through the application of wisdom. It is, in a simple sense, a form of 'know how' and equivalent to the practical wisdom (i.e., *phronesis*) spoken of by the Greeks.[84, 87]

Finally there is the virtue of *xin*. This virtue suggests faithfulness and integrity.[89, 90] However, while faithfulness can be interpreted in a number of ways it is perhaps best translated according to keeping one's bond and therefore acting with integrity, if not honour. For Confucius it was also the basis on which to construct a stable government and, for us all, a well-functioning family and workplace.

Question 1.6

If you have been brought up in a Confucian culture what influence has it had on you? Are Confucian virtues simple, or hard, to implement in daily life?

We have now completed the final part of our cross-cultural survey and to my (i.e., Tom) mind the most interesting. While Asian virtues can sound a little daunting they provide us with ways to live and work not available if we followed only a rationalist Western mindset. For now we have a way to incorporate qualities like intentionality, intuition and extend notions of wisdom to consider questions of both reality and wholeness. In short, we recommend them to you.

So which virtues are the most important?

The business of this chapter has been to identify key virtues from around the world and thus extract a small set of foundational virtues which, together, represent who we are as humans in a deep and lasting way. But how are we going to sift all the good and noble qualities we have come across? To do this we will use the three criteria mentioned at the start of this section (p. 7–8). That is, foundational virtues must be:

1. practical, thus imparting a survival advantage,

2. found cross-culturally and over long spans of time,

3. and be few in number.

Using these criteria, and thinking back on all we have learnt, let's begin by excluding some qualities immediately. For example, although *Ma'at* has some value for us as the earliest recorded way of understanding right relationships we have only a limited historical record from which to interpret it. From across the world Confucius' concept of *yi* is also similarly vague. While some Hindu and Buddhist virtues are trapped within such specific philosophical systems as to isolate them from the larger corpus of virtue ethics.

On the flipside, what we can say is that a small group of qualities keeps getting named time-and-again as virtues. These must be the strong contenders for what, in the end, we will name as foundational virtues. For example, how often has wisdom been mentioned in one form or another? The same for temperance, justice and courage. The four cardinal virtues figure in just about every virtue system we can find. But so does honour. Be it expressed in terms of right relationship with others, or as a matter of personal integrity, honour appears to be a ubiquitous virtue. But there are other virtues often noted as well. What about diligence? Although not always mentioned explicitly it is inherent in the practice of one's religion (e.g., Jews and Muslims) or in diligently working towards enlightenment (e.g., Buddhism). One could even pair diligence and courage in much of the literature of Medieval Europe. And then there is a virtue which is never given a single name but goes by *ren*, benevolence, love, charity, mercy, generosity and even includes forgiveness. It pops up time and again. For ease of description we will simply name it 'kindness'. So, in sum, we now have a putative list of seven candidate foundational virtues.

But there is also a problem with this list. When applied to particular circumstances, or in the context of decision-making, temperance does not work the same way as the other virtues. Whereas courage, diligence, wisdom, honour, justice and kindness are thoughtful ways to orientate yourself to the world temperance is often about the control of strong, if not impulsive, emotion. In this way temperance acts on other virtues. More particularly, temperance appears to guide wisdom. This idea being particularly appealing given that a temperate decision is so often a wise one. For these reasons we have chosen to subsume temperance under wisdom rather than consider it foundational in its own right. Although a little controversial we believe this accounts for the available evidence much better.

Having now reduced our list of candidate foundational virtues to six we now have to test if each has a survival advantage associated with it. If not, then the virtue in question is likely to be peripheral at best. To recognise the survival advantage in having courage, showing diligence and in demonstrating wisdom is fairly obvious. Without courage panic takes over and we crumble in the face of danger; without diligence we achieve nothing of worth in this life and in an earlier age we would likely have starved; and if we are foolish, and hence not wise, then life will likely be either short or miserable. But what of honour, justice and kindness, in what way might these virtues have a survival advantage? In answering this we need to recognise that these three virtues are all relational. That is, they exist between and amongst people. This is important for humans are a communal species. We lack claws, fur, or sharp teeth so must band together to cope in a hostile world. These three virtues assist us to do just that. Without going into detail honour organises relationships between people to produce both cohesion and a common purpose. For the individual honour also motivates them to play their part as a valued member of their community. Justice, on the other hand, is the mechanism which prevents a community ripping itself apart. For justice distributes fairness and heals broken relationships. Finally, kindness is an interesting virtue for it appears to defy evolutionary expectations in so much as grace is shown to the criminal and compassion to the undeserving. What survival value could there be in this for a community? Indeed communities can exist without kindness with ancient Sparta being a classic example. But if a community is organised this way three significant problems arise. Without a belief that one will be cared for crime rises as people develop a selfish attitude. This can fracture a community. In addition, unkind communities fail to harness their greatest resource — their people — for no potential is ever seen in the small, the weak or the injured. Finally, unkind communities will fail because they have little capacity to ask for help in times of trouble, nor might any help be forthcoming even if a plea was made. As such, kindness is of immense value for it ensures a community's survival for today and tomorrow.

So, these six virtues — Courage, Diligence, Wisdom, Honour, Justice and Kindness — are a small set, found cross-culturally and possess inherent survival advantage to those who master them. They are our foundational virtues and our keys to achieving excellence in the art of living.

Question 1.7

How have the six foundational virtues affected your life and made you who you are?

Activity 1.3

The six foundational virtues are all around us. In fact they are so much a part of who we are that we project them into the world in obvious, and not so obvious, ways. For example:

a. Pick a big cultural narrative or even a piece of literature. In it, look for characters and circumstances that speak to the six foundational virtues. If you are interested in Jungian Psychology think about how the six foundational virtues can be extended to become archetypes?

b. Or go for a wander around your city's art gallery. Look at how colonial painters of the 19th century, and fascist/communist art of the 20th century, represented Courage and Diligence. In what ways do statues of the Buddha represent Wisdom? How do the courtly paintings of van Dyck show off personal honour? How do images of the Last Judgement typify Justice? And what do representations of the bodhisattva Guanyin say about Kindness?

c. Finally, our public institutions such as Parliament, universities, the Church, military, courts of law and police also represent the same set of foundational virtues. See if you can align each foundational virtue with an institution.

Chapter 2

Courage

> Courage is the quality which guarantees all the others
> — Winston Churchill

Courage: Are we sure we know what it is?

We are all familiar with great stories of courage and triumph. Be it the sportsman who scores the winning point in the dying seconds of a match, or the decorated soldier who saves his mates through some superhuman act of bravery and self-sacrifice. This sort of mythologising is so much a part of our culture that we scarcely give it much thought. But in doing so we are probably promoting a particularly masculine ideal of Courage while also confusing it with heroics. In doing so we miss other examples of equal worth thus creating a lopsided view of this unique virtue. For instance, alongside great acts of physical courage we must also acknowledge the quiet courage of the person undergoing major surgery who knows their recovery will be slow and painful. Or what of moral courage? While we remember Dr Martin Luther King Jr for his civil rights activism this could not have happened without him being an exemplar of moral courage. A courage that remained steadfast even as an assassin laid in wait.[1] Only when we add these and other stories to the media's perception of Courage can we begin to understand this foundational virtue in all its magnificent totality.

Studying Courage

If we want to study something we usually need to bring it into a laboratory. But to do this for Courage is difficult. We could, for example, ask volunteers to handle a rather large and friendly spider as a measure of Courage. But this would, in truth, be an experiment about fear. Or, we could ask volunteers to hold their hands in a bucket of ice water as long as possible. But would we be testing for Courage or pain tolerance? Therefore Courage is a slippery thing to grasp.

What we need is a different approach. The one which recommends itself best is to ask people about their experience of Courage. To read their stories and listen to what they have to say. In doing so we learn of Courage directly and begin to pick up on important issues. But we must nevertheless select our stories of Courage carefully and to this end we have settled on two first-hand accounts of physical courage. What is particularly nice is that one story pertains to a man of great strength while the other is about a pair of daring young women.

Hazel Findlay and Emily Harrington: Rock climbing superstars

I (i.e., Tom) first heard of Hazel Findlay and Emily Harrington one day when watching a TV show about extreme rock climbing. Here were two diminutive young women in their 20s about to climb a shear kilometre high cliff in the Atlas Mountains of Morocco. The story of their 16-hour climb was also blogged by Emily and it forms our first account of Courage,

> We woke up at 3.30 am to begin our climb. We forced down some food and caffeine and hiked an hour and a half to the base of the route, beginning the first pitch at 6 am, just after first light.
>
> The first half of the wall is characterised by difficult technical slab climbing — meaning very few holds, spaced bolts, and little room for error when it comes to balance and technique. We were also onsighting which meant we had no idea where the holds were. There was no chalk on the wall because no climbers had been up there recently. It was the ultimate unknown challenge: just a 2,800-foot blank wall before us.

We climbed slowly through the first six pitches ... I fell at the very end while trying to onsight the hardest 7c+ (13a) pitch. After 45 meters [sic] of battling I failed, slipping off in a zone where no holds seemed to be (there were, I just wasn't finding them). I let out a heartbroken scream followed by a few sobs. There would be no repeating this pitch. I was already feeling tired and my skin was thin. We had far too much climbing left to keep moving so slowly ... We climbed onto a steeper, orange head wall ... The change in angle was welcoming for our skin and toes, which were aching from all the slab climbing, but now the pump was setting in and our forearms began to suffer ... The climbing was confusing and there were bushes and loose rocks intermingled among the solid stone. I finally committed to the run outs — actually grabbing one draw after I placed it because I felt off balance while trying to clip. I arrived at the belay on a massive ledge, confidence shattered and nerves fried. My mind and body were wrecked. I couldn't think straight. It was nearly 7 pm already. We had five pitches of hard climbing left and only one hour of daylight.

It was still my lead ... Hazel offered to take the lead but I said no. I wanted to turn it around. I focused and set off. I ignored the runouts, committed to the small holds that had begun to feel like razor blades, and just kept moving up in the fading light. I reached the anchors with a renewed attitude and psyche. But it was short lived. Hazel seconded and then took over the lead.

Now it was dark and freezing cold. I shivered and tried to be supportive as she quested up the next 7b pitch in the dark. Three times she broke a hold and came flying off the wall — a fit of frustrating screams and cursing. She kept trying again though, and eventually succeeded ...

In the end, she clipped maybe two bolts and placed a sketchy wire before reaching the anchors. I followed on top rope, feeling weird and shaky and desperately wanting to stand on horizontal ground after nearly 15 hours on the wall. When I reached the belay Hazel expressed that she felt it was too dark, and we were too cold and tired to safely continue ... There were only two pitches remaining ... and it looked like another cryptic horror fest. We opted to walk along the ledge until we reached a class 3 gully we had previously scrambled up when we climbed another route on the same wall the week before.

> We quickly but safely simul-climbed up the gulley, reaching the top at 10.30 pm — 16 1/2 hours after leaving the ground! Relief melted through me. We had reached the end. Our priority had been to free [climb] all of the pitches, but our main objective was to get to the top — a proud feat in itself.[2]

What a story! Simply climbing a ladder can give some people 'the willies', let alone 16 and a half hours on a cliff face. Holding this story in mind let's now turn to our second tale of Courage.

Mawson: A man on the edge

As to our second story of Courage …

> Sir Douglas Mawson was a bright and well-connected young Australian who, by the age of 30, was both an Antarctic veteran and ready to lead his own expedition. He was also described as having a '… splendid physique, [and an] astonishing indifference to frost'.[3]
>
> Mawson's great adventure, one which almost cost him his life, began on December 2, 1911. After a month's journey south he and his party arrived on the Antarctic coast at Cape Denison. This is when trouble first began. Rather than enjoying getting off the ship and stretching their legs the men could waste no time in constructing their hut as Mawson had found perhaps the most windswept place on Earth.
>
> Soon enough long summer days shortened and gave way to the long night of winter. Nevertheless Mawson and his men were snug enough in their little hut and could shut out the almost continuous blizzard. As winter finally gave way to the approaching summer Mawson readied his kit and organised his men. Ultimately he set out on a scientific study of King George V Land with two companions, Ninnis and Mertz, while other members of his party went in different directions.
>
> For five weeks Mawson, Ninnis and Mertz moved at speed mapping the coastline and collecting various rocks and fossils. However, events turned quickly. Some 500km out from base Ninnis, his sledge and dogs fell to their death when an ice bridge covering a crevasse gave way. In the midst of shock Mawson and Mertz quickly realised their own predicament, for Ninnis had most of the food and the tent.[4]

Turning for home Mawson and Mertz made a 27-hour dash for a discarded tent cover which would have to make do as their only form of shelter for the coming weeks. But worse was to come. Soon the remaining rations dwindled and the men were forced to butcher their dogs for food. This was a fateful decision for now they would have to do more of the heavy pulling while, unbeknown to them both, the rich dog livers they were consuming were slowly poisoning their bodies. Mertz fell sick all too soon and the last line of his diary simply reads as a tragic understatement, 'The dog meat does not seem to agree with me because yesterday I was feeling a little bit queasy'.[5] Soon he was beset with nausea and abdominal pain followed by dysentery. Mertz would ultimately lose skin, hair and finger nails as he withered away. His death was a bad one, for insanity and rage took over to the point that he bit off the tip of his little finger before finally collapsing.[6] And all the while Mawson had to watch his friend suffer and die realising, at some level, he too was not far behind.

Having buried Mertz, Mawson was now alone on the ice with a 160km left to trudge before the shelter of Cape Denison. Of his chance of survival he wrote, '… there is little chance of my reaching human aid alive …' (9th of January, 1913).[7] But he chose to live as long as possible. Having come so far but now alone, and so sick that the soles of his feet were beginning to lift, Mawson nevertheless decided to press on for home. As to the last part of that journey, when Mawson was at his weakest, the worst thing of all happened,

> A few moments later I was dangling on end of rope in crevasse … I had time to say to myself 'So this is the end' … [But] the sledge stopped without coming down [on me], I thought of [Divine] Providence again giving me a chance. The chance looked very small … my finger ends all damaged, myself weak … With the feeling that Providence was helping me I made a great struggle, half getting out, then slipping back again several times, but at last just did it. Then I felt grateful to Providence. (17th January, 1913)[7]

In many respects Mawson underrepresented what happened in his diary note. Not only had he nearly died in the initial fall but the climb out was a full 5m up a thin hemp rope. His struggle also took four-and-a-half hours!

Thankfully, 47km from Cape Denison Mawson came across a small stash of supplies left by some of his men. There was also a note with the food. It mentioned that their ship, the Aurora, had arrived a fortnight before ready to take everyone home again. Could he hope that it was still anchored and waiting for him? Mawson was now close enough to scan the horizon, but saw nothing. And so he walked on. Three days later he reached an ice cave, called Aladdin's Cave, which overlooked Cape Denison. Thankfully more supplies were left and so Mawson could rest and eat, preserving what little strength he had left. Yet, although close to safety a storm now blew up forcing Mawson to retreat into the cave for days. When he did finally make the decent down to Cape Denison he was just in time to see the Aurora's funnel smoke on the horizon. It had left for home that very morning. Nevertheless, six men volunteered to stay behind for another winter and there were rations aplenty. Mawson was safe, although unrecognisable to his men as he approached. So much so that one of them apparently greeted him with, 'My God! Which one are you?'.[8]

What have we learnt about Courage?

From the above two stories we can infer much about what it takes to be courageous. For example, training for Courage is a must, as is a 'can do' attitude. But so is a clear reason to be courageous which is, in turn, supported by a value system or even a faith.[9] Yet inference is always open to conjecture. What we need is a first-hand account gained through lived experience. Lucky enough Hazel Findlay has spoken directly to Courage and her words provide an excellent backdrop to all that we will cover in this chapter. On climbing and Courage she says,

> I am interested in the mental side of climbing. ... I really like the problem solving element of climbing, reading the rock, reading your own body, and making decisions based on information you get from both. Also the mental challenge of being afraid, when you're at risk, or in an uncomfortable or frightening position. Then there's the mental challenge of dealing with your ego, and dealing with how other people perceive you, and all of that. It's not just like there's this one mental challenge; there's this whole host of mental challenges associated with climbing.

Having discussed problem-solving her way through tricky situations Hazel moves on to consider her attitude to climbing and the self-honesty needed for success,

> I get that a lot of the time: 'You're so lucky to be so brave' or 'How is it that you are so brave; were you born that way?' It's a massive pet peeve of mine,

because you're not born with that capacity. You'll never be a mentally strong climber if you think that it's something that's given to you. It's really just to do with them letting themselves off the hook to actually work towards that. It's them saying, 'I will never be that good because I can't be that good,' or that brave, or that strong, or whatever ... [I] actually just equate [bravery] to how much you want to do something. I really like that way of thinking because it's actually a better depiction of what's going on in your brain, and it's more beneficial. So if I say to myself, 'I'm not brave enough to do Indian Face,' what I'm really saying to myself is, 'I don't really want to do Indian Face.' Because, if you do [want it] enough, then you'll be brave enough. ...

Finally, Hazel makes some interesting remarks about her relationship with fear,

> Fear has all these negative connotations that modern society has latched on, massively. I definitely feel everyone's a bit bogged down in the fear thing ....' There really isn't much risk at all, but people ... [are] limited [by it]. It's crazy ....[10]

Taken together, Hazel Findlay teaches us much about Courage as only an expert can. For her, Courage is not a choice. It is actually a series of choices that sum together. First, there is the choice for hard work and preparation which allows the potential for Courage. Then there is the choice to accept reality as it is, not how you'd like it to be. Next comes the choice to problem solve your way out of a situation rather than go to pieces. Finally, Courage forces a choice with respect to how you wish to consider fear.

 Question 2.1

    a. Describe a time in your own life when you had to display Courage. What was it that helped you to be courageous? Were these qualities similar/different to what we learnt about above?

    b. In reading Hazel Findlay's account of what it takes to be courageous which choices for Courage are you good at and which do you need to work on?

Philosophical enquiries into Courage

While the stories above set the scene for our investigation into Courage they are of limited benefit when we want to understand this foundational virtue at a deeper level. To do so we must turn to the academic literature which, on this topic, spans more than two millennia! But before we all give up even before we've started, have Courage, persist, it's not as daunting as it seems. To help, we'll divide our task two ways. First, we will touch on the philosophical literature about Courage and specifically ground ourselves in the work of the ancient Greeks. Second, we'll tackle the contemporary psychological literature. What makes our large task possible is that pretty much all current investigations into Courage are a footnote to the work of Plato and Aristotle.

In his dialogue titled *Laches* Plato set up an encounter between his teacher Socrates and two older men, one of whom was Laches.[11] The dialogue reads as a debate in which propositions about Courage are put forward and tested. Although Courage is never actually pinned down Plato does make a number of useful points. For example, Courage is credited to a soldier who holds his position in the heat of combat. However, it is also recognised that this is only one form of Courage. To understand Courage more generally Plato, through his characters, posits that Courage must be a '… a certain endurance of the soul …'. However, everyone recognises that this definition is too vague. Returning to military matters Plato then turns Courage on its head by commenting that for a soldier to persevere in the face of overwhelming force may not be Courage at all, but stupidity. In the end Plato leaves us with a rather unsatisfying answer to what Courage is, even if some of its qualities and complexities were teased out.

To help us further we need the more practically minded Aristotle who went on to develop a number of Plato's ideas in his *Nicomachean Ethics*.[12] For example, in Book III, Chapter 9, he wrote plainly that, 'Courage is … [concerned with] confidence and fear …'. In accordance with modern research and therapeutic practice Aristotle also stated that fear is a normal part of life but that the courageous person will endure it, apply rational thought in the midst of it, and so sustain confidence through it. Doesn't this sound like what Hazel Findlay taught us only a moment ago?

However, it is the implications of Aristotle's work that are most interesting. For he: (1) scoffs at the untested bravado of young men; (2) dispels the feats of the hero, unless voluntary choice guided their actions; and (3) leads us away from the boldness of soldiers and athletes given that their Courage is often the result of repeated successes. For Aristotle, being courageous was thus something quite specific.

As to how one attains Courage Aristotle was quite emphatic on the importance of training. He believed that having been trained to avoid cowardice through punishment, and to act bravely through rewards, a soldier could be made courageous. As such he prefigured operant conditioning by two millennia. In contemporary terms he would have made an excellent drill sergeant for the army handing out token rewards and grubby punishments with equal measure.

Even so Aristotle was interested in only one type of Courage. What, for example, do we make of the quiet courage of ordinary people? Consider a person who finds themselves in such a difficult position that their ability to act is either limited, or thwarted, yet they display great Courage nonetheless. This form of Courage was first recognised by the Stoic philosophers of ancient Greece and represents an important parallel tradition worth commenting on.

To give you a better understanding of the Stoic position we can turn to one of their later philosophers — and Roman Emperor — Marcus Aurelius. In the 2nd century AD he wrote the following on what it means to be stoic,

> [Recognise] that in almost no time [you] will have to leave all this behind and depart from the world of men ... [Therefore do not] give a thought to what others will say ... [and show a] glad acceptance of [your] present lot.[13]

Although perhaps a little dismal Marcus Aurelius' approach to life, and to Courage, has much to offer people trapped by circumstance. For instance, a well known example of stoic courage comes from the Vietnam War.[14] As a young man James Stockdale flew as a Navy pilot. While leading a mission over North Vietnam in 1965 his plane was shot down and, although he survived, was held prisoner for eight years. Four of which were in solitary confinement. Being imprisoned and tortured Stockdale was at the mercy of his captors and therefore unable to act courageously in the common sense of the word. Yet, to the extent that he could control how he perceived his situation, how he responded to torture, and in taking small opportunities to assert control, Stockdale used a Stoic mindset to both maintain his mental health and to be courageous.

Although useful the Stoic position is, unfortunately, not a completely fulfilling one. Not only did the Stoics limit themselves to quiet courage but the burden of their position on the average person is often too great. For how many of us can handle pain and strife with equanimity? For these reasons, and many more, Aristotle still holds the field in the study of Courage.

Question 2.2

> Which of the ancient philosophers best resonates with your view of Courage?

The psychology of Courage

Given that Psychology grew out of Philosophy it makes for a natural extension to our discussion. As Psychology is also the accepted way to understand how we think, feel and behave, it stands to reason that it should also be the focus of our discussions. Yet psychologists can't even agree on what Courage actually is.[15] Nevertheless do have some sympathy, for Courage is a complex thing to study and a good starting point is to differentiate it from both heroism and bravery.

Heroism, bravery and Courage

In 2012 Weinstein published an enlightening study on heroism using undergraduate students and military cadets.[16] Somewhat surprisingly nearly half the young people surveyed claimed to have acted heroically at one time or another. Looking into this Weinstein discovered that these heroic individuals were also typically male, saw themselves as risk-takers and self-reported low levels of fear. While we might therefore describe heroism as being consistent with age, gender, impulsiveness and a blunted response to fear it is perhaps better to simply turn back to Aristotle and suggest heroism often equates to foolhardiness. In this way it has very little to do with Courage.

The implications of this realisation are important, especially in the workplace given the high regard we have for all sorts of community heroes. While not wanting to denigrate the excellent work of first responders, emergency doctors, and so on it is important to realise that according people 'hero status' perpetuates a myth and, at worst, drives bad behaviour.

Take, for instance, the person who can be described as a 'rescuer' and so joins a hallowed profession. Taken to the extreme such people can indulge heroic rescue fantasies which can put themselves, and others, in danger. For these rescuers downplay risks and act impulsivity.[17] Worse still, rescue fantasists will even seek out those organisations and jobs where they will be positively reinforced for taking undue risks. They may even manipulate situations to *cause* risk so that they can be seen as the heroic rescuer with all the adulation that provides. In the end, heroes are lucky and hero rescuers downright dangerous. Best to avoid them both.

Chapter 2 Courage

Question 2.3

   a. If you are a psychologist, counsellor or social worker what are some of the dangers of a rescuer:

      (1) entering the helping professions;

      (2) marrying a person who needs to be rescued?

   b. In your workplace, or perhaps in a community organisation you are involved with, could there be the risk of employing a rescue fantasist? What risks might such a person pose to the organisation, to its staff and to those people it serves?

   c. How might you go about recognising a rescue fantasist before trouble strikes?

   d. If you believe you know of a rescue fantasist in your organisation what should you do about them?

Activity 2.1

Take, for example, the common workplace situation in which you are part of an interviewing panel to hire new staff. Write out some questions to determine if any of the candidates may be a rescuer or even harbouring a rescue fantasy.

Moving away from heroism, let's now briefly examine something less toxic, and a whole lot more useful — bravery. While bravery and Courage appear synonymous they are not. To demonstrate the difference let's quickly take an extract from Hartley's 2011 study in which he asked military veterans to describe the differences between a commander's courage and their bravery,

> Bravery was seen as an immediate response to an imminent threat to the individual, and may be a reflexive response by someone who in other circumstances would not be considered to possess courage. Courage, on the other hand, was seen as a long-term character quality that served as a foundation for brave acts. Commanders with command courage were capable of facing physical threats, but also responded to moral and ethical risks, and in facing those risks considered the mission and the welfare of the troops ahead of their own. The commander's courage was defined by the participants as an individual trait that is revealed over time.[18]

Although only one study bravery was disambiguated from Courage quite clearly. Not only is it an immediate response to danger it can be shown by a person who, otherwise, lacks Courage.

This now brings us to Courage itself. In recent years Cynthia Pury and her colleagues have sought to understand Courage in various ways. For example, they have put forward concepts such as personal vs. general courage and talk of 'persistence, integrity, and bravery' or even 'volition, risk and value'.[19, 20, 21] Yet trying to pin such ideas down, let alone connect them, is extremely difficult.

A better way is to take a less cerebral approach and come to an understanding of what Courage is by simply asking people.[22] This approach led to Courage being defined according to seven criteria:

- Courage comes with training.
- The action of being courageous implies a risky situation.
- There also needs to be volition if an act is to be considered courageous.
- To be considered courageous one has to be motivated to act accordingly.
- Courage necessitates confronting, or enduring, through difficulty.
- Fear is part of acting courageously and has to be managed.
- Courage uses a range of cognitive processes to appraise risk and to problem solve various solutions to the situation at hand.

Although accurate this list of what constitutes Courage is also exhausting. For this reason it is better to use two similar, and vastly more succinct, definitions. Courage can thus be summarised to bravery with persistence or better still, '… perseverance despite having fear …' (p. 214).[23, 24] So, as we move forward, keep these twin pillars in mind for fear and perseverance are at the heart of Courage.

Fear
'Courage is resistance to fear, mastery of fear — not absence of fear,' said Mark Twain, and he was right. But this does not help us much if we first don't understand what fear is. In simple terms we may consider it to be a response of our brain and body designed to keep us safe. In this way we think fearfully and feel it too. Put simply, fear starts in our mind as we appraise some situation as risky, even dangerous. This then sets off a cascade of responses in the body from an immediate activation of the Sympathetic Nervous System to make our heart beat faster and lungs breath deeper, to a longer-term response which involves the release of a hormone called cortisol from our adrenal glands.

Chapter 2 Courage

Question 2.4

From what you have read above, is it better to use mindfulness breathing to control fear or to use better thinking to appraise a situation more appropriately?

Beyond these statements what can we learn about how fearful people respond to situations when compared to courageous people? In a delightfully simple experiment Marshall and colleagues compared 29 'fearless' vs. 21 'fearful' people based on their uncomfortableness with heights.[25] Most importantly, each participant was interviewed immediately after experiencing heights to capture their thinking in as much detail as possible. From these interviews it was discovered that fear-based thinking seemed to centre on one particular type of unhelpful thought pattern called 'catastrophisation' which begins with the 'What ifs ...' and ends by blowing the situation out of all proportion. In essence, the fearful participants turned a somewhat stressful experience into a catastrophe whereas the fearless/courageous participants did not.

But, as we just learnt, fear is also felt in the body. As early as 1983 Cox sought to understand this by comparing two groups of experienced bomb disposal operators.[26] One group of soldiers having been decorated for gallantry but the other not. The implicit assumption being that the soldiers who had been decorated were the more courageous. Interestingly, when the data was analysed the decorated soldiers 'maintained a lower cardiac rate when making difficult discriminations under threat ....'.[27] Nor were these findings a one-off, being replicated by O'Connor two years later and also by McMillan over a generation later and, as such, appear robust.[28, 29] The implication of these studies being the importance of people learning to regulate their heart rate when managing fearful situations.

 Activity 2.2

Think about something which causes you a little fear.

a. See if you can appraise the situation differently and thus remove the fear. If not totally successful what thoughts are going through your mind? Do you use catastrophisation or other fear-based ways of thinking?

b. In addition, what's happening in your body as fear commences? Does your heart begin to speed up? Do you feel queasy in the stomach? These and other responses are likely to be your

Sympathetic Nervous System kicking in. How might you go about learning to control these responses?

However, the study which teaches us most about fear and Courage was undertaken by McMillan back in 1988 and involved soldiers undergoing parachute training.[30] In brief, trainees were asked to describe their experience of 'jump training' and from these descriptions three personality profiles were developed. Trainees were profiled as being either 'courageous' (i.e., optimistic but with some fear through which they persevered), 'fearless' (i.e., confident and had low levels of fear) or 'overconfident' (i.e., < 10% of participants characterised by underestimating fear and risk). Looking at what distinguished the courageous group of trainees from the other two we find out that they:

- were willing to acknowledge a moderate degree of fear before jumping,
- only had a satisfactory level of confidence, not too high nor too low,
- could correctly estimate their level of fear during each jump,
- could manage their bodily reactions to fear.

Therefore the courageously labelled trainees could perceive, predict, express and manage their emotional state better than either the fearless or overconfident trainees. As such, courageous soldiers do not have an absence of fear but a level of personal insight, if not emotional intelligence, to hold their fear in check.

 Question 2.5

    a. What lessons about fear have you gleaned from what we have discussed?

    b. If you are a psychologist or counsellor what methods do you use to help clients control their fear?

Perseverance

Three words, and one foundational virtue, come to mind when I (i.e., Tom) think about perseverance. They are psychological grit; the personality trait of Conscientiousness; resilience; and the virtue of Diligence. To simplify matters, let's consider psychological grit to be such a recent term as to yet be fully embraced by researchers. We will therefore put it aside. As for Diligence this will be the topic of our next chapter and within it we will discuss Conscientiousness. So we'll also put these topics aside for the moment. In the end we are left with resilience. While only part of the puzzle explaining perseverance it's important nonetheless and therefore worth considering.³¹

Although the details are debated within the literature, resilience is about one's ability to adapt well to adversity and therefore 'bounce back'.³² Although resilience is a large topic we can summarise some key points fairly easily given that many of the factors which make a person resilient are also shared by those who are courageous. For example, resilient people have a strong self-concept, or value system, as we learnt when we read about Mawson at the start of this chapter. Resilient people also have a strong social support network. This we saw when Hazel Findlay climbed her high cliff in the Atlas Mountains *with* Emily Harrington. In addition, a resilient person is one who is both a realist and a good problem solver and, as such, avoids 'emotional coping'. Isn't this also what Hazel Findlay said in her interview about Courage? But alongside these qualities resilient people also have hope.³³ Indeed, hope sustains Courage.

In sum, to become courageous learn to persist through fear. Except for overwhelming fear learn to be ok in its presence, treat it as a caompanion in life, even a friend.

 Question 2.6

    a. Are you a person who perseveres?

       (1) If so, what allows you to do so?

       (2) If not, what prevents you?

    b. In thinking about hope, what gives you hope? How can you harness this to be more courageous?

 Activity 2.3

    If you are a psychologist or counsellor read on Snyder Hope Theory. How might this contribute to your practice?

Moral courage is different

Having now made some headway in our discussions of Courage we can now move into deeper waters. So let's discuss moral courage given that it is particularly virtuous.

Although some authors disagree, Putman has made the useful observation that there are three forms of Courage — physical, psychological and moral.[14] Not surprisingly each relates to a different type of stressor. For example, physical courage relates to a fear of physical harm, if not death. This is certainly true for a police officer, mountain climber or Antarctic explorer. Psychological courage, on the other hand, is about facing those fears which lurk in the recesses of your mind.[34] But moral courage is more complex for it applies to the risk inherent in making ethical or moral choices.[35, 36] And as for what that risk is? Moral courage is about the risk of social disapproval, if not exclusion.[34] In fact moral courage is probably the greatest form of Courage because many of us fear loneliness most of all.

To describe just how hard it is for a person to show moral courage let's consider a person's ability to dissent from their peers. To do so we'll briefly review a classic experiment from the history of Psychology.

Back in the 1950's the world was still reeling from the horrors of World War II. At this time psychologists were particularly interested in why good Germans complied with the orders of their Nazi bosses. To investigate this question Solomon Asch performed a series of experiments which had profound implications.[37] Although the experiments varied a little depending upon what the researchers were interested in the basic methodology always remained the same. Small groups of participants were presented with a card which had a black line on it. They were then given another card showing three black lines, of which only one matched the length of line printed on the first card. The question then posed by the researchers was laughably simple: 'Which of the three lines on the second card matched the line on the first card?'. However, this being a psychological experiment something was purposely amiss. In fact Asch constructed his experiment in such a way as to form groups in which only one participant was real and the rest were his confederates. Specifically, the confederates in each group were asked to be either unanimously correct in their response to the question about line length or unanimously wrong. The confederates were also asked to answer the question about line length before the actual participant to provide increased peer pressure. So here we have a wonderful test of conformity and thereby dissent. Unbelievably, given the ease of the task, when the results were tallied a significant proportion of actual participants concurred with the unanimously incorrect answers given by the confederates! Now imagine the likelihood of people dissenting when something important is at stake. This is why moral courage is so impressive, for it goes against so much that we hold as important about community life.

Given that dissent is difficult for people, but often a social good, studies have since focused on how to increase the likelihood of dissent and therefore of moral courage. This is particularly important in professions where decisions can have life-and-death consequences, such as in nursing and medicine, in aviation or in the military. While we will deal with the development of Courage more fully at the end of the chapter let us take a brief digression and make a few pertinent statements about growing moral courage.

Increasing people's capacity for dissent, and therefore moral courage, is easier than you think in spite of both evolutionary forces and social conditioning.[38] Simply by being exposed to alternate views, or minority opinions, increases the probability of a person feeling able to dissent. Moreover, having observed dissent, people often feel that they have permission to dissent as well. For teachers and parents this demonstrates the overwhelming value of engaging young people in debate and giving them moral exemplars as a way to grow moral courage (see Chapter 6).

However dissent is not always possible given that some workplaces, or organisations, are very adept at pushing aside questions from employees and stymieing alternative perspectives. For this reason it is also important that educators provide students with a grounding in ethics before they enter the workforce so that new employees know what is appropriate or not.[39] But in saying this we do not mean for students to study ethics by memorising a code of practice or learn how close they can get to the edge of what is legal before slipping over. For us, ethics education is ultimately about asking, 'But is it good?' and having the intellectual tools to reason out a course of action from this starting point. From this solid foundation moral courage becomes possible even if those in power hope to quell dissent.

 Question 2.7

- a. Have you ever had to be a dissenter (e.g., a 'whistle blower'), or make a morally tough decision which would be criticised by others? If so, what allowed you to make that decision?
- b. If you are a teacher, lecturer or trainer, how do you encourage debate and counter orthodox perspectives in what you teach?

Yet moral courage, as seen through dissent, may only be half the story. Can a person be said to have moral courage if they dissent but nevertheless fail to act to prevent wrong? In short, is dissent is enough? To illustrate this point Linn and colleagues used the example of the My Lai massacre by US soldiers during the Vietnam War to persuasively argue that moral courage is not just about dissenting from doing evil, but must also be paired with doing good.[40] In this instance they argued that care for the civilian wounded was a necessary minimum for dissenting soldiers to demonstrate moral courage. As such, moral courage is also about moral action guided by the foundational virtue of Justice (see Chapter 6).

In many respects moral action appears similar to a host of prosocial, or helping, behaviours. If this is so then psychologists are already well armed to help people be more morally courageous. However when moral action was investigated three important differences to prosocial behaviour emerged.[41] The main difference between prosocial behaviour and moral action was that while there is often a benefit to the person who acts pro-socially moral action may be very costly. Interestingly, moral action can also be disambiguated from other sorts of helping behaviours as it is not dependent upon the number of bystanders present. In most situations the more bystanders there are then the less likely any one person is to help. It's called 'diffusion of responsibility'. But this does not apply in situations of moral action. Finally, people often help when they feel in a good mood. Yet, when studying moral action mood played almost no part. Situations in which moral courage was needed were identified quickly and acted upon without reference to how one was feeling at the time except, perhaps, that anger made moral action more likely. Therefore, while moral action and helping behaviours may be related moral action is very much its own thing.

Having now understood key factors related to moral action we can deal with the most important issue ... What brings it out in people? In this way we go to the heart of moral courage. Yet this question is a difficult one. For why does one person, in the moment, rush to the aid of another while other people stand about trying to ignore what's going on? In fact the answer may not lie in the unfolding situation, but way back in childhood. For example, researchers have noted the immense value of developing empathy in children as a precursor to moral action.[42] The assumption being that if a child can be brought up to feel the distress of others then, as an adult, they will be more likely to respond to distress and so act with moral courage.

As for a parenting style likely to develop empathy in children, if not moral action, Bronstein provided the following advice,

> Supportive, responsive parenting ... predicted girls' willingness in late adolescence to speak up or take action when they witnessed or experienced injustice or harm. In contrast, parenting that was harsh and restrictive predicted both girls' and boys' later reticence ...[43]

But Bronstein went further and made a bold claim worth noting. Even if a child was parented harshly all was not lost. As children develop self-esteem, and for girls social competence, then these new abilities appear to moderate the effects of poor parenting when it comes to empathy. In this way schools, sporting clubs and other community organisations (e.g., Scouts) that aim to build character have an important role to play in building both empathy and, ultimately, moral action.

 Activity 2.4

> If you are a teacher, coach or Scout leader, for example, use what you have learnt above to design an activity to build self-esteem and social competence in the young people you work with. In this way you build deliberately towards moral courage.

So, to conclude this section on moral courage, let's just say that it is not substantially different from Courage generally defined. There is risk, one needs to manage fear and persist in some good action. If there is a difference it is simply in how difficult it is for people to be morally courageous. Therefore, when you see signs of moral courage in a person applaud it, reinforce it, encourage it! Do good where and when you can.

Can Courage ever be a bad thing?

It was David Hume, in the 1700s, who first recognised that if a society pushed too hard to express one virtue then it risked destabilisation, if not destruction, given that virtues often counter-balance each other. For example Courage, taken to its warped extreme as iron-hard strength, will typically push aside the counter-balancing virtue of compassion, hence Kindness (see Chapter 7).[14] This we have seen all too recently in European history with the rise, and fall, of Nazi Germany. Their many displays of muscular strength were inevitably accompanied by an absence of compassion that led from forced sterilisations of the 'feeble minded', to so-called mercy deaths for the disabled, and eventually to the Holocaust itself.[44, 45] So Courage can be a bad thing if left unchecked.

In addition to a simple excess of Courage we also have the ugly phenomenon of 'bad courage'.[46] Either some people will do horrendous things under the banner of Courage, and so misappropriate the term, or a type of Courage will prevail whereby reward outstrips virtue. For example, in the first instance terrorists will often describe themselves as being courageous, or some people talk of suicide as a courageous act. No they're not. The first is evil and the second sad. As for reward outstripping virtue we see this when, '... soldiers who displayed the most courageous behaviour received the greatest admiration from their comrades'.[47] While offering admiration, or awarding medals, is not a bad thing in itself the danger of accolades presents when a person becomes addicted to the rewards of Courage and so, like any addict, shifts their behaviour to seek ever greater highs. On the battlefield a soldier caught in this spiral may even begin to shift from acting courageously to acting heroically, with all the risk-taking and bravado that that entails. In more typical settings this same accolades addiction is felt most strongly by those in professional sports. Money and fame cause injured sports stars to return to the field too soon, to brawl, and even to take performance-enhancing drugs. Therefore Courage has its dark side and vigilance must be maintained when anyone wants to push Courage before all else.

 Question 2.8

    a. Have you ever seen any examples of Courage taken too far, or people addicted to the rewards of acting courageously? If so what were the key issues driving the person's behaviour? What was the result?

    b. In understanding that rewarding Courage too strongly can have bad outcomes how might a sports coach motivate their players to achieve great things without falling into accolades addiction?

Building Courage

It's all well and good to talk about Courage, but if we don't build Courage what's the point? Therefore, in this final part of the chapter we will tackle this vital question alongside how we identify people with the capacity for great feats of Courage.

Finding courageous people

We all have a capacity for Courage even if it's demonstrated in different ways. While an athlete might have physical courage children, for example, are wonderful truth tellers and so have a moral courage all their own. Or, in a more subtle way, those people who attend Alcoholics Anonymous (AA) demonstrate great personal courage in dealing with their problems. As such, Courage belongs to us all. To demonstrate this point in a different way only 10% of candidates who apply to become very courageous bomb disposal operators are turned back.[48]

But to find people who may show unusually high levels of Courage typically requires both psychological training and some sort of survey or inventory.[24, 49, 50, 51] In other words it's not very practical for you or me. Perhaps an easier way to assess a person's Courage is to consider their personality traits and three in particular.[41, 52] Given what we have learnt about perseverance it is not surprising that people who rate high on the trait of Conscientiousness will be more likely to show Courage. Nor is it a surprise that those who score high on the ominously named trait of Neuroticism will likely fail to show Courage. However this is not the whole story. A third personality trait also appears to be important. Those people who display high levels of Openness to experience also appear to be more likely to exhibit Courage. The reason being that this third personality trait is probably useful in problem solving through the generation of unique solutions to otherwise difficult issues. Looking for people who show Openness to experience may also be particularly useful when moral courage is sought for these people appear able to manage the disapproval of others better than the rest of us. Therefore in looking to see who might be particularly courageous perhaps all that is necessary is to assess three traits: Conscientiousness; Neuroticism; and Openness to experience.

But to assess personality traits, even in an *ad hoc* way, needs a keen eye and some level of judgement. Again, this makes it difficult for the average person. Yet certain personal qualities do hint at Courage and they are not hard for the average person to pick up on. For instance, those people who can manage fear may be more courageous. Even better is to identify people who have both a strong capacity for problem solving and who demonstrate resilience. Although expressed in a different way it was these same qualities that gave the original Mercury astronauts the 'right stuff',

> They were all married men in their early 30s who had grown up in middle-class families in small towns or on farms. They were Protestant, enjoyed outdoor living, had university degrees in engineering, were of superior intelligence (mean IQ 135), and were inclined to action.[53]

Taken together, Courage is a foundational virtue and thus shared by all people. However, because of nature and nurture some of us are more likely to be courageous than others. The problem is, of course, that the media has primed us to consider only the powerful and strong as courageous. Don't be fooled. Courage comes in many forms and sometimes from the most unlikely people. As such, look for Courage broadly and scratch below the surface of a person's story. You'll often be amazed at what you find.

Activity 2.5

a. Assume you are part of a recruitment panel for a job vacancy. The job in question requires the successful candidate to have Courage. Now knowing all about this virtue what attributes will you look for in the candidates? What questions or scenarios will you put to them to see which of these attributes they have? How will you go about choosing the best, i.e., most courageous, candidate?

b. On the page opposite is the Current Courage Checklist (Table 2.1). It represents a brief synthesis of all the major points mentioned in this chapter. Feel free to use this checklist. To complete the Current Courage Checklist all you need do is look at each item in turn and tick the appropriate response box. Responses are graded from 'Strongly disagree' to 'Strongly agree'.

To understand how to interpret the checklist let's begin by recognising that the 10 items are split into two domains. The Personal domain is all about how you 'do' life generally, while the Cognitive/Emotional domain relates to how you handle specific situations.

In the first instance consider each item individually and so recognise your strengths and weaknesses.

Alternatively you can score this checklist to get an overall understanding of your current capacity for Courage. To do so, every tick in the 'Strongly disagree' column gets a score of 1. For every tick in the 'Disagree' column give a score of 2 etc. until you get to the 'Strongly agree' column whereby each tick gets a score of 5. Therefore the lowest you can score on the checklist is 10 (i.e., 10 items x 1 point), whilst the most you can score is 50 (i.e., 10 items x 5 points). By corollary, an overall score of 30 represents the halfway point. Did you score above, or below 30?

Developing Courage

Whether you want to develop Courage in a general sense, or take a person with Courage and 'max them out' this section considers important ways forward. Nevertheless, for those of you who are a bit 'old school' let's commence by saying that training in Courage is not about throwing a child into the deep end of a swimming pool and expecting them to swim. Nor is it about taking teenagers out bush and have them abseil from great heights without sufficient

TABLE 2.1
Current Courage Checklist
For each item tick the response which best describes you.

	Strongly disagree	Disagree	Neutral	Agree	Strongly agree
Personal domain					
I have a clear value system or am motivated by a religious or ethical principle.	☐	☐	☐	☐	☐
I have good social supports.	☐	☐	☐	☐	☐
I have all sorts of resources to call upon to assist me through tough times.	☐	☐	☐	☐	☐
I look after myself.	☐	☐	☐	☐	☐
I am a hopeful person.	☐	☐	☐	☐	☐
Cognitive/Emotional domain					
People have said that I have acted with courage in the past.	☐	☐	☐	☐	☐
I am a good problem-solver.	☐	☐	☐	☐	☐
I think of others when solving problems.	☐	☐	☐	☐	☐
I can manage my own feelings of stress well.	☐	☐	☐	☐	☐
I persevere to get things done.	☐	☐	☐	☐	☐

preparation. These 'crash on through' methods just increase fear and therefore reduce the likelihood of Courage. Nor is training in Courage about learning how to wear a uniform better. Outward appearances of Courage often hide insecurities which will bite a person in the end. By contrast, growth in Courage comes from a deliberate training schedule in which people begin to understand themselves deeply, are supported by others along the way and progressively get introduced to stressful situations. In this way we build Courage from the inside out.

To grow in Courage takes the development of a number of personal qualities and begins with understanding your value system.[54] If a person knows what they believe, and why they should persist through some frightening experience, then they are more likely to do so. But values work at a number of levels. There are, for example, cultural values. In Australia, the two most prominent ones are 'mateship' and a 'fair go'. Both of which are about how we relate to others. People also have family values, perhaps centred around hard work or success. Then there are personal values. These might be ethical or religious but can be more general relating to what you hold dear and how you treat yourself, your family and your friends. But whatever values you hold it is important to articulate them and live by them. When this happens Courage has a fertile soil in which to grow.

 Activity 2.6

> Name your personal values, family values and your cultural values. How do they influence who you are?

As we have said many times courageous people are good problem solvers.[14] But this doesn't mean they are just clever. It's the way they look at problems that matters. Courageous people take a realistic stance towards problems and so avoid the dangers of self-deception and rationalisation. They even avoid procrastinating on a solution. Therefore, and in general terms, courageous people solve problems in such a way as to take responsibility for their lives.

 Question 2.9

> Do you use any of the above 'bluffs' to avoid a difficult problem? If so, which ones?

Courageous people also develop good relationships with other people.[54] By identifying friends, family, colleagues and others within your network, and knowing when to call on them for help, you can persist through the hardest of trials. But often recruits, junior professionals, trainees etc. require a special form of relationship to help them towards Courage. In this way mentoring becomes a vital relationship.[55] However, mentoring is not straightforward. It is a complex relationship with both tangible and intangible qualities about it. Nevertheless a good mentor provides teaching, promotes risk-taking and is personally encouraging. Moreover, when rigorous training is paired with good mentoring then Courage will be almost inevitable.

Chapter 2   Courage

 Question 2.10

> Have you ever been mentored? What was the experience like? What aspects of the relationship helped you in your journey towards Courage?

 Activity 2.7

> a. Write out a list of people in your social support network. Now, for each member of your social support network rate the extent to which you can call on them for help. In this way you now know those people who will simply be supportive of your journey versus those people who will actually help you along the way.
> b. If you do not have a mentor go and get one! But choose wisely ...

Finally, developing Courage is about mastery experiences. These are opportunities for technical training and simulated experiences which, when repeated time-and-again, build up a person's confidence and therefore their propensity to act courageously. Of the Mercury astronauts it has been written,

> Prior to their journey into space [the trainee astronauts] had dealt with dangerous situations in which fear was appropriate and found that they were able to function despite its effects. The astronauts benefited from these mastery experiences and were confident that they had the skills and knowledge necessary to overcome realistic threats. ... These people [therefore] had particular psychological competenc[ies] and the resources for coping effectively with danger.
>
> During the journey into space, they experienced remarkably little fear. Before the flights, there was little evidence of significant anxiety or elevated physiological arousal ... The astronauts felt that as a result of their intensive training and past experience, they were prepared to handle any emergency.[56]

Or take for example another type of mastery experience. Although perhaps apocryphal, I (i.e., Tom) once heard that junior neurosurgeons at one major US hospital had to do 1000 craniotomies before being allowed to operate on the brain itself. During this early part of their training these doctors were referred to as 'can openers'. While a somewhat disparaging term it undergirds a training method dedicated to both mastery experiences, the loss of fear and exemplary practice.

We can even adapt mastery experiences to meet the demands of moral courage. For example, Osswald and colleagues developed role plays to do just this.[41] They argued that role playing has the effect of providing participants with better problem solving capacities when they encounter a situation 'on the street' which may require intervention. For example, having learnt in role playing that heroism is not clever a person may decide to refrain from rushing in to help someone, looking instead for other bystanders to also assist, or simply choosing to call the police instead. Both actions being courageous in their own way and practiced in advance.

 Question 2.11

> What sort of mastery experiences have you been involved in? Did you find them useful in boosting your Courage? Why, why not?

 Activity 2.8

> Use what you have learnt in this chapter to design a mastery experience for people in your organisation. Remember that it has to help people to manage their fear and problem-solve their way through a situation. How often might this, or other, mastery experiences have to be repeated to get improved problem solving and lower fear responses in these people?

And this brings us to our last point when discussing training in Courage ... Courage must be demonstrated. Until we are tested we don't know if we have yet got the 'right stuff'. While some try to test their mettle on the sporting field this can be a hit-or-miss affair — pun intended. What we need are formal tests of Courage. Now we're certainly not advocating for traditional, or *ad hoc*, initiation rites or hazing but we do suggest that good options exist which should be used.[57] For instance, completing an adventure-based program is an excellent demonstration of Courage for both adolescent boys and girls. For girls, especially, such programmes have been shown to increase both physical and moral courage and so have multiple benefits.[58] Or, did you ever think about the virtue-basis of exams? Here is a simple and common way for students to show Courage.

Courage then is a journey for us all. On any journey wear strong boots. These are your values and they will keep you upright. Look at the map regularly. That is, problem solve your way ahead. Also, take good friends with you for a journey is always better shared. 'Be prepared' too! Mastery experiences will give you the confidence to complete your journey. Finally, complete the journey. Having potential is not enough, Courage is not real until it is demonstrated.

 Question 2.12

> What options do you have to demonstrate Courage?

In closing

Courage shines brightly. Be it a corporate executive holding firm in the face of a deteriorating share price, a military commander staying calm whilst small arms fire rattles about, or a mother looking after a chronically sick child. But the light it gives is not yours alone. Courage is a gift to others. For in having Courage you hold back the dark, protect those whom you care about, and give a sense of peace to all. It is truly a virtue worth developing.

Let us now finish on a particular note. I (i.e., Tom) love poetry and the following few lines from Kipling's *If* say to me in sharper clarity than any psychological study what we need to know about Courage. I hope these lines also resonate with you …

> If you can keep your head when all about you
>   Are losing theirs and blaming it on you,
> If you can trust yourself when all men doubt you,
>   But make allowance for their doubting too;
> If you can wait and not be tired by waiting,
>   Or being lied about, don't deal in lies,
> Or being hated, don't give way to hating,

Then that is Courage …

The Freedom of Virtue: Navigating excellence in the art of living amongst a world of instant gratification

Chapter 3

Diligence

> An overnight success is ten years in the making
> — Tom Clancy

The unseen virtue

In 2015 tennis great Martina Navratilova paid Novak Djokovic a significant compliment when she said of him, '[It's just] his work ethic, diligence, his preparation, his willingness to keep working on his game and keep getting better ... He deserves that he finished No. 1'.[1] Yet while Diligence may be the key to success it is also the hidden virtue. We may sit in the grandstand and cheer each winning point but we are only spectators to the last moments of years of preparation and dedication. We see the trophy held aloft, but never the blisters.

Indeed Djokovic said of his own training regime,

> I usually spend four hours [a day] on court doing drills and intense match play, then do an uphill run, some agility training, and then yoga and massage. ... I [also] run for long distances at high altitudes. If you keep doing it, your fitness will be able to endure in any sort of altitude. ... [I also won't eat pizza] ... I love pizza. I eat it maybe three or four times a year now, but I promise that if it wasn't for tennis I would eat it every day.[2]

So, in the first instance, Diligence is about hard work and self-denial in preparation for winning.

But Diligence also has a second meaning. People can be considered diligent who are precise. Let's take an example from a radically different discipline to demonstrate this point. Marie Curie (1867–1934) was a Polish–French chemist who could not initially pursue a university education in Warsaw for the fact that she was a woman.[3] Yet Marie Curie became the first woman to win the Nobel Prize, and then won a second after that! Even more extraordinary, she won her two Nobel Prizes in different scientific disciplines (i.e., Physics, 1903 and Chemistry, 1911) and along the way founded the science of radioactivity.

However it was Curie's Diligence with respect to precision that concerns us. While Henri Becquerel had discovered 'uranium rays' emanating from particular minerals that would expose photographic plates even in the dark they remained a mystery.[4] Marie Curie looked into the problem testing 24 different minerals for their radioactive properties using an electrometer developed by her husband, Pierre. Most importantly she found that radioactive minerals, such as pitchblende, differed by less than one billionth in electric charge from ordinary minerals. If that wasn't precise enough she felt compelled to explain this tiny anomaly rather than shew it away as an artefact. This, in turn, required her to extract the radioactive component of pitchblende. The time and effort to do this was truly astounding, especially given the drafty old shed she worked in. Moreover, nobody would have thought that from tonnes of ore, in the end, she'd be extracting only grams and milligrams of radioactive material.[5,6] Now that's Diligence!

Diligence, therefore, is not one thing but two. While hard work can exist without precision, we cannot think of an example where the opposite is true.

The benefits of Diligence: School success, career achievement and longevity

Although becoming a world champion athlete or a Nobel Prize winner requires Diligence, so does every other major life goal. Whoever graduated a degree without showing Diligence in their studies? What CEO has gotten to their position of authority without putting in long hours at work over many years? In a slightly different vein, what parent has not raised a wonderful child without unwavering dedication to their welfare? Diligence is thus a key ingredient to successes in life and, usefully, Psychology has much to say about it.

In 2002 Arthur conducted a comprehensive study of over 450 boys and girls and found, not surprisingly, a statistically significant correlation between Diligence and academic achievement.[7] Most importantly, for students 14 years of age or younger Diligence was actually found to be a crucial factor in promoting their educational success.

Four years later Arthur followed up his original study by recruiting 380 university students. In this investigation he clearly noted the importance of Diligence to university success and identified a number of Diligence-related study behaviours. More bluntly he stated, 'The most striking implication [of this work] is that students are in control of their academic lives. Diligence, study habits, and classroom participation, [are] all modifiable behaviours ….'.[8] Consequently Diligence is a choice some people make for success.

Question 3.1

Homework is now a contested issue in some schools. What do we learn about the value of homework when we consider the importance of developing Diligence in students?

Shifting from university life to career success Diligence is also necessary in professions such as Medicine. However, in explaining this point we must be aware of a slightly different word that psychologists use to describe Diligence, for they call it Conscientiousness and typically regard it as a personality trait. For this reason we will use both terms throughout this chapter to describe the same idea but change the word according to whether we are discussing virtues or psychology. We hope this will not be too confusing for you. So, returning to our discussion, it has been written that '[t]he main personality characteristic repeatedly identified in the literature [related to success in Medicine] was Conscientiousness.'[9] While the esteemed British Medical Journal published an article in which the following virtue statement was made: 'from our reading of the literature we distil three broad attributes that doctors should have — cognitive ability …; humanity …; and diligence ….'.[10] Not only do the authors now name Diligence but also elevate it to a core competency alongside intellectual ability and emotional intelligence. High praise indeed for this foundational virtue.

Yet Medicine is a unique career. So we must ask whether Conscientiousness, as the psychological equivalent of Diligence, is as useful to the rest of us? Interestingly, when personality was considered alongside workplace performance across a wide range of jobs (e.g., police, managers, sales staff etc.) only the trait of Conscientiousness stood out as crucial for *all* occupational groups.[11]

More surprising still was that Conscientiousness in childhood actually predicted career success decades later.[12] Using the gold standard research method of a longitudinal study Kern and colleagues analysed data from participants in the Terman Life Cycle Study. What made these individuals particularly interesting was that they were all chosen for their superior intellect (i.e., an IQ = 135+) which, in a simplistic way, should have predicted life success across-the-board. However, this was not always the case with some participants being high achievers and some low. Using data derived from 693 males for whom there was both childhood personality data and a vocational success rating Kern found some unexpected outcomes. Of course intelligence was broadly correlated to career success. No surprises there. But career success was also correlated to a cluster of childhood attributes such as motivation, ambition and, of course, Conscientiousness. Who'd have thought career success was set up so early in life!

But most surprising was Kern's findings regarding Conscientiousness, health and longevity. Although there was already a link Kern used the Terman Sample once more to derive precise outcomes.[12, 13] When the researchers looked at data related to mortality they found that the most successful individuals were the least likely to die irrespective of age; and consistent with this they also found that greater levels of childhood Conscientiousness correlated with lower mortality. Yet for those people rated as the most unsuccessful in the sample, and therefore at risk of dying early, all was not lost. Boosting Conscientiousness at any age was seen as a positive step to turning one's life around.

So, to close this initial foray into Diligence what can we say? Three points come to mind. First, Diligence is the engine room of virtue. With it all things become possible. Second, levering off the old proverb about 'training a child in the way they should go …' we now know the importance of instilling Diligence in the young.[14] In this way chores, homework and all those other little jobs we remember from childhood take on new significance for they are an excellent training in Diligence. Third, and finally, the value of Diligence probably extends well past career success, health and longevity — for what marriage could survive without it? So while we may all get excited about developing Courage, as we learnt about in the last chapter, it is the quite virtue of Diligence that will probably make for us a happy life.

Question 3.2

a. How diligent are you? Given that people often differ in their response depending upon which aspect of life they are thinking about try answering this question with respect to:

(1) study;

(2) work;

(3) housework;

(4) parenting;

(5) catching up with friends/family;

(6) sport; and

(7) community engagement.

b. Having answered Question 3.2a, what impacts, good or bad, might there be for your quality of life?

c. In thinking about Kern's work what implications are there for parents and teachers?

d. More broadly, what are the implications of Kern's findings for government policy, healthcare professionals, community-based caseworkers and others who assist people struggling with life?

 Activity 3.1

In an area of life in which you may lack Diligence devise a plan to improve. How will you hold yourself accountable?

If the psychological trait of Conscientiousness is so valuable what holds us back?

If a person has high levels of Conscientiousness, and therefore Diligence, then they have been given a great gift, but these people are relatively rare. For the rest of us we show glimpses of Conscientiousness from time to time but often have trouble in sustaining effort for a variety of reasons. Let's now look at why this happens and what we can do about it.

Two factors which hamper Conscientiousness: Family of origin and childhood bullying

Childhood Conscientiousness is so important to outcomes later in life. Although many things may affect how a child develops in Conscientiousness we will highlight only two. The first pertains to one's family of origin and focuses on parenting. The second issue which can hamper a child's growth in Conscientiousness is bullying no matter if it is in the schoolyard, online, or in the home.

Beginning with a child's family of origin we can quickly make some pertinent statements about Conscientiousness, and therefore Diligence, by simply comparing parenting in high and low socio-economic status families. While parents who are high status often value a parenting style which breeds independence in their children, those of low status seem to value conformity. It has also been observed that mothers of higher socio-economic status provided earlier age estimates for when their children will attain developmental milestones as well showing a capacity for overestimating their children's abilities. Moreover, parents of high socio-economic status also tend to want from their children earlier mastery of skills/abilities that the community considers valuable.[15] In this way parents of high socio-economic status likely inculcate the value of Conscientiousness in their children from a young age by simply having high expectations while teachers, coaches and others reinforce the messages from home.[16]

In addition to socio-economic status family of origin also includes other factors such as parenting style which impacts the level of Conscientiousness a child may develop. Amongst the worst sort of parenting, if Conscientiousness is your aim, is to be a helicopter parent.[16] These are the sort of parents who love their children so much that they suffocate them. They try desperately to protect their children from all sorts of real, and imagined, dangers often to assuage their own anxiety or lessen some misplaced sense of guilt. But children learn Conscientiousness, and thus Diligence, only through managing difficult situations. If a parent is always there to prevent their child from trying something new, or ready to pick up the pieces after a small mishap, what message is being conveyed to the child? It is certainly not a message of 'Just try harder next time.'.

By contrast, we cannot underestimate the value of authoritative parenting for children, either in the development of Conscientiousness or for a host of other life skills. In this style of parenting, which should not be confused with being authoritarian, children and adolescents are engaged by their parents in such ways as to promote their maturity.[17] As such, authoritative parenting equates to emotional warmth but also has within it limits balanced against expectations and freedom of choice. Accountability for actions is also upheld and punishments are meted out appropriately. Ultimately, authoritative parenting provides a clear structure for family life in which a child feels safe and supported while having room to grow.[18]

Question 3.3

a. How were you parented? How might this have impacted your own level of Conscientiousness and therefore Diligence?

b. If you are a parent, has the information above caused you to reflect, if not alter, some of your parenting habits? How so?

c. If you work with parents who struggle, how might you go about improving Diligence outcomes for their children?

In discussing what hampers a child's sense of Diligence we must also consider the schoolyard. In this regard Dombeck wrote persuasively about the harm that bullying does to children in both the short-term and long-term. Although he does not name a loss of Conscientiousness directly he did allude to a range of harmful emotional/behavioural outcomes from bullying consistent with damage to this vital trait. For example, he writes,

> … the second ugly outcome [of bullying] unfolds more slowly over time. Having a wounded self-concept makes it harder for you to believe in yourself, and when you have difficulty believing in yourself, you will tend to have a harder time persevering through difficult situations and challenging circumstances.[19]

Taken together, early life events can hamper a person from developing high levels of Conscientiousness and therefore Diligence. Nevertheless, I (i.e., Tom) can also think of people whom I've met over the years who have developed good levels of Diligence in spite of growing up in relatively deprived households or being subjected to victimisation. Although these people do not necessarily have high-level careers they still have gone on to live fulfilling lives. So, have hope, from the worst beginnings people can grow into marvellous human beings.

Question 3.4

In thinking about the short- and long-term impacts of bullying what interventions may be needed to help a child recover a sense of Conscientiousness?

Activity 3.2

Write down those personal strengths you have which can be used to harness your Conscientiousness. In thinking about your answer aim for about 5 strengths. Now put them into action.

One big problem that thwarts Conscientiousness: Procrastination

Thankfully, most of us grew up in loving families with food on the table and parents who gently pushed us towards doing our best no matter the circumstance. Even if we were bullied at school it was probably brief so that our self-concept was not badly shaken. In this way most of us do not have deep-seated problems with Conscientiousness, or, for that matter Diligence. However, that we all struggle from time to time with getting moving, getting jobs finished and with worry suggests other factors which limit the full expression of this most useful virtue.

In this part of the chapter let's just deal with one factor that thwarts Conscientiousness for many of us, namely procrastination. The reason for highlighting procrastination is not just because it is the antithesis of Diligence, but because: (1) it is so common affecting a fifth of all people, and half of all students; (2) there is a strong correlation between procrastination and low Conscientiousness; and (3) psychologists have recently begun to understand its causes.[20] In this way procrastination represents an important problem, but one that we can now treat effectively.

Procrastination is often thought of as a cycle. It begins when we are given a task to complete and ends when that same task is either finished in a rush, or simply given up. According to Burka we begin any new task with all good intentions recognising that procrastination has hurt us in the past and we are genuinely determined not to let this happen again.[21] But without fundamental change nothing will be different and deep-down we know this too.

Moving into the procrastination cycle we start our work by tinkering around the edges but appear happily oblivious to the time and effort involved. The first part of the procrastination cycle ends when we acknowledge the enormity of the task and a feeling of dread hits us in the pit of our stomach. What happens now is that pressure builds. Although the deadline is not imminent the time for an early start, where information could be gathered and processed with ease, has gone. So let the mind games commence! We now wonder, 'Can I be bothered to start?', 'Who cares anyway?', or worse still 'I'm going to be in so much trouble if I don't get this ******* thing done!'. Don't we also self-recriminate at this point in the cycle, emphatically stating that we should have begun the work sooner. But typically the response to this is simply more avoidance, often by diverting to other tasks. Less helpful is when a person now engages in seriously maladaptive coping behaviours such as comfort eating, drinking to excess or smoking dope.

The final part of the procrastination cycle now plays out when we are forced to confront the monster in the corner. We simply have to go over to our desk, sit down and do something … anything. In being forced to confront the looming deadline we must also reckon on another failure. What could have been good work just won't be. This elicits the last gambit of the procrastinator. While it takes many forms it is most obviously seen in university students who feign illness when an assessment is due. In getting that extension they have a day or two reprieve. But, in the end, what does it matter? The work will still not be good enough and it's just better to forget the whole damn mess (Figure 3.1)!

Question 3.5

a. Are you a procrastinator?

b. In answering Question 3.5a it may be best to consider specific life domains given that we tend to procrastinate in selective ways. For example do you procrastinate about:

(1) study;

(2) work tasks;

(3) seeing family;

(4) making friends;

(5) making important decisions; etc.?

Activity 3.3

If you are a procrastinator, work out the specific parts of your procrastination cycle. In doing so you'll find out when it is about to commence and the little bluffs you use to maintain it. In doing so you'll have the information needed to short-circuit it in the future.

Although depressing, I (i.e., Tom) think many of us — myself included — can identify with this cycle and relate to the many bluffs we use to put off to tomorrow what we could have done today. But what good does it do us? Sure,

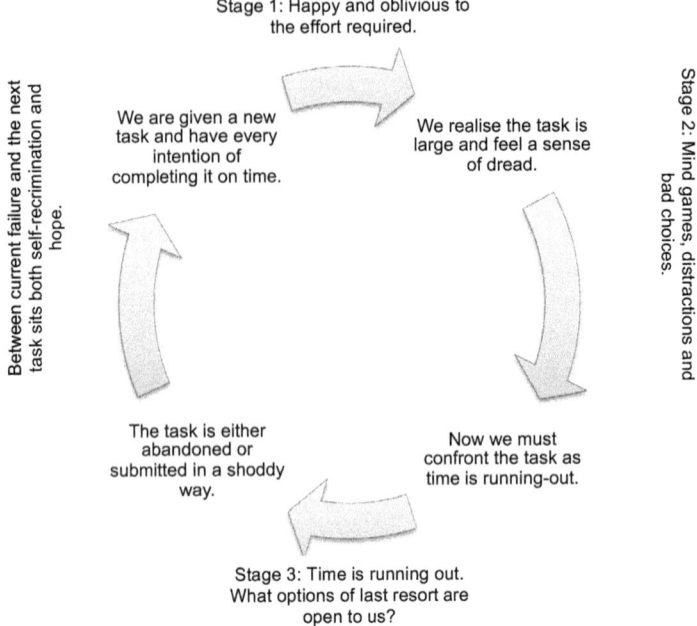

FIGURE 3.1

The procrastination cycle commences with all good intentions but builds when we begin to use small gambits to avoid work. It completes when the work is done in a blind rush or when we just give up.

some friends will be impressed by our supposedly 'chilled' attitude to work. More than a few colleagues may even be astounded by the veritable frenzy of effort we are capable of as the deadline closes in. And don't we love the sympathy when we get that extension due to 'illness'. Some procrastinators even enjoy the special pleasure of being rescued by a naïve workmate or even a spouse. In the end this is all infantile. Better to understand the root cause of procrastination and fix it.

Turning from how procrastination builds to what might be at its root cause research by Rozental and Carlbring has overturned many common assumptions.[20] While procrastination had always been paired with worry these researchers only claimed a moderate correlation. For this reason they explored other causes. For example, people who were prone to procrastination did so regarding unpleasant or difficult tasks. Procrastinators also appeared to be particularly achievement focused, if not perfectionistic. They even appeared to perceive time differently. But most interestingly, Rozental and Carlbring suggested that procrastinators, '... defer tasks and assignments to a greater degree than others do because of self-doubt and a lack of self-efficacy ...'.[22] This is such an important statement given that it reconfigures how we think about procrastination. Rather than being about worry, if not anxiety, it turns out to have more in common with concepts related to low self-esteem.

Question 3.6

    a. If you are a procrastinator, do Rozental and Carlbring's findings ring true?

    b. If you are a psychologist or counsellor what have you found to be the root cause of procrastination in your clients? What skills and strategies helped them change their behaviour?

The dark side of Diligence

As we learnt at the start of the chapter Diligence can be about either hard work or precision and both are wonderful in moderation. But there is also a dark side to Diligence in which it lessens as a virtue and becomes more of a vice. For Diligence taken to extremes can alienate a person from their family and compromise their health. To this end let us now consider both burn-out and perfectionism.

Burn-out

So far we have asserted that Diligence, and by corollary Conscientiousness, is good. And so it is. A diligent student will get into a good university degree and be set-up for life; a motivated athlete will win competitions; and a detective with a 'never give up' attitude will solve their cases. But as a person's capacity for Diligence increases what we see is ever diminishing returns for the effort put in. While, at first, lots of Diligence leads quickly to success, past a certain point a similar expenditure of energy provides only small improvements. Indeed some people even find that as they push past Diligence into something approaching obsession the quality of their work goes backwards. This is the danger zone where Diligence can spiral out of control leading to burn-out.

Question 3.7

    Have you ever seen a colleague burn-out? Perhaps you may have had burn-out yourself. What was it like?

In using burn-out as an example of Diligence taken way too far what we can say is that burn-out is not just exhaustion, nor is it simply feeling depressed, although these are some of the common symptoms. In fact burn-out is both subtle and multifaceted. To understand its various elements we can do no better than consult Herbert Freudenberger who, in the 1970's, first identified the condition. Of it he wrote:

> [My clients] had originally entered their professions with interest and enthusiasm, bursting with ideas and the desire to implement them. These were fields they had chosen, jobs that they had studied for.
>
> ... Yet they now found themselves fatigued, depressed, irritable, bored and overworked. Each day they seemed to have less to contribute and more in the way of physical symptoms to cope with.
>
> ... [They showed] rigidity, an ever increasing resistance to new concepts and programs, and inflexibility ... People who are in the throes of burning out often fail to see their situation ... Instead they find fault with everything and everyone ... [23]

Although he goes on to detail various other aspects of burn-out Freudenberger nevertheless highlighted several key points in this brief description. For example, a person with burn-out:

- loses their *joie de vivre* and instead feels 'stuck',
- shows physical symptoms of fatigue,
- demonstrates emotional changes such as depressed mood,
- becomes ridged in their thinking and a fault-finder, and
- loses a degree of self-insight which would have otherwise prevented burn-out (also see Wisdom — Chapter 4).

However this is only a brief sketch of burn-out. As research has accumulated over the intervening decades burn-out has come to be thought about in other ways.[24] Most commonly it is now ascribed three elements which, together, link the person to their environment. Specifically, burn-out is now thought to be about: (1) emotional exhaustion; (2) depersonalisation (i.e., a distorted perception of self/world leading to a loss of empathy[25]); and (3) a lack of accomplishment. But no matter the diagnostic details it simply remains the dead-end of Diligence.

Beyond this basic description it is of particular value to ask who is at greatest risk of developing burn-out? In answering this question we could look through many psychological lenses but perhaps the simplest is the lens of personality. This is a useful approach for it parallels our earlier discussion of Conscientiousness which, after all, is a personality trait.

Personality is often thought about using the Big Five model which brings together five personality traits. Of these five we have already considered how Conscientiousness, Neuroticism and Openness to experience contributed to Courage (see Chapter 2). We have also said that Conscientiousness is the personality trait which is most similar to Diligence. So, it should come as no surprise that burn-out is all about Conscientiousness taken to extremes.[26] In particular, very high levels of Conscientiousness are what contributes to the emotional exhaustion experienced in burn-out.[27] But things are never so simple in psychology for Conscientiousness may also moderate the effects of burning out under some circumstances given that highly conscientious people ' … are characterised by careful planning, effective organisation, and efficient time management ….'[28] But, be that as it may, Conscientiousness burning too brightly, for too long, will lead to burn-out.

Yet Conscientiousness is only half the story. There is also a role for the undesirable personality trait of Neuroticism. Although we all have some level of Neuroticism people who over-express this trait see the world through 'negative eyes' and so cope less well with stress than the rest of us. Interestingly, these people are also more likely to expend energy on managing how they feel rather than on the job they are meant to be doing. In this way they rob themselves of limited energy and so burn-out.

As to the signs of impending burn-out friends and family will often see these weeks and months ahead of the person who is sliding down into the pit. But in so far as you might want to do a self-check on how you're going Henderson wrote of four general warning signs albeit in *Forbes* business magazine. They are,

> [1.] You can't get enthusiastic.
>
> You've got plenty to do, but you just can't seem to make yourself do it.
>
> [2.] Your self-care is suffering.
>
> If you're living off Fritos and coffee, skipping the gym, or battling nightly insomnia, you're on a bad trajectory.
>
> [3.] Your mood is affecting others.
>
> If your uncharacteristic demeanour is starting to affect your interactions and relationships with others, it's a strong signal that you're approaching the end of your rope.
>
> [4.] Your free time is all about recovery.
>
> Do you stagger to the end of Friday like you've just completed the mental equivalent of an Ironman? We all veg out occasionally, but if you seem unable to escape recovery mode, it's a sign that your batteries are about to die. … Take heed.[29]

Finally, what can we do about burn-out?[30] Be it in prevention or recovery one foundational virtues stands out above all others, Kindness (see Chapter 7), and in particular self-Kindness. To show you some different ways in which self-Kindness might be applied to a situation of burn-out Table 3.1 details 16 general tips for prevention and recovery. Nevertheless, while useful, these tips are no substitute to seeking help from an appropriately qualified professional.

 Question 3.8

    a. Consider Table 3.1, what else can you do to prevent, or to recover from, burn-out?

    b. If you are a psychologist or counsellor what do you consider to be the most effective treatments for helping a burnt-out client?

Perfectionism

Until now we have more or less spoken of Diligence as being about the capacity for hard work and discussed the negative side of this as burn-out. But, as we learnt at the start of the chapter, Diligence is also about being precise which, if taken too far, becomes perfectionism. While we should expect a degree of perfectionism from our doctors, pilots and engineers, for their skills keep us safe, perfectionism for the rest of us is at best a bugbear and at worst a mental health issue.

Just like in burn-out, the personality traits of Conscientiousness and Neuroticism also play their part in perfectionism and this is not surprising when we consider those people most at risk.[31,32] Take, for instance, gifted children who are often very conscientious if not also a bit highly strung. They are known to have rates of perfectionism at between 43.5% and rising to over 90%![33]

As to the other factors which contribute to perfectionism Margot and Rinn examined a number of likely culprits such as parenting style, birth order and gender. While they found '... first born/only children and males [to be] at the highest risk for negative or unhealthy perfectionism',[34] their most important findings were summarised as,

> Parental expectations and criticisms may be important in the development of perfectionism ... Children whose parents have high expectations, strict rules, and a focus on academic perfection, and whose parents criticise their children when they fail to meet their high expectations are at risk for developing perfectionism ... [35]

TABLE 3.1
General tips for managing burn-out through self-Kindness

Prevention	Recovery
Lifestyle	
Having consulted your doctor, exercise both for its own sake and as a way to achieve goals that you decide upon.	Having consulted your doctor, exercise both for its own sake and as a way to achieve goals that you decide upon.
Eat a balanced diet.	Eat a balanced diet.
Sleep well.	Sleep well.
Have hobbies.	Have hobbies.
Work	
Understand what is expected of you and ask yourself if this is reasonable. If not, do something about it.	Reintegrate back into work gently. Have a clear return-to-work plan.
Solve problems early while they are small.	Assess what went wrong and what you can do differently next time.
Pace yourself. A working year is a long 48 weeks without even factoring in a busy family life.	Put in place clear workplace goals and lines of reporting.
Take leave and use weekends to renew yourself.	Plan for the mid-term so that you can recommence your career in a more measured way.
Family and friends	
Use your family and friends to support your wellbeing. They should be a good sounding board.	Use your family and friends to support your recovery. They should be an encouragement to you.
Attend family functions and social events.	Assess, and perhaps adjust, your responsibilities at home.
Speak about emotions, especially if you are struggling. Ask for help.	Speak about emotions, especially if you are struggling. Ask for help.
Make time for fun and silliness!	Be around good people who enliven you to the joy of life.

continued over the page ...

Yourself

If you are prone to thinking negatively about your workplace performance then use evidence, not feelings, to assess yourself in relation to reasonable expectations.	See your doctor for a check-up.
If you are prone to feeling anxious about situations then learn techniques to calm your breathing.	Learn to rest
If you feel overly responsible for situations and outcomes assess what proportion of responsibility is yours vs. others. Advocate for yourself.	Understand what personal strengths/weaknesses you have. Play to your strengths and put in place ways to limit your weaknesses.
Delegate!	Begin to set small personal goals and achieve them (e.g., exercise, gardening, car maintenance etc.).

Here then is an apparent contradiction with respect to Diligence. We have previously said that high expectations placed upon children are good for building Diligence yet it now appears that this may not always be so. Importantly, the difference lies in what Margot and Rinn said about criticism. It is when high expectations are paired with criticism that perfectionism grows.

The good news is, however, that perfectionism can be treated effectively. For example, four strategies come to mind.[36] First, perfectionistic thinking should be identified and challenged quickly. 'If I don't get this right my mother will kill me!', said one child. No she won't! Second, a more flexible thinking style should be developed which often comes down to devising multiple options for any given scenario. In this way 'success/failure' thinking is replaced with 'curious' thinking as seen when a person asks, 'What if …?' or 'What about …?'. Third, perfectionism can be lessened when a person recognises the benefits in lowering their standards. For example, replacing the expectation of an A+ with an A- gives a child the chance to see more of their friends without compromising their status as a high achiever. Fourth and finally, perfectionists often need to feel better about their apparent failures. In this regard psychologists recommend strategies such as mindfulness meditation in which a feeling is present but not judged. In this way fear of an exam, just is, and the anger felt at missing a goal becomes an empty vessel.

So, as you can see there is hope for those of us who tend towards perfectionism. While it is always best to avoid such problems in the first place effective, and simple, treatment strategies exist.

Question 3.9

a. Think about a person you know who is a perfectionist. In what way is their thinking faulty? For example, do they use 'I must ...', or 'I must not ...' sort of statements?

b. If you are a psychologist or counsellor what do you consider to be the most effective ways to help a perfectionistic client to change?

Activity 3.4

If you are a teacher, psychologist, counsellor or parent take one of the four strategies above and think how it could be applied with a person you know to be a perfectionist.

So, there you have it — the dark side of Diligence. Be it burn-out or perfectionism, you don't want either. If you recognise the risk do something about it now. Practice self-Kindness and perhaps get help from a professional. As for Diligence, perhaps it is best to close this section of the chapter by describing it as a lion best kept tethered.

Growing Diligence in healthy ways

As we commented at the start of the chapter, to possess the virtue of Diligence is to give yourself the best shot at a long and success life. While we obviously have to guard against burn-out and perfectionism Diligence is, on the whole, is a very good thing. Having said this it is surprising to learn that there is precious little about growing Diligence in the psychological literature. For this reason we will keep our discussions broad but nevertheless suggests some useful strategies to develop Diligence in the young and old alike.

Beginning with children, why not use stories? Children are naturally receptive to stories and use them to make sense of the world as well as their place within it. From a virtues perspective age-appropriate literature, such as *The Hobbit*, represents a particularly useful vehicle through which Diligence can be taught.

Closer to home, a child's own set of family narratives has a particular potency worth capturing. Not only do they impart crucial information about people, place and culture but also set up family norms and expectations. From our perspective, stories about immigration, drought, saving to buy the family home etc. are all stories which can teach Diligence. They also stand in stark opposition to the ever-present media narrative of instant gratification.

Question 3.10

a. What are some of your family stories which show the value of Diligence?

b. In addition to *The Hobbit*, what children's books, or books for adolescents, have you come across with a strong theme of Diligence?

Moving beyond stories, which tend to tick away in the recesses of a young mind, we also need tools to build Diligence. Three come to mind almost immediately. Let's deal with the least fun of these first.

Regular homework breeds Diligence. Be it piano practice, spelling, or learning one's times tables, Diligence is about sticking at something to achieve a worthwhile end. Although this may sound old-fashioned, if not mildly controversial, a good education has always had both explicit and implicit components. Explicitly education is about knowledge and skills; but implicitly the best teachers also impart a way of doing life well. In so much as virtue underscores the implicit purpose of education, and accepting Diligence to be an important part of this, then homework has a value beyond fact-based learning.

However, homework is often boring. A more fun way to teach Diligence is through sport. By regular training, and by competing each week, a child learns that effort breeds reward. Hopefully by end of season their team is in the finals and Diligence has paid off handsomely.

Finally, given that some children just don't like school and are not sporty we need other ways to teach Diligence. While being responsible for the care of a pet is certainly one way to breed diligence there is perhaps even a better way. Having a veggie patch is a great way to inspire Diligence in a child. Not only can they get as dirty as they want but in preparing the soil, planting seeds, watering them, and watching the veggies sprout all takes Diligence. Finally, imagine how proud a child will feel picking their veggies and bring them in for dinner!

Question 3.11

a. If you are a parent what other activities could you use to breed Diligence in your children?

b. If you are a teacher what school-based activities could be harnessed for Diligence?

Let's now shift our discussion towards adults and focus our context on the workplace.

A relatively recent study by Chokkalingam and colleagues found that low Conscientiousness in the workplace appeared to be the result of an inability of staff to manage their emotions.[37] The good news for those workers studied was that Chokkalingam was able to fix the problem with a relatively simple intervention. What they did was to take about 50 employees and teach them yoga! Not only did yoga help each employee to regulate their emotions better but in doing so workplace Conscientiousness, and therefore Diligence, improved. Moreover, it did this to a surprisingly high level. From this study we might even conclude that yoga should become part of the normal day for workplaces generally given that employees feel better able to cope and employers see higher levels of Conscientiousness. It produced a classic win–win outcome.

However it is sometimes necessary to construct more elaborate workplace interventions to increase the general level of employee Diligence. Levering off anti-smoking interventions which require participants to develop high levels of Diligence to 'kick the habit' we learn that interventions of this type must contain the following elements to be effective:[38]

- A clearly stated goal must be named so that employees know what they are aiming for,
- Employees need to recognise, and take hold of, their personal strengths,
- Accountability to others is vital, and
- Strategies to manage obstacles along the way and even setbacks must be found so as to maintain hope.

Together, these four points are your way to design effective Diligence interventions.

 Activity 3.5

Design a training package to increase Diligence in your workplace using the above four points.

Yet one workplace intervention is more successful than all the others in boosting Conscientiousness and it is on this point that we will conclude our discussion. The intervention to which we elude is simply to create a workplace culture of continuous improvement.[39, 40] Moreover, a culture of continuous improvement has been demonstrated to show increased outcomes irrespective of whether an employee began their work with high, or low, levels of Conscientiousness. It works, not because it pushes employees by way of unrealistic KPI's, but because it treats them as responsible individuals and as partners in a shared mission. We recommend it to you.

 Question 3.12

> If you are a manager, or in HR, what interventions could you introduce into your workplace to (a) improve employees' emotional self-regulation; and (b) provide opportunities for continual improvement?

A parting thought

Diligence breeds success in life, even bringing forth genius. Michelangelo spent four years up a rickety scaffold paining the ceiling of the Sistine Chapel. Along the way he had to learn the intricacies of fresco painting, suffer the stifling heat of Roman summers and the dictates of a cantankerous pope. And while he had talent in abundance, Diligence was always the midwife of his success.

Chapter 4

Wisdom

> Why do smart people do dumb things?
> — adapted from Feinberg and Tarrant

Moving from smart to wise

Wisdom is a subject so broad in its sweep that it's really too much for a single chapter. Indeed people can spend their entire careers writing books about Wisdom. So how should we proceed given the limited space we have to understand this quintessential virtue? We could, for example, discuss Wisdom from the perspective of various world religions and in so doing focus our attention on morality and ethics. We could also consider Wisdom from the position of Philosophy which bares its name (i.e., *philos* + *sophia* — to love Wisdom). But perhaps of greater use is to consider Wisdom from the perspective of our professions. In this way we not only treat Wisdom as practical, but also focus on wise decision-making.

Therefore the territory that we will chart will be small but focused. We will first look at misadventure, folly and foolishness to get an understanding of what Wisdom is not. In doing so we will also learn why Wisdom fails us every now and again. Then we'll briefly touch on some of the academic themes around Wisdom as a launch pad for a longer discussion about wise decision making. In so doing we'll come to understand that Wisdom is not just an intellectual pursuit, for the smart are not always wise. Instead, Wisdom uses our brains but also requires our humanity too. It is a subtle, but excellent, way to engage the world.

But first, what not to do in life …

Most of us are well acquainted with misadventure, folly and even a little foolishness from time to time. For this reason we all understand what is *not* wise and this, surprisingly enough, is a strong beginning in our exploration of Wisdom. So, as you read the three stories below think about your own life. But don't be too harsh on yourself. Misadventure can lead to Wisdom if lessons are learnt; folly is a very human vice; and even foolishness, which has a tendency to hurt others, can be forgiven.

Misadventure

Misadventure is not the opposite of wisdom so much as a failure of execution. In fact misadventure and Wisdom have much in common. Not least of which is that the lessons learnt from misadventure are often the fertile soil in which future Wisdom grows. Let us illustrate this with a brief story.

> Jessica Watson was a teenage sailor who wanted to sail solo around the world. This was a remarkable goal for one so young and a journey that would begin in misadventure.
>
> Nobody attempts a solo voyage of over 20,000 nautical miles without great preparation. For example, Jessica had been sailing since childhood and had completed 12,000 miles in both coastal and ocean waters before her 'round-the-world' attempt. She was also well prepared having certifications in first aid, radar, radio, and ocean survival. Even her yacht, Ella's Pink Lady, was refitted appropriately for the journey.[1]
>
> However, Jessica's preparations almost came to naught during a simple test voyage down the East coast of Australia when Ella's Pink Lady collided with a massive bulk carrier in the dark of night. Although demasted no one was injured and her yacht was able to return to port under motor. But, in their report the Australian Transport Safety Bureau concluded that both Jessica and the crew of the bulk carrier had made mistakes and so must share the blame for the collision.[2] Needless to say that being

unable to clear home waters without misadventure created a media circus and the whole journey was nearly called off.

Nevertheless, Jessica had her yacht repaired and sailed from Sydney leaving its sheltered harbour on 18th October 2009. She crossed the equator on 19th November, reached Cape Horn by mid-January and, by late February, had sailed passed the Cape of Good Hope. Jessica retuned to Sydney Harbour and to a hero's welcome on the 15th May 2010 after 210 days at sea.

The lesson of the story … While Jessica began her circumnavigation of the world in misadventure she learnt from her mistakes and finished in triumph.[1]

Question 4.1

Can you think of a misadventure in your own life? What happened to cause it? What did you learn from it? Did you become wiser as a result?

Folly

Compare this now to folly. One of the best examples of folly revolved around the later life of Harry Selfridge (1858–1947) who founded Selfridge's department store in London.[3]

Harry's childhood held within it the seeds of his eventual downfall. His father abandoned the family soon after the US Civil War and to make 'ends meet' Harry's mother was forced out to work. Without a father in the home young Harry and his mother formed an unusually tight bond which was further strengthened after the death of both his siblings. This loving bond between mother and son was to last a lifetime and ultimately trigger Harry's downfall.

As for his rise in business, Harry Selfridge was a self-made man through his legendary ability for retail. Indeed the phrase '… days to Christmas!' was one of his rallying cries to shoppers. By the early years of the 20th century Harry decided to move his retail operations from the US to London and so capitalise on the growing English middle class. In time this would make him a very wealthy man.

But although Harry had the Midas touch it could not last. In the years following World War I his wife and mother died, the Great Depression hit like a tsunami and the taxman came calling. But the saddest part was that this impressive man, now on the brink of a luxurious retirement, took up with the 'bright young things' of London society. Harry's womanising, gambling and general spending were so out of control that, at one point, he owed the colossal sum of £150,000!

Sad was Harry's demise. In 1941 his own board of directors cut him loose and, in the remaining few years of his life, old Harry could be seen out the front of his much loved department store wearing ever more dishevelled clothes and never allowed to enter.

The life of Harry Selfridge is a sombre example of person with tremendous capacity, brilliance even, but who lost it all through folly. He was unwise, to be sure, but not a bad person and this is the regret of folly.

 Question 4.2

Think of a time of folly in your own life. What motivated it? What happened? How could you have acted more wisely?

Foolishness

Finally, let's discuss the antithesis of Wisdom — foolishness. By this we don't mean everyday foolishness so much as that special form of insanity when a person has the capacity to do right but choses wrong, especially when this choice hurts other people.

While stories of foolishness abound one of the worst came to light during the Global Financial Crisis (GFC) and it did not involve just one person, but an entire country. Greece is rightfully a proud country having given much to the world. But in the matter of their national debt the Greeks behaved foolishly and people got hurt. Let us explain …

Greece has traditionally run a generous welfare state and, of itself, this is not necessarily a problem. However, no household or country can escape the basic rules of economics. Foremost amongst these being that if your outgoings exceed your incomings there will be a time of reckoning, and this is how Greece got into trouble. Wanton spending and inadequate tax collection measures by successive governments resulted in a national disaster which is still being felt years later.[4] To give you an idea of the scale of the problem, by 2005 essentially half of all companies inspected by the Greek taxman were found to be evading their responsibilities while former Finance Minister Evangelos Venizelos concluded that, '[a]round 15,000 individuals and companies owe the taxman 37 billion euros.'.[5] In the years leading up to the GFC it was as if tax evasion had become a national sport!

However, for our purposes we simply need to note the foolishness of the Greek State and the pain it has caused the Greek people.

Question 4.3

Have you seen acts of foolishness? What were the consequences to the foolish person and to those around them?

So what then is Wisdom?

To ask 'What is Wisdom?' is one thing, to answer it is quite another. Nevertheless, as you read on keep in mind the following four points about Wisdom, and wise decision-making, for they will guide your thinking:

- Wisdom grows over time. As you accumulate more knowledge, even from misadventure, your capacity for wise decision-making will improve.

- Although wise decisions often require knowledge, remember that knowledge has to be used in the right way.

- Wisdom goes beyond knowledge for otherwise smart people would also be wise people. In this way Wisdom also requires emotional, intuitive, empathetic and moral faculties to be effective.

- Finally, there are few absolutes with Wisdom. Your frame of reference is the arbiter of what appears wise and what does not. Therefore Wisdom changes over time and may look very different to other people. Accept this.

Wisdom as a philosophical enquiry

Given what we learned in Chapter 1 about the stark differences in Wisdom between Eastern and Western cultures we must make a choice in how to proceed. For this reason let's couch our discussion in the Western tradition for it is both easier to understand and often more practical.

The Greeks had two words for wisdom, *sophia* and *phronesis*.[6] *Sophia* was the more abstract term and often related to Plato's work. In many respects *sophia* was a word that spoke to harmony, truth, or a deep appreciation of something. By way of some examples, we glimpse *sophia* when we see the honesty in a Rembrandt portrait, realise that $E = mc^2$ captures a great truth about nature and just know that Justice and goodness go together.[7]

By contrast, *phronesis* is that sort of Wisdom we use in the conduct of our lives. As such, *phronesis* is of prime importance to us in this chapter. Historically, we first come across *phronesis* in Plato's *Apology* which, amongst other things, is a compelling piece of journalism.[8] In it Plato, via Socrates, suggests *phronesis* to be about the application of intellect to problems of society. But of wise people Plato notes that although they use knowledge to solve problems they set limits upon their wisdom according to their expertise. Moreover, they also tend to be reflective and able to admit their mistakes. Finally, Plato considers wise people to be good at tolerating both ambiguity and uncertainty, whereas foolish people rush at solutions. Ultimately, in this *tour de force* Plato set much of the agenda in Wisdom research, even into modern times.[9]

Nevertheless, Aristotle built on Plato's work when he wrote his *Nicomachean Ethics*.[10] Concentrating on Book VI, Aristotle discussed both *sophia* and *phronesis*. However he now grounded *sophia* in scientific, rather than metaphysical, terms. *Phronesis*, on the other hand, remained dedicated to the practical Wisdom needed to sort out life's problems.

But Aristotle could not help himself and so shifted our view of *phronesis* in the following way. He writes, '... [I]t is held to be the mark of a prudent man to be able to deliberate well about what is good and advantageous for himself ... as a means to the good life in general.'. In this way Aristotle linked *phronesis* to 'the good life' and also to the individual, not to the community *per se*. Moreover he put a sting in the tale when we realise that to discern what the good life is requires that a person have the capacity to think about their life, consider what's important and what the future may hold. To some degree this means that we have to develop *sophia* before *phronesis*. To complicate matters further, Aristotle also recognised that a person's ability to apply *phronesis*, and so get what is good in life, is also a function of their freedom to act within given social/economic constraints. The implication of all of this was to place *phronesis*, and the good life, in the hands of elites who had the intellectual ability, the time and the money to get what they considered good. The outcome of which is that Aristotle's position is not entirely satisfying for the rest of us.[11] In the end, the best way to overcome this problem is to cleave Wisdom from the good life, to separate it from happiness for the most part. Indeed this position makes more sense when one realises that in being wise one often finds a degree of heartache. Yet in spite of these shortcomings Aristotle became the backbone of investigations into Wisdom right through the Middle Ages, via Aquinas, and even holds sway in our own time.[9, 12]

Question 4.4

   a. Think of a time when you stumbled across *sophia*.

   b. When have you had to apply *phronesis* in your own life?

   c. What does the good life look like to you? Is Wisdom the way to get it?

The psychology of wise decision-making

Given that the practice of Psychology and Counselling is all about better life choices, health and wellbeing it is remarkable that Wisdom does not feature more prominently in either the research or professional literature. In fact it is almost absent! It is as if psychologists have forgotten that much of their work with clients *is* Wisdom work.

Question 4.5

   If you are a psychologist, counsellor or chaplain in what ways do you help your clients to develop a sense of Wisdom? Think about this question in terms of (a) psychoeducation about their problem; (b) managing their problem; and (c) doing life in general.

Nevertheless there are people, here and there, interested in Wisdom from a psychological perspective. Moreover, many of these researchers are also interested in wise decision-making and hence what they have learnt is of interest to us. To this end we will summarise the work of Paul Baltes, Robert Sternberg, Dilip Jeste and Monika Ardelt.[13, 14]

To begin with, Baltes and his colleagues defined wisdom as, '… excellence in the conduct and meaning of life ….'.[15, 16] This is, on the surface, a first-rate definition for Wisdom. Not only does excellence suggest virtue but, as we have learnt, Wisdom is often practical. They have even successfully tested their perspective of Wisdom using what has come to be called the Berlin Wisdom Paradigm. From this work five criteria were developed which were thought to encapsulate Wisdom.[17] They are:

- An extensive factual knowledge about human nature and life in general.
- A well-developed procedural knowledge which gives options and strategies for dealing with life problems.
- A knowledge of how life changes with age.
- A knowledge about how people value aspects of life differently based on personal and cultural differences.
- A knowledge about the unpredictability of life and how best to deal with this given that our own knowledge is finite.

Although comprehensive, Baltes' conception of Wisdom is particular. By being knowledge focused, even if that knowledge is of different sorts, it emphasises 'head before heart'. This is something that may not always hold true in being wise. In addition, and more subtly, Baltes' model may imply that only the smart, well educated, well travelled, well connected and the older amongst us can be wise. It is, in the end, a biased model. While Baltes has demonstrated that his model works we do wonder, given the above criticsm, if it excludes other forms of Wisdom such as the penetrating wisdom of the young or the life-wisdom of the seriously disabled? It is, in the end, a model likely in need of further refinement.

The next model of Wisdom we need to consider was that put forward by the eminent psychologist Robert Sternberg. For him, Wisdom is the '… application of intelligence, creativity and knowledge to the common good ….'.[18] However, this rather lovely definition of Wisdom is a bit of a *mélange*. For what is the relationship between knowledge, creativity and intelligence? Why do these three aspects of Wisdom feature so prominently in his model? And, why *must* these three qualities be used for the common good and not for individual advancement? Although enticing, Sternberg's work appears somewhat incomplete.

Nevertheless, Sternberg usefully places Wisdom within the context of his own Balance Theory which gives us a way in to understand how wise decisions are made. That Balance Theory is also a modern spin on Aristotle should make us reasonably comfortable with it. However, while Aristotle would have simply placed Wisdom between two extremes (see Chapter 1) Sternberg argues that wise decisions are achieved by balancing intra-, inter- and extra-personal outcomes for the short- and long-term.[19, 20] Yet an enthusiasm for balancing so many factors causes problems. By way of a simple example take a policing or military scenario in which personnel are required to use force to prevent great harm. This necessitates a mission-focused mentality which is, in the circumstances, wise. But the ramifications are to prioritise a short-term goal over numerous possible long-term outcomes. In addition, being mission-focused also forces one to downplay a variety of inter-personal factors. Therefore, in some instances, Wisdom may actually be found by disrupting, not achieving, balance.[13]

Perhaps a more useful interpretation of Wisdom comes from Dilip Jeste who has done much to link this foundational virtue with philosophy, psychology and neuroscience. In this way his approach is very much in keeping with the intent of our book. By scouring ancient texts and considering the work of others Jeste was able to recognise a number of oft' mentioned Wisdom attributes. It was these which came to represent his six core elements of Wisdom which he describes below.

> ... [The first dimension of Wisdom] is 'Social decision-making.' This is the concept of the 'village elder', or 'Solomonic wisdom.' When people have a debate going on and they don't know what to do, they would go to the wise person and the wise person would make the right choice. That's social decision-making.
>
> The second one is 'Emotional Regulation' — control over one's emotions. Think of it as the exact opposite of teenagers! Their emotions change from hour-to-hour, minute-to-minute, whereas a wise person would have pretty stable emotions. Not absence of emotions, but having control over the magnitude and the variation in emotions.
>
> ...
>
> The third one is 'Prosocial Behaviours' — things that we do for others rather than for ourselves — compassion, empathy, altruism. I think this is probably the single most important component of wisdom.
>
> Then comes 'Insight' — knowing yourself. It includes self-reflection. You are trying to analyse yourself and understand yourself. Understanding yourself is much more difficult than people think it is.
>
> ...

> The fifth is 'Acceptance of uncertainty', which also means 'acceptance of diversity of views.' I may have strong feelings about something, but I understand why somebody else might have different feelings about it.
>
> ...
>
> The last component ... [is] being 'Decisive', in that you accept uncertainty, you accept diversity of views, and yet you cannot sit on the fence all the time. You cannot be ambivalent all the time. You have to make a decision. You have to be decisive and act upon it. A wise person is not somebody who will spend all the time thinking about the pros and cons of everything. That needs to happen initially, but it needs to then end at some point, and a decision has to be made. Even after making the decision, you might continue debating internally, but you have to act.[21]

Although a consensus approach to the study of any psychological phenomenon is not always optimal, Jeste was nevertheless able to develop these six propositions into something worthy of further study.

Considering Jeste's Wisdom propositions more closely we immediately realise that a number appear intuitively correct. For example, few people would argue against the inclusion of emotional regulation or having insight. Yet others propositions appear slightly odd. For instance, why is social decicision-making and prosocial behavior separated when they have so much in common? Furthermore, why does social decison-making have to end with recourse to a village elder? In addition, while wise people do manage uncertainty well Jeste may have done better to swap uncertainty with ambiguity which has been part of various wisdom traditions for millennia. Finally, Jeste includes decisiveness as the last aspect of Wisdom. While we do not disagree with this we do feel that decisiveness could be problematic for 'fools rush in where angels fear to tread'. Taken together, Jeste's Wisdom propositions have much to recommend them for they are freed from Baltes' fixation on knowledge and Sternberg's reliance on balance.

Finally there is also Ardelt's model of Wisdom. While it too attracts some criticism her tripartite approach might just represent our best hope for identifying the basis of this most important virtue.

To understand Ardelt's thinking we need to be aware that she began her academic life as a sociologist who fell into psychological research. She also developed her model of Wisdom out of an interest in productive aging. As such, her approach to Wisdom has nuances not found by those who'd have taken a straighter path. Of her work she says,

> [My interest in Wisdom] goes back to my dissertation research, actually. I was interested in Life Course research ... and I wanted to know what predicts successful ageing ... [My belief was that somebody] who has

become wise over the years would have an easier time to age well because ... they know how to deal with the vicissitudes of life.

But then I said, 'Okay, but how do you measure this? There's no way to measure this!'. I had to go the library to pick up this book related to the data that I was going to use and right next to it was the book by Sternberg that had just come out *'Wisdom: Its nature, origins and development'* and I was like, 'Wow! There are actually people who have studied this.' I had no idea. So, of course I got the book, and I read it, and I was as confused at the end as when I started because everybody defined wisdom in a different way. It was all over the place, but a lot of people referred back to this chapter by Clayton and Birren that they wrote in the 1980s, 10 years earlier. So I got the chapter and they had defined wisdom.

... [Clayton and Birren] had done this multidimensional scaling analysis where they asked people of different age groups 'What do you think are characteristics of wisdom?' ... and they came up with those three dimensions — cognitive, reflective and the affective dimension of wisdom ....[22]
(paragraphs inserted for the benefit of the reader)

While Ardelt has done good work in limiting Wisdom to only three component parts — and in justifying the value of these in terms of the cognitive, reflective and affective domains — what she fills each domain with appears somewhat boutique.[23, 24, 25] For instance, Ardelt considers the cognitive domain to be about '... see[ing] the grey [inherent in a problem] rather than the black and white ...' and '... the desire to know the truth ....'[22] As such, her cognitive domain goes beyond knowledge acquisition, or even problem solving, to focus on nebulous ideas about human nature, ambiguity and the existential realities of life. This domain is rendered more complicated still when problems about social cognition are posed for now it includes notions about one's self *and* others. By contrast Ardelt's reflective domain highlights the degree to which a person can engage problems from multiple perspectives and so not be self-centered. This she says is a precondition for developing insight for now subjectivity is minimized. Although useful, mixing reflection with perspective-taking and the development of insight does appear to pack a lot into this one domain. Finally, the affective domain has since been renamed the 'compassionate domain' for better or worse. That it emphasises both positive affect (i.e., emotions) and '... sympathetic and compassionate love ...' is not wrong but risks being too focused on productive aging.[26]

Yet, to her credit, Ardelt is not precious about her model and this provides opportunities for refinement. Operationalised as the Three-Dimensional Wisdom Scale she says of it that, '... [the scale] has actually behaved quite nicely, at least in a Western, North American, European context. Now, if you go to other places, I think the jury is still out on that one!'.[22] In other words her model of Wisdom does not yet demonstrate universal validity.

That Ardelt's model is a work in progress is valuable for it allows us to adapt it. From my (i.e., Tom) work as a counsellor in which I have born witness to all sorts of misadventures, follies and foolishnesses the adaptions I would make are as follows. Why not make the cognitive domain to be just about problem solving and so give it broad utility? I also wonder why the reflective domain doesn't just focus on a person's ability to reflect on their motivations and feelings? Finally, Jeste was right when he pushed emotional, or affective, control as a central aspect of Wisdom for it restrains so many vices. So why not limit the affective domain to this alone? Taken together, Cos and I both hope that these simplifications to Ardelt's model, although significant, will give it greater appeal.

So there we have it, four psychological models of Wisdom each with overlapping and unique features. Now let's apply what we've learnt.

 Question 4.6

Reflect on all that you have learnt about Wisdom. What psychological attributes of Wisdom do you think are core, peripheral or could be excluded? In this way develop your own model of Wisdom.

So how do we learn to be wise?

If only we could think and act wisely ... How many mistakes would we avoid? How many arguments would it save? And how many bashful apologies would never need to be uttered? Not that becoming wise will prevent all our misfortunes, but it will at least minimise them. So while Wisdom is not a panacea, it is a wonderful thing to cultivate. To show you how to do this we will lean both on Ardelt's insights and on our reconstruction of her three Wisdom domains.

Living wisely
Before we name those skills which you should develop to enhance Wisdom let's set the stage. Ardelt has also had much to say about living wisely. In particular she has recognised that Wisdom can flourish only under specific circumstances.[22] For her, the wise society looks something like a place:

- where '... people have the freedom to develop the way they want',
- where people have '... enough money ... [to] live on ...',

- which allows for reduced work hours thus enabling '… time for your personal development',
- in which parents raise children and '… don't plop them in front of the computer or the TV or the smartphone', and
- where people can '… be more social …'.

In other words, what Ardelt is advocating for is a society in which people's growth needs are balanced against family demands and the necessities of work. It is a place where quality time with family and friends matters.

 Activity 4.1

> Write out a timetable for each day of the week noting all the duties, work and activities you do and the time they take. Do you have enough personal time? How might you re-organise your week to get the time you need for self-development? In addition, name the activities you would introduce into your week if time permitted which would enhance your personal growth.

Thinking wisely

Having now put forward a context in which Wisdom can flourish let's turn to specific skills you'll want to develop along the way. To begin with, Wisdom is often about problem solving. However this this a large topic in its own right for there are many classes of problems; from those that require an understanding of analytics to those which require a deep appreciation for the needs of people. In this way depending upon the problem you face slightly different skills will be required whether it is expert knowledge or a facility for empathy.[27,28,29,30,31] Nevertheless we can still make some useful, albeit general, points about problem solving to help you along the way.

In the Western tradition most theorists pair knowledge and Wisdom. And it is true that without some knowledge of the world we cannot hope to make competent, or wise, choices. By way of an example, experts exemplify this point given that their vast knowledge on a topic leads to outcomes the rest of us perceive as wise. However, knowledge and Wisdom are not the same thing. In our experience teaching in tertiary education Cos and I have both seen bright students who have immense amounts of knowledge but little ability to use it well. They are smart, but not wise.

What wise people do is take their knowledge and use it to problem solve effectively. Although problem solving is a large area of investigation amongst psychologists we can, in short order, make a few salient points that will help you in your own life. For instance, expert problem solvers have at least four traits:

- They know a lot about their chosen topic including how facts link together, even in surprising ways.

- They also know a lot of problem-solving strategies.

- When given a problem they spend time identifying key issues before working on a solution.

- They check their progress as they move towards a solution adjusting outcomes as new information comes to light.

In these four ways expert problem solvers maximise their talents and so appear wise to the rest of us.

Question 4.7

Use the four criteria above to assess whether you are a good problem solver. In what ways could you improve?

Activity 4.2

Think of a workplace problem that needs to be solved. Use the four criteria above to select the right person for the job. How did it turn out? Was the problem solved efficiently and accurately?

Having discussed the traits of expert problem solvers let's now touch on some of the details of excellent problem solving itself.[27] Be it in education, in the workplace, or even at home, problem solving is foremost about strategy. The process begins by you identifying the 'geography' of the problem before settling on a method of solution. For instance, what is the desired outcome? What are the key issues which need to be considered? Have any boundaries or limitations been imposed which will restrain the sort of solution method you may want to use? And what resources do you have access to that can help you solve the problem?

 Activity 4.3

> For a problem you are confronting list all your resources. These may be intellectual, personal, relate to other people who can help, or even the money/time available to produce a solution. With a little thinking you'll be surprised how many resources you have. How best can you deploy these resources in the solution of the problem?

However, excellent solutions never occur by chance. They all involve a specific solution process. While problem solving strategies are often particular to a discipline or context we can, at least, suggest two broad options from which you can choose. These are deductive or inductive reasoning.

If you need an exact answer to a problem then consider using deductive reasoning. In particular apply this strategy by asking a series of 'If … then …', or 'True/False' statements to narrow options down to a specific conclusion. For example, consider the sad situation of a business in decline which has to lay off one employee amongst five possible employees. The CEO can use deductive reasoning to identify who is to be made redundant. To use this strategy all the CEO need do is simply look at each employee in turn and ask '*If* I let … go *then* what will be the ramifications to my business?'. In this way the employee who will cause the least disruption to the business is identified and the decision made.

However, if your problem requires that you make a prediction, and therefore invoke probability, consider using inductive reasoning. In this way you'll want to look for things which occur together, or change together, and from these observations make some assertion. For example, a teacher has recognised that one of her students, Aarav, has become disruptive in class. To work out why she uses inductive reasoning. In particular, the teacher knows Aarav to be a good boy. She also recognises that only recently he was befriended by the class clown, George. By implication Aarav's teacher thinks George may be the problem and makes sure the two boys do not sit together in class anymore. To demonstrate the accuracy of her inductive prediction Aarav's behaviour soon improves.

 Activity 4.4

> Identify a problem which requires deductive reasoning to solve and another which needs inductive reasoning. Have a go at each method of solution. Did these methods work well?

However problem solving is, in the end, a mechanical process. What makes it fascinating are the errors and missteps that we are all prone to make along the way. In fact only excellent problem solvers — and the wise amongst us — avoid these. For example, we are all subject to a range of false beliefs, fallacies, cognitive biases and shorthand ways of thinking (i.e., heuristics) on a daily basis. Not only do these channel our energies down dead ends, but they also blind us to better alternatives and, as such, should be identified and rooted out.

Take, for example, a common false belief in which one electrician within a large business is seen by his manager as more able simply by the fact that he puts through more jobs each week. Not only is he considered the better employee, but perhaps also gets a bonus for the extra work done. He may even get a promotion in time. Yet looking only at jobs completed is not enough when we want to understand the value of this electrician to the business. In actual fact his manager may be harbouring a false belief about the value of this tradesman by not investigating further. Without analysing the types of jobs the fellow is doing, and whether they are simple/quick to complete, it is unfair to call him the better employee. In fact another electrician may be far better but puts through less jobs in a week because he is called out to solve more complicated problems. In this way we come to realise that false beliefs are common and often the result of surface-level thinking.

Question 4.8

Can you think of other examples of false beliefs leading to erroneous conclusions?

Activity 4.5

Investigate how false beliefs by government have either sent countries to war, or cost elections. To help, consider the recent example of the 2018 Malaysian election in which the government was unexpectedly toppled. Who held the false beliefs and why?

Or what about common fallacies that we all fall prey to from time to time? These are ways of thinking which sound plausible even although they are illogical. For instance there is the burden of proof fallacy and the oddly named fallacy fallacy; both of which turn on a claim being accepted not because it is correct, but because alternative arguments are insufficient. There is also the ever popular gambler's fallacy in which two independent events, such as spins of a roulette wheel, become linked in a person's mind for better or for worse. In fact some people's thinking can become quite magical when they take this fallacy too far.

Then there's the black and white fallacy and the middle ground fallacy which infects strategic thinking such as in business and politics. In the first instance we accept the simplistic position that there can only be two opposing solutions to a problem and thus deny the value of debate and negotiation in delivering a nuanced, and optimal, outcome. By contrast, the second of these fallacies would have us incorrectly settle for the comfortable middle ground on some controversial issue and so deny that there is either a right, or wrong, way to proceed.

Then there are fallacies with society-wide consequences. For example, in the context of the current 'culture wars' we often hear commentators make use of the moralistic fallacy when discussing matters of equality. Indeed this fallacy can drive public opinion and shift government policy. To explain this error of thought let's present the argument which undermines it. In simple terms, '[just because] everybody *ought* to be treated equally, [does not mean that] there *are* no innate ... differences between people.'[32] Therefore at its heart the moralistic fallacy represents a forlorn hope where *ought* is confused with *is*.

By way of a second example of a fallacy which affects entire communities let's consider the warden's fallacy. Not only does this error of thought underpin much of our 'safety culture' given how grim the nightly news is, but the warden's fallacy can turn deadly when imbibed by police. Presented as a story, the warden's fallacy reads that having been around violent criminals all day the prison warden comes home in the evening and feels agitated, falsely believing his community to be fundamentally unsafe. In this persistently heightened state he now insists that the children don't walk to school, that an extra lock be fitted to the front door and that the family invest in a dog called Brutus. Ultimately, the warden has made the illogical leap that the jail in which he works and the community in which he lives share a similar level of threat.

Taken together, we are awash with social media, TV, public announcements, sound bites and spin. Whenever an argument sounds plausible don't assume it to be. Ask if a logical fallacy is built in to what is being said. And if someone is trying to persuade you of their position assume a fallacy to be present unless determined otherwise.[33]

Activity 4.6

Turn on the TV and listen to how the media reports and commentates on stories. Can you find examples of logical fallacies?

TABLE 4.1
Some common cognitive biases[34]

Cognitive bias	Description
The bandwagon effect	When you assume incorrectly that your colleagues, family or friends know better and you just follow along.
Confirmation bias	When you hear only those pieces of information that already agree with your position. In this way you try to be right, even when you are wrong. Surrounding yourself with 'yes men' or listening to only one sort of media are good examples.
Illusion of control	When we try so hard to believe that we have more control over a situation than is true. In this way we fail to plan for other contingencies.
The Semmelweis reflex	When we deny new evidence because it conflicts with a cherished belief. Or put another way, 'I will be right no matter what!'.
Causation bias	This is when we invent a link between two events when no such link exists. Either we are indulging in magical thinking or haven't explored all possibilities as to why B followed A.
The overconfidence effect	This bias occurs when one is overconfident about their understanding of a situation.
The false consensus effect	Sometimes we just like to believe that others agree with us more than they might. This sort of false consensus is diabolical in business or political decision-making.
Fundamental attribution error	This bias involves having you attribute other people's actions to them as a person but to attribute your own actions to the situation. In this way you let yourself 'off the hook' and get to blame others all the time.

In addition to logical fallacies our thinking is also skewed by those cognitive biases we harbour in the dim recesses of our minds. But cognitive biases are quite different to logical fallacies and so operate on a different premise. Whilst we can consider a logical fallacy to be about sloppy thinking, a cognitive bias often comes about when a fragile ego, or emotion, gets in the way of a reasoned outcome. Some common examples of cognitive biases are provided in Table 4.1. Given the breadth of this topic we'll say no more except to note that the wise always understand that their thinking is never completely rational.

 Activity 4.7

> Have a look online for a description of logical fallacies and cognitive biases. Which ones could you be most susceptible to?

Finally, we must also deal with heuristics. Although not illogical, nor a sloppy form of thinking, heuristics do bring us to grief from time to time for they represent shorthand ways of thinking. As such, heuristics trade off the amount of data assimilated for improved speed of processing. A necessity in our complex world, but a fraught calculation in social settings where small details provide context and understanding.

For example a common heuristic is to assume that either a tall person, or an older male, is the senior person at some corporate or political function. I wonder what Germany's Chancellor, Angela Merkel, would make of this sort of shorthand way of thinking?

Yet more serious is when a heuristic is used to stereotype a group of people. While this can have uncomfortabe consequences, as when an older lady in a hospital's emergency room asks for an Asian doctor for 'they are the smartest ...', stereotyping is often more painful. Be it racial profiling by law enforcement, our perception of 'illegal immigrants' or the sad necessity of the Black Lives Matter campaign, the heuristic of stereotyping is ugly.

So, in sum, wise cognition is not just about learning problem solving strategies, but learning to *avoid* errors of thought. Be it false beliefs, logical fallacies, cognitive biases or heuristics don't let these trip you up.

 Activity 4.8

> Read about the work of Nobel laureate Daniel Kahneman and his colleagues on cognitive biases and heuristics and how they influence both business and government decisions.

The final part of our discussion on the cognitive components of wise decision making is possibly the most crucial. What seems to separate the wise from the simply clever is their capacity for insight. That is, some people have the ability to see right into the heart of a problem, or into another's soul.

In thinking about insight let's lean on the work of Sternberg.[13, 20, 27] So what makes for insight? First it is about knowledge, the more the better. But insight goes further. Insightful people also have the capacity to redefine a problem in new and better ways. For them, the glass is neither half full, nor half empty, they ask simply for a different glass. In many respects this is where Wisdom, creativity and genius overlap.

Beyond having a penetrating intellect, and an uncanny ability to redefine problems, insightful people also understand the future implications of their actions. As such, the quality of a solution to a problem is not judged for what it provides now, but also for what it will mean for people in the future. Although harking back to Sternberg's Balance Theory it is not that insightful people necessarily seek to balance short- and long-term outcomes, but can at least envisage the long-term consequences of their actions rather than trusting to 'lady luck'.

Taken together, wise people do demonstrate particular cognitive advantages over the rest of us. Nevertheless we can learn from their example and become wise ourselves. To do this we must: (1) become structured in our thinking about how to solve problems; (2) avoid making, or falling prey to, sloppy arguments; and (3) learn to become insightful.

 Activity 4.9

> a. Building insight is crucial. However, like any skill it must be practised. Riddles, puzzles and cryptic crosswords are a great way to do this. Have a go.
>
> b. If you are a teacher how might you adjust your curriculum and teaching methods to grow your students in Wisdom?

Reflecting wisely

Before acting outward in the world we should look inward. Sometimes simply taking a reflective pause before making a big decision can change your thinking and thereby avert a disaster. But more than this, we are asking you to begin to understand the psychological forces at play inside your head. What motivates you? When do you feel fear? What about desire? Who are you trying to impress? These, and many other questions, motivate our behaviour even although we are barely conscious of them. In so many ways they either enhance, or detract from, our capacity for Wisdom. Just ask Harry Selfridge.

While it is not our intention to have you go into therapy it is nevertheless worthwhile to point out one particular trip-wire in the jungle of your mind which is likely to turn Wisdom into folly. We now speak of the power of projection. Projecting is actually one of the most common problems we all have in sorting truth from fiction and fact from fantasy. As such, those who have learnt to look inwards and recognise their projections are often the people most able to render a wise decision.

In *Psychology and Religion,* Carl Jung gave us the best introduction to what projections are,

> You can find them spread out in the newspapers, in books, rumours, and ordinary social gossip … We are convinced that certain people have all the bad qualities we do not know in ourselves or that they practice all those vices which could, of course never be our own.[35]

Projections are thus the nasty little qualities we each possess, but which we refuse to acknowledge and so cast off onto other people. But they nevertheless show up in how we act. Be it snide remarks, blame, innuendo, glee at another's misfortune, accusations, or as malicious gossip, projections can do great damage.

To demonstrate this let's look at two examples. First, in the corporate world recruiters are particularly susceptible to projections because they are making important judgements about people. Taking this one step further, it is not hard to imagine a job interview where a bright young graduate fails to impress a recruiter. Not because he is poorly qualified, but because the recruiter has projected something of his own inner world onto this graduate. The recruiter may go back to the employer and refer to the graduate as 'Not up to the task', 'Too young', or say something silly like 'I just get a bad feeling …'. What's really going on is that the recruiter has felt his age creeping up on him, the plateauing of a career and perhaps job insecurity. Unfortunately for the employer, who is none the wiser, they just accept this advice and move onto the next candidate letting a perfectly good catch get away.

The second instance of projection worth mentioning relates to the 2016 US Presidential Election. So many pundits got the outcome wrong simply because they projected their own value system. In essence, these commentators filled gaps in their knowledge with assumptions that did not hold true for middle-America. Or, to put it another way, they swapped what was happening for what they wanted to have happen. What's more, in large and small ways the same commentators have often kept on projecting their own inner demons onto President Trump rather than always providing a balanced critique of his policies.

In sum, the reflective domain is all about waiting and watching. Not other people, but how you are responding to a situation. Let your ability for reflection be a way to engage greater depths within yourself and be the springboard for wise decision-making.

 Activity 4.10

    a. When you have a big problem to solve practice sitting quietly and relaxing before doing anything. Become aware of your thoughts and the feelings they bring up. Ask what these feelings are about. In this way you'll become aware of your deeper motives. At this point consider a wise solution to the problem at hand.

    b. Managers also need to know when colleagues and subordinates are projecting. To begin to filter out the projections of others you can take a leaf from the intelligence community who deal with this sort of problem all the time when assessing the value of human intelligence. For instance ask yourself:

        (1) Do the people who I'm listening to have an agenda?
        (2) Are these people calm by nature?
        (3) Has the information been compiled in a rush?
        (4) Can I corroborate the information through an independent source, or by comparing it to numerical data?
        (5) What information have my people highlighted, devalued, or excluded in their reports — and why?

    c. Finding a wise mentor can also be a great way for you to avoid projecting as they will hold you accountable. See if you can find such a person.

Acting wisely

As we learnt above, Ardelt thought the affective domain to be about compassion but this seemed a little narrow for everyday use. Of greater utility was Jeste's concept of emotional (i.e., affective) control and we agree.

But how do we proceed in understanding affective control? While Psychology and Psychiatry have had much to say about disorders of mood and emotional dysregulation this may be a bit too clinical for what we are after. Luckily, affective control has also been a central theme within virtues traditions the world over. In fact affective control is nothing more than the virtue of temperance placed within a psychological context.

But temperance is not easy to grasp at. For instance, we could consider it to be a break on behaviour and thus an 'operator' in much the same way as the virtue of hope (see Chapter 2), albeit acting in the opposite direction. Many would also claim temperance to be a cardinal, or core, virtue and thus having equality with virtues such as Courage, Justice and Wisdom. Even so we respectfully disagree. Indeed we have chosen to subsume temperance under Wisdom because a wise decision is often indistinguishable from a temperate one. In this way temperance now defines the affective domain and becomes a part-player in Wisdom.

As for how we develop temperance the idea is to start young with parents and teachers playing a vital role. For example, using data from the Jyväskylä Longitudinal Study of Personality and Social Development (JYLS) it was found that coming from a low socio-economic home, and having parents who drank or smoked were predictors of intemperance later in life.[36, 37] While little can be done about family circumstance such findings nevertheless suggest that parents can do simple things to model temperance to their children.[36] While managing alcohol and cigarette consumption is one thing, parents can also model temperance in the way they communicate to each other and in how they resolve problems. Indeed temperance can even be modelled in the food choices a family makes, how much screen time is allowed, how credit cards are managed and even in what sort of holidays are taken. In many respects temperance is a lifestyle choice.

As for teachers and school welfare staff they become vital in identifying children at risk of intemperance. For instance, boys who demonstrated aggression by age 8, who had weight issues and poor school performance before the age of 14 were at higher risk of intemperance later in life with all the bad choices that entails. Whereas for girls, weight gain and school performance were a risk factor by 8 years of age and aggressive tendencies by 14. Interestingly, as both boys and girls matured into their teens they began to share risk factors for life-long intemperance including drinking alcohol early and leaving school prematurely. For teachers these are key signs to look out for.

But how do we shift a person from intemperance to temperance and thereby improve their life choices? One answer comes from an unlikely set of studies. If we assume poor delayed gratification links to intemperance through impulsivity then we have a way forward. Although delayed gratification has a multitude of factors feeding it including genetics, age, intellect and unexpectedly the misperception of time it is, in the final analysis, about safety! People wait for a future reward only if they feel safe to do so.[38, 39, 40, 41, 42]

To justify this claim Liu and colleagues had participants view scenes of poverty and then measured how well they then did with delaying gratification.[43] When offered a small reward now versus a large reward later-on participants invariably failed to delay gratification and took the small reward. By implication the images made the participants feel unsafe and thus they needed to act impulsively. Michaelson and his team of researchers also found the same effect in a different way.[44] By engaging with stories of apparently trustworthy, neutral and untrustworthy people participants were less likely to delay gratification if the untrustworthy person was involved.

So, in an unexpected way affective control is about temperance; temperance is about delayed gratification; and delayed gratification is about feeling safe. In this way not only do we discover intemperance to be a really clever, albeit unwise, survival strategy but one born of necessity. To this end, although it is easy to put a moral value on temperance we should not rush in. It appears, after all, that people can only be temperate if they feel safe enough to be so.

 Question 4.9

    a. What might the research on intemperance and delayed gratification suggest about ADHD?

    b. If a feeling of being safe undergirds temperance what does this say about working with prison inmates?

 Activity 4.11

    If you are a parent or teacher think about some small ways in which you can model affective control, and thus temperance, to the children in your care.

While affective control, and thus temperance, is good we can also have too much of a good thing. As Aristotle first noted, all virtues live on a continuum and temperance is no different. While we have already linked intemperance to being unwise, if not vice-ridden, what is the outcome of being too temperate? In highlighting the dangers of taking temperance too far the famed mid-20th century psychologist Karen Horney wrote of excessive self-control in the following way,

> The tendency towards excessive self-control can be so strong ... Persons who exert such control will not allow themselves to be carried away, whether by enthusiasm, sexual excitement, self-pity or rage ... They will not permit alcohol to lift their spirits and frequently prefer to endure pain rather than undergo anaesthesia. In short, they seek to check all spontaneity ... Such persons are held together merely by their idealised image ... [And since] the most disruptive impulses are those of violence prompted by rage, the greatest degree of energy is directed towards the control of rage. Here a vicious circle is set in motion; the rage, by reason of being suppressed, [now] attains explosive strength ...[45]

Therefore, and in sum, a little temperance goes a long way towards being wise.

Question 4.10

If you have trouble with temperance where can you be safe? To whom can you turn who is trustworthy and thus represents a safe person?

Bringing the three domains of Wisdom together

Wise people are insightful people. This is the hallmark of Wisdom. But under the general heading of insight wise people can also be shown to manage some problems better than the rest of us. One sort of problem requiring great insight is when we have to deal with ambiguity. Moreover ambiguity often pops up when we have to confront the big questions of life such as accepting one university offer over another, choosing to marry and not think about your ex, or even coming to terms with matters of gender. For this reason learning to contend with ambiguity in the wisest way is of great importance. What characterises wise decision makers in such circumstances is that they do not rush to judgement, but speak in nuanced tones, maintain friendships in spite of differences and accept that some things in life will never be right. In other words they accept, and work with, ambiguity rather than trying to force simple binary answers. What's interesting is that to manage ambiguity is not the preserve of any one Wisdom domain but takes all three. So, to conclude this chapter let's look at ambiguity, and thus Wisdom, but from an integrated perspective.

From speaking with people Nicolaides learnt a lot about coming to terms with ambiguity.[46] She learnt the importance of (a) metaphor as a *cognitive* picture allowing ambiguity to be clearly seen; (b) endurance as the *affective* capacity akin to temperance required for people to work through ambiguity; and (c) *reflection* as a way to be in 'communion' with ambiguity. She even discovered a fourth element to do with awakening from ambiguity which relied on all three Wisdom domains working together. Let's now tease out these ideas a little more …

Before ambiguity could be dealt with participants in Nicolaides' study remarked on the need to generate a useful metaphor to assist their movement from a place of knowing into the experience of unknowing. In particular, metaphor was used to make a cloudy problem clear, to give it boundaries, if not shape. More subtly, developing a good metaphor helped participants by bringing some features of the problem to the fore while forcing other aspects to recede into the background. Not only did this allow participants to concentrate on what they considered important but, by the choices they made, they brought their value system into play. Yet the metaphor generated by participants also did something else. For some participants metaphor became a way to draw closer to ambiguity, but for others it allowed ambiguity to be held at a safe distance. In this way the cognitive domain which was generating the metaphor was also responding to affective needs.

Beyond creating an effective metaphor participants also spoke of the need to endure through ambiguity if a satisfying solution to their problem was to be found. This obviously suggested an important role for Wisdom's affective domain. For example, affective control may be used to quell disabling emotions such as shock, as noted by one participant. Affective control was also important in managing frustration when potential solutions were judged and rejected. But, surprisingly, affective control not only appeared to be important in enabling people to persist towards a solution but also to let go of their preconceptions without feeling overwhelmed.[46]

Finally, having sat with their ambiguity for some time various participants in Nicolaides' study then talked of an experience by which they came to be in communion with their ambiguity and this speaks strongly to a role for the reflective domain. Here notions of intimacy, if not vulnerability, were conjured up and limits to any solution had to be admitted and accepted. Some participants even had to accept a position of 'not knowing'. One participant, in particular, commented on the experience of this describing it as 'grief' while Nicolaides added '… loss, … wrath, … [and] sweetness' and finally 'surrender' to the description.[47] Ultimately the act of communion was expressed in a willingness to trust.

Finally, participants who had engaged metaphor, endured and communed with ambiguity also talked of an awakening. In overtly religious language one participant expressed their solution to ambiguity as 'co-creating' with God.[48] What's fascinating about this response is that it represented a solution to the problem of ambiguity, but one opposed to nearly everything we are taught by society. For co-creating is not time limited, finite, or necessarily concerned with categories of right and wrong. It emerges, flows and flourishes. Such solutions are, in essence, both adaptive and utterly wise for they utilise all three domains.

So, in closing, while it is tempting to think of Wisdom as a purely intellectual process this is incorrect. Nor is it adequately understood by speaking to both 'head and heart'. While engaging cognitive, reflective and affective capacities do represent the bare bones of Wisdom Nicolaides also teaches us that Wisdom is greater than the sum of its parts.

Activity 4.12

> Reflect on a time when you were confronted with a problem that held ambiguity within it. Map the ways in which your cognitive, reflective and affective domains worked together to help you find a satisfying solution.

Moving to the next level …

Wisdom is the central virtue. That is why we placed it half way through our book. For Courage without Wisdom is rash, while Diligence without Wisdom is self-imposed slavery and, as we will come to see, Honour, Justice and Kindness without Wisdom lead to all manner of foolishness. Therefore Wisdom represents a unifying force. It conducts the orchestra of the virtues. It is, in the end, the one virtue which is truly indispensable when living to excellence.

The Freedom of Virtue: Navigating excellence in the art of living amongst a world of instant gratification

Chapter 5

Honour

> [Honour is] pervasive in human society
> — William Lad Sessions

From me to us ...

All virtues are social in so much as they either help you find success within your 'group' (e.g., family, organisation or community), or regulate how that group is managed. However, up until now we have focused on only those virtues which pre-empt individual success. All things being equal Courage, Diligence and Wisdom are all you need for people to label you a leader, a change-maker, or in some quarters even a genius. Using a sporting metaphor, Courage proves you will not stand on the side lines of life but take your place on the field. Diligence means you will always 'go hard' for the ball. While Wisdom allows you to play with panache. Except for a little luck there really isn't much more to individual success.

Yet, from Chapter 1, three other foundational virtues remain to be discussed. They are Honour, Justice and Kindness. These virtues are alike, but differ from those already discussed for they are overtly relational. While one can have Courage, show Diligence and express Wisdom without anyone else present the same cannot be said for Honour, Justice or Kindness. In addition, that we have three foundational virtues which are relational is important because we live in community. Not as a matter of convenience, but as a matter of survival. So to have some virtuous mechanism to regulate our relationships is of the greatest importance. This is what Honour, Justice and Kindness do.

Why don't we talk of Honour anymore?

Honour is the lost virtue. While it guided the conduct of individuals within their families and villages for millennia it now appears to be something confined to arcane military colleges, or just the movies. This is a shame because Honour is powerful stuff. An honourable person is the most dangerous sort; for they know what they hold to be true and will defend it, often in spite of stinging opposition. The same applies to a group of people bound together with Honour. They become cohesive and mission-orientated if not unstoppable. For this reason Honour is the key ingredient in welding a football team into champions, turning a military unit into legends, or creating a company which becomes an industry leader. It also makes for a family that has pride in who they are.

 Activity 5.1

> Name a leading business or organisation. How did its values lead to its success? Were these values Honour-related?

The problem in coming to this chapter is not that Honour doesn't exist in the 21st century, but that it is complicated by an array of factors which muddy the waters. Let us consider three of these: (1) the breakdown of traditional communities; (2) a failure to see the signs of Honour about us (e.g., the handshake); and (3) a particular media skew when portraying Honour.

Unlike past generations we live in a globalised world of unimagined wealth. To capture the smallest amount of this bounty rural peasants the world over are leaving behind their attachment to family and place, moving either to big cities in search of work, or casting themselves adrift as refugees. The effect of this has been to disperse families and break down communities that were often honour-based. Sadly we are then often presented with a particular perspective on migrants and refugees. What we see is not the stable honour cultures from which these people came, but the almost chaotic attempts new migrants make to re-establish community in a new land. This being said, an understanding of Honour thus has significant implications for governments, welfare agencies and even police when helping immigrants to establish themselves anew. It even goes some distance in explaining the dire predicament of some indigenous communities.

Question 5.1

>   a. In what ways could a teenage gang be seen as an attempt to form an *ad hoc* honour culture?
>
>   b. How might police and community services utilise foundational virtues, such as Honour, to divert teenagers away from gangs?

Governments have also contributed to Honour receding from view in two significant ways. First, by passing laws that now penetrate nearly every aspect of life, including the previously private domains of family and religion, meaning that responsible adults have had taken from them their natural ability to manage conflict and negotiate relationships. Second, while governments have rightly introduced generous welfare systems across the Western world this too has led to a fading sense of Honour. As hardship strikes families and communities, except perhaps in rural areas, now feel little need to band together. They simply access government services instead. What's interesting is that the corporate world has followed suit. By creating vast HR departments and Employee Assistance Programmes (EAP's) the corporation now controls employees' relationships rather than trusting to people's natural ability to regulate their own affairs.

Less ominously, most of us do not see Honour at work because we do not know what to look for. Let's give you two simple examples of honour-based behaviour that we see every day. The simplest example is that members of a group tend to dress in a similar way. This is not by accident. Wearing a club uniform on the sports field is no different to wearing corporate attire, for both signal that one belongs to a particular group which holds specific values and has a defined purpose. Or, more subtly, what about shaking hands? This too is honour-based for it signals the meeting point between people and indicates trust. The Japanese take this one step further when they bow on greeting. For in the depth and length of the bow two individuals also establish hierarchy which is an essential element of Honour as we will learn shortly.

Question 5.2

a. Have you ever analysed how a handshake works? For example, how do men and women shake hands in similar/different ways? Or how does a CEO shake hands compared to a person of lower status? What do these differences tell you?

b. What other common behaviours, or social interactions, signal Honour? Can you think of ones in the home, at work, at a local sports club, or more generally in the community?

Finally, Honour is a complex topic to discuss because it has been given a bad name by the media. For example we are confronted, almost nightly, by media stories out of the Middle East — and none of them good. As such Honour is often talked about only as it pertains to war, returned veterans or, at worst, 'honour killings'. All of which provide a blunt, or inaccurate, perspective on this important foundational virtue.

Question 5.3

In what way is Honour understood differently for men compared to women?

However, perhaps the greatest difficulty when trying to discuss Honour is not when it is used, but how it is used.[1] The problem is a linguistic one. At the simplest level Honour is frequently confused with a number of similar words such as integrity, dignity, reputation and glory. To give you an idea of this sort of problem let's look at integrity. While Honour is measured against an ideal of excellence, integrity is outcomes-based. So, when a businessman borrows a lot of money the honourable thing is to repay the money in accordance with the details of the loan. To do so demonstrates his integrity. In this way Honour relates to one's word and integrity to how one acts.

More confusingly, different languages use the word Honour differently and in English it can even have a multitude of meanings. For example, we respect a person who '… honours an agreement …', even deeming them '… honourable …'. An athlete or scholar may also '… win honours' and '… be honoured …' for doing so. There are even titles given to important people such as judges or senators including 'Your Honour' and 'The Honourable'. In England one can even be called 'The Right Honourable …' just to give it a little more kick! The word Honour can also be applied to groups of people. There are, for example, honour cultures across the world and even the Mafia sometimes go by the name of the 'Honoured Society'. Therefore, if we are not careful, Honour can come to mean so many different things that it can lose its status as a singular virtue.

Opening the door to Honour

Unless we can find a way to knit together all the above meanings for Honour we will soon get lost. At a broad level our task is to somehow link the personal attributes of Honour, such as being honourable, with its social aspects. For Honour belongs to both the individual and their group. To do this we present two examples of very different honour cultures. The first example comes from the observations of Professor Frank Stewart who, as a younger man, lived with the Bedouin of the Middle East.[1,2,3] The second relates to the honour culture that my co-author, Cos, grew up in. Not only have Cos' personal insights influenced this chapter, but his lived experience in a Calabrian-Australian community presents a perfect foil to the work of Professor Stewart.

Bedouin honour culture

The Bedouin people have, traditionally, been nomads who lived within kinship groups and moved their livestock from well to well, trading as they went. If you have ever watched Peter O'Toole in *Lawrence of Arabia* you have some idea of what we are describing. Being nomads the Bedouin were not subject to the systematic control of 'the State', as we are in urban centres, and so developed community-based notions of good and bad, of how to wield authority and administer justice. And this was all encapsulated in their honour system. Therefore, Honour represents a general feature of community life and Justice a specific virtue alongside.[2] It is for this reason our chapter on Honour precedes our chapter on Justice (see Chapter 6).

In Bedouin culture Honour (i.e., *Ard*) is '… the right to be treated in a respectful fashion.'.[1] Whereas to lose one's honour is to lose the right to be considered an equal in the community. Most curiously, however, Bedouin Honour is not simply gained or lost as we might think of such things in the West. It can also be placed in jeopardy, forfeited, sullied, or even placed under protection. Hence the Bedouin honour system is very nuanced.

To demonstrate this sort of complexity let's recount one example from Prof Stewart's work.[1,2] For the Bedouin Honour is only attached to men. Neither women nor children have Honour in their own right. But women do play an important role in managing a man's Honour. Therefore women are not excluded from the community's honour system, just that they have a particular function within it. To put this in context, a romantic misadventure by a man's unwed teen daughter is an issue of Honour. In saying this however we must consider three particular, if not peculiar, elements to Honour. First, a problem only arises if the daughter does not seek her father's approval, for he is her 'guardian'. Second, the father's Honour is only affected if he finds out about her tryst. Third, his Honour is not lost by her actions, only jeopardised.

Assuming that the young woman's father does find out about the unsanctioned romance then a legal process commences within the community's honour system. In the first instance the father must react to the assault on his Honour. If he doesn't he will lose the community's respect which may have significant implications for him and his family. Interestingly, the legal process that follows is actually designed to help him re-establish his Honour in the eyes of the community and therefore differs to what we may think of as law in the West. Within this legal process there are also differences. For example, the action taken by the father is not against his daughter but her boyfriend. Even although she was the one who imperilled her father's Honour. In addition, although a local magistrate hears the case he acts more like an arbitrator than a judge. As for the punishment metered out to the love-struck young man this is more about public shaming than retribution. In this way the father's Honour is restored and his place as a respected member of the close-knit community once again assured. Importantly, what sits behind this pantomime of Honour is a very precise ritual designed to re-establish trust between the father and his community, it is only by extension about crime and punishment. In this way Honour for the Bedouin becomes the currency of trust.

 Question 5.4

 a. What were your reactions to reading about the Bedouins' honour culture? What things struck you as useful, strange, or unhelpful?

 b. In the West we often talk about the Law not being just. Could justice for victims be more about upholding their Honour? If so, how might our courts include notions of Honour in how they treat victims and deal with offenders?

Calabrian-Australian honour culture

Compare the Bedouin experience to that of my co-author Cos who grew up as a second generation Australian born into an immigrant family of Calabrian Italians. Cos' father Joe came to Australia during the economic boom of the post-War years. But along with his suitcase of clothes he also brought the culture of a small Calabrian village. In Cos' own words,

> Like many immigrants, my father became time-locked in the thoughts and ways of his place of origin, in this case village life in southern Italy. For me, I also had the unenviable position of being the eldest son of an eldest son, so heir to the clan (i.e., family) leadership as well as being a 'half breed' due to my Australian mother. So I got to be both a participant and observer to culture.

Because Cos' father settled amongst other immigrant Italians Cos therefore grew up in an honour culture that was not only stuck in a time warp of decades, or centuries, past but was also self-reinforcing. In our conversations I asked Cos what this was like and his response surprised me,

> [To be] raised in an honour culture, a culture filled with a complex pecking order, endless jostling and no outwardly discernible rules of engagement, is hard to describe. The first thing to understand is that *there is always an underlying tension* ... which is why we [Italians] seem so loud and abrasive. Everyone is always checking that they haven't breached another's standards while checking their own boundaries for slights and outright offence.

As an Anglo, I was somewhat taken aback. I'd always considered the bantering of Italian friends to be just an expression of good-natured, if not disorderly, family life. I never thought it had a function. But Cos said it was more subtle even than this. Relationships were like a game of 'snakes and ladders' in which people would rise in Honour as their reputation grew, but could fall just as easily. To demonstrate this point he gave the following example,

> Many years ago one of my many cousins brought her fiancée around to [each of] the relatives' homes to properly introduce him ... So over lunch we got to meet 'The Greek' as he had been nicknamed. While this description may seem a little racist, and it is, it noted one important aspect of Honour ... to exclude those without reputation (e.g., outsiders including those from other cultural groups) and hence who have no place in the pecking order.
>
> [Over] the course of the meal 'The Greek' spent most of his time fawning over my father's stories and flattering him shamelessly. It got so bad my cousin said to her beloved 'Really? Would you like a roll of toilet paper ...?' [to which] my mother piped up, 'He [i.e., Joe] has such a big head he won't

even notice'. Now The Greek made the mistake of snapping back, 'That's no way for a wife to speak to her husband!'. Without hesitation my father snarled, 'You ever speak to my wife like that again and I'll throw you out into the street!'.

[So family life is a] confusing mess prone to error, overstepping the mark and swift discipline. To the outsider it can seem like a brawl, just one step above a back alley fight. But make no mistake, ... [the family] is a cohesive ... group with strong bonds of love and respect.

In explaining this story Cos introduced me to several important aspects of how an honour culture works.

First, Honour is about inclusion and exclusion. It concerns a group of individuals often tied together by blood, but perhaps also by shared tradition, who together can effectively whether life's storms. Therefore, a new person has to be introduced into the culture by their attachment to a pre-existing individual. In this case The Greek was introduced as the fiancée of Cos' cousin. Second, one always begins at the bottom of the hierarchy which is made known to the individual, in this case by a mildly dismissive nickname. Then it is up to the individual to begin their long journey of integration and movement up the pecking order. Third, we also see the importance of a senior person in regulating the social hierarchy. While The Greek was clever enough to lavish attention on Cos' father as a way to ascend the hierarchy he also felt a quick rebuke when he overstepped an unwritten boundary. As Cos put it,

> There's an old saying, 'The only thing wogs like more than fighting with each other is to fight with outsiders'. And while this may appear harsh, what was actually happening in the rough exchange around the dinner table was disciplining the outsider [i.e., The Greek], returning him to his initial position in the jostling hierarchy — at the bottom.

I then asked Cos why it was so important for an outsider to enter into the group from the bottom? For in Anglo culture if a young woman brought her fiancée home for the first time and he was, for example, a doctor he'd almost immediately be accorded some level of respect. The bluntness of Cos' reply took me aback appearing to be something a Borgia would say,

> The reason why a person comes into a family at the bottom is without reputation there is no way to take the measure of the person. What are they good at? Are they honest? Are they a risk taker? What are their loyalties like? All of this is missing at the beginning. No reputation has been earned yet. If you think about it in purely evolutionary terms honour cultures, such as from Calabria, were about communities on the brink of starvation. You had to know who to trust if you were all going to survive. That's why terms such

as glory and honour are important. They are your 'bullshit filters' against people who lack either, while reputation is your scorecard.

For me this was fascinating as I now could link reputation to Honour and had, for the first time, understood the importance of winning glory in the eyes of others.

But how did glory and reputation work in the community that Cos grew up in? While modern society distains glory-seeking, except in war or sport, this is not so with honour cultures,

> … honour cultures accept this (i.e., glory seeking) as a necessary stage of growing up and provide channels that really work to ensure that the vast majority of young people emerge with little or no damage and plenty of stories to tell, showing they have the spirit in them to weather life's trials, as well as take up the burden of Honour. Qualities such as loyalty to a friend, honesty, stamina and fortitude, as well as a bit of fearlessness for the bad times ahead are all seen as good.

I then pressed Cos on his notion of glory and how it worked. With a wry smile he told this tale,

> As a young man I owned a high-powered customised car, so of course speed and reckless driving was going to feature … I was never interested in drag racing, but did a 'rollercoaster run' once. … [There] were three passengers [in the car] including a lovely young lady on my lap while I raced down the highway out of town in the middle of the night swerving around traffic islands. Was it stupid? Yes. Was it risky? Of course. Was it worth it? To my twenty-something self in search of glory — definitely. To my friends I was now the hero!

Now by no means are we saying that driving recklessly is a good thing. However, because it involved risk, if not considerable danger, it did bring Cos the glory that he required at that age. Pressing Cos a little further on glory he then commented,

> … glory is only the start of Honour. It allows … [young men] to demonstrate their 'fitness' often for the purpose of attracting a mate. This is why young men seek glory. Sadly it is this wildness that the 'Nanny State' has tried to stamp out. Yes, glory is wild, reckless and obviously dangerous at times, but it is part of our psyche and part of our evolutionary history. If we don't provide avenues for 'relatively' controlled glory-seeking it won't go away, it will just turn into rebellious teenage outbursts.

He went on to say,

> While glory is for the young man Honour is for the older man and shows the community he is 'fit' to make a home, raise children and take responsibility for his life.
>
> In an honour culture there are moments where you are ushered from glory to Honour. In my culture we observe marriage to be one of the great turning points and the transition from glory to Honour ... I married late in life, in my late forties. My father had recently died and his last wish was that his passing not stop our wedding ... [So it] fell to my *Compari* [i.e., Baptismal Godfather] to stand in the role of my father and issue the traditional 'pre-marital warning'. 'Now you look after her, we like her, ...' he admonished at the end of the pre-wedding dinner as all the men went off to drink and talk ... It was a lovely, archaic, unnecessary — but a vital — gesture [in moving from glory to Honour]. I'm sure my father would have approved of how well his Honour was protected. [*paragraphs inserted for the benefit of the reader*]

Therefore Honour follows glory. While glory may prepare a young man for the duties of Honour, and attract a mate, Honour itself is an altogether more serious business. An honoured person is a full member of the community, worthy of respect and able to provide for their family.

Finally, Cos was insistent to have me understand one last point about growing up in an honour culture. Honour must be maintained and this is done by maintaining your reputation. As he spoke what I realised was that the rules for maintaining one's reputation were quite different to that which I had experienced growing up in Anglo culture. For instance, while Anglos may baulk at a person having an affair, in an honour culture this may be tolerated without loss of reputation so long as the man's wife is not insulted. In this way you'd never take your mistress to a public celebration for that is an occasion properly belonging to a husband and his wife. Therefore, the idea of 'insult' becomes the chief means by which a person loses their reputation. Cos illustrated this with one final story,

> A young guy I knew had three flaws: (1) he drank too much; (2) he had an ego; and (3) a temper. Ordinarily enough this would just make him an unpleasant person but not cost him his reputation. He had even recently won some glory by qualifying as a tradesman. Things were good for a little while until he thought he could improve his reputation further by getting 'one-up' on an old senior member of our Italian community and who was also a customer [of the business he worked for]. The old man wasn't happy with some of the work done which would have been ok if the young tradesman hadn't gone 'off-tap' at him. The older man rightly felt insulted ... What the young tradesman hadn't reckoned on was the reach [into the community] that a 'slight of Honour' has with the wrong person. With no apology forthcoming his employer saw business drop off and was left few

options but to fire him. The tradesman ultimately had to move 400 km away to a major city to get regular work!

Listening to Cos had my head spinning at times. His childhood seemed to have more in common with Machiavelli than rural Australia. I also became aware of how nuanced terms such as 'reputation', 'insult' and even 'face' were and how these shade our perception of Honour. For me, Honour was now much larger and more complicated than I had ever envisaged.

Question 5.5

> a. What features of Bedouin honour culture are similar to the honour culture Cos grew up in? What features are different? In recognising cross-cultural similarities what then are the key elements of an honour culture? What purpose(s) do they serve?
>
> b. Now extend these ideas out to think about a local sporting club. How does Honour function at this club?
>
> c. Are there even elements of an honour culture in your workplace?

How the professionals look at Honour

Although Honour is an age-old concept our current understanding goes back a little over 50 years making it a relatively new topic amongst academics. That honour is also remarkably complex means that it has to be studied using tools from a variety of disciplines. Therefore we can do little more than survey key ideas and extract a few overarching principles to guide our discussions. To do this we will rely on the excellent work of Oprisko who wrote *The Phenomenology of Honour*.[4]

Taking their lead from Darwin, Honour was first conceptualised as a political tool by people such as Hans Speier. It was through the coercive power of Honour that a group of people came together and organised in such a way as to effectively meet an external threat. Therefore, its virtue was wholly practical and resided in the group's continued survival rather than in any notion of personal excellence.

By the 1960's a new cluster of academics became interested in Honour and chief amongst them were J. G. Peristiany and Julian Pitt-Rivers. Together these two scholars would publish a number of seminal texts including *Honour and Shame: The Values of Mediterranean Society* and *Honor and Grace in*

Anthropology.[5, 6] In doing so Honour shifted from the cold tool of political authority to being something invested in community life. In essence, Honour came to be synonymous with how a person valued themselves and, in turn, how they were valued by their community.

In more recent times the study of Honour has shifted again taking on decidedly new, and useful, twists. For example, there is now a move away from just seeing Honour as a 'European thing', or as the preserve of men. Younger academics such as Sharon Krause have also moved Honour towards discussions of character, if not human dignity, thus making it virtuous.

But what is Honour? This is the fundamental question and is answered differently by each academic according to their life experience and training. However the work of four scholars stand out.

Liepmann considered both 'objectified' and 'subjectified' Honour. The first being about what the community considers to be my worth, while the second is what I consider to be my own worth. The implication being that Honour can be a brutal valuing process which cleaves apart a person's value from their virtue.

Stewart again divides Honour two ways. For him, 'horizontal honour' is the equality in respect that all full members of a society recognise and share. Like dignity it cannot be increased, but it can be diminished if the person breaks a social norm (i.e., a taboo). 'Vertical honour', however, is Stewart's way to engage the idea of authority in so much as people who have demonstrated excellence have the right to special treatment and the ability to direct the behaviour of others. In many ways his views make sense of George Orwell's paradoxical statement in *Animal Farm*, 'All animals are equal, but some animals are more equal than others.'.[7]

Krause takes another approach to Honour by looking at it in three ways: 'public honours' (i.e., a reward for good citizenship, such as a medal); 'codes of honour' (i.e., a way to define sub-group membership within a larger society); and 'quality of character' (i.e., the extent to which one internalises Honour as a virtue). Krause considers the first two as lures for individuals to sublimate themselves to the wider community while quality of character is that which allows each person to remain themselves and not be crushed by the expectations of their community.

Sessions, however, provides the most fine-grained analysis of Honour by first discussing 'personal honour' which, to him, is '... distinctive in the premium it places on commitment to principle (the honor code), loyalty to others (members of the honor group), and the kind of concern it has for the regard of those honorable others ...'.[8] He then goes onto discuss how five other forms of Honour work in relation to personal honour. In particular he discusses 'conferred honour' and 'recognition honour' as being about respect; 'positional honour' in relation to power and authority; and finally 'commitment honour' and 'trust honour' being founded in agreement and sealed in trust.[9]

In spite of the complexities of jargon, and no matter the theorist, Honour remains ' ... the most lasting cultural mediator between the individual ... and his social group.'.[10] It therefore always has two parts. There is an internal valuing component and an external valuing component. While the language shifts between academics the internal aspect of Honour is typically associated with notions of human dignity, self-respect or virtue. For Krause it is even seen as a motivator that propels a person to assume greater responsibilities, and risks, than they otherwise might. By contrast, the external component of Honour is akin to ideas such as 'vertical honour' or 'positional honour'. It is based in a person's abilities and track record of achievement. Given that this public aspect of Honour represents a person's social value it is, by far, the more pragmatic side to Honour. It is also necessary if a group, or community, is to organise in such a way as to maximise its strength to counter threats.

Question 5.6

    a. Of the different theorists who have researched Honour with whom do you connect the most? Why?

    b. If Honour has two components, one internal and the other external, how do they play out in your own life, especially at work?

    c. Do you know of any people who value themselves highly but are not seen this way by the world at large? For this sort of person what may be the consequences to their life both personally and professionally? What might the private and public sides of Honour teach us about narcissism?

    d. By contrast, can you think of an example whereby a person does not value themselves at all highly but is nevertheless well esteemed by others? For this sort of person what may be the consequences to their life both personally and professionally?

    e. Honour appears to be founded in our evolutionary past when communities were under constant threat of starvation and pillaging. Given that we now live in cities with plentiful food, sanitation, excellent medical care and effective police forces how might this lessening of threat affect honour systems?

The dynamics of Honour

Having now discussed some of the structural elements of Honour let's now see how it functions. But to do this is not simple, given that Honour is a Janus-faced virtue. From the perspective of the community Honour is about cohesion and purpose. It is also based in trust amongst community members. However, people are themselves honourable or not. We must therefore also look at Honour from the perspective of the individual. In this way whenever with think about Honour we must always hold two perspectives in tension. To help we'll call these two parts to Honour 'personal honour' and 'group honour'.

As to potential topics we could cover in this section there are a host to choose from. We could, for example, talk about the importance of a 'headman' or 'elder' in an honour system. We could also discuss elaborate ceremonies in which positional honour is given to a person as they take office. But to do so would be to admire the chess pieces, or the checker-pattern board, without ever playing a game. To avoid this problem we will cover some of the key dynamics of Honour. Chief amongst these being glory, promotion/demotion within the social hierarchy and finally the ugly topic of dishonour. In this way you will come to see how an honour culture and the people within it function.

Glory comes before Honour

Glory and Honour get confused when Hollywood script writers get adventurous with the truth. While tragic heroes, epic battle scenes and stirring music might fill cinemas they do little to help our understanding of these two distinct, although related, concepts.

While Honour can be approached from a number of perspectives Oprisko suggested that glory is simpler since it has only three basic qualities: (1) it comes about through trial; (2) its outcome is binary (i.e., you either fail miserably or succeed wildly); and (3) it has a lasting quality about it. In so many way glory is a precise concept that clearly belongs to the gladiator and the Olympic gold medallist. Except …

Glory is also something that we must all attain if we wish to be honoured (i.e., respected). Or, in Cos' words, 'You pursue glory before being given respect'. Now please don't confuse glory and heroics (see Chapter 2). Glory has an important personal/social function, whereas heroics is often simply impulsive. By winning academic honours, a sporting trophy, or earning a Queen's Scout badge, for example, an adolescent stakes their claim on the world and signals to their community that they are capable of adult responsibility and therefore ready to be respected. This is the function of glory.

But there are actually two parts to glory. There is, in the beginning, glory seeking; and, in the end, the attainment of glory.

In the context of adolescent boys glory seeking, as opposed to simply risk taking, provides them with a proper outlet for their energy and opens them up to what is possible in the world. It provides a means for boys to step out into the world, muck-up and deal with the consequences thus developing resilience as a precondition to being able to cope with the duties of group honour. In another way glory seeking also helps adolescent boys differentiate between the self-imposed boundaries learnt at their mother's knee and the wider boundaries of society. In the end, it is through glory seeking that adolescent boys grow into capable young men. In terms of Honour, and specifically personal honour, glory seeking is also the means by which a young man's self-respect grows and character is formed.

As for the attainment of glory, this only needs to happen once to be effective. But, having said this, it also needs to be recognised by the community at large. As such, while glory seeking is an individual matter, the attainment of glory is a community concern. For instance, in the town where Cos grew up the adults understood that glory seeking signalled that an adolescent boy was nearing the point when he was ready to enter into the honour culture as a full member. By this observation the community could prepare for the transition and ultimately celebrate each young man's attainment of glory through marriage.

Question 5.7

a. In your own adolescence what sorts of glory seeking did you do?
   (1) How did it make you feel both before and afterwards?
   (2) What did you learn from it?
   (3) What sort of social status did it confer?

b. If you are a parent, what sort of glory seeking do you encourage in your own children?

c. In what way might glory be a gendered concept? What does glory look like for adolescent girls? How might menarche be seen as the attainment of glory?

d. Do contemporary educational practices hamper the development of boys by not allowing them to seek the glory they need?

But what happens when glory goes wrong? At one end of the spectrum an adolescent may not be capable of pursuing the smallest amount of glory perhaps because of a serious illness, or is prevented from glory seeking by well meaning, albeit overly protective, parents. At the other end of the spectrum a fully grown adult may be addicted to glory seeking and so remain quite adolescent even into middle age.

To people trapped by the first of these problems there is no easy answer. Illness and disability do limit opportunities for glory seeking, especially in societies which promote sport and the physical prowess of young men. Perhaps the only thing to do is push and shove anyway. Yes you will cause consternation with some — but seek glory nonetheless. While, for the second group I (i.e., Tom) want to say, 'You should know better at your age!', but I won't. Fast bikes, adventure holidays and copious selfies do have their place, but remember glory is a stage to pass through. To loiter can diminish you in the eyes of others and even engender a level of disrespect. Glory, after all, only opens the door to life.

Question 5.8

- a. For adolescent girls, could teenage pregnancy be an example of glory seeking gone wrong?

- b. Although we have talked of glory seeking in adolescence as a stage to embrace, and pass through, is glory seeking needed at other times in life? For example, in what way(s) does one need to earn one's glory before being admitted to a profession or accepted by a team?

- c. Having attained glory what responsibilities should a young adult take on? Should responsibilities be given over incrementally?

Activity 5.2

- a If you are a parent, teacher, coach or Scout leader, for example, design an activity for the adolescents in your care which specifically helps them seek, and attain, their glory.

- b. Using what you have now learnt, design a rite of passage ceremony that publically acknowledges the attainment of glory for an adolescent.

The snakes and ladders of living in an honour culture

Having attained glory, and having been accepted as a full member of the honour culture, one learns quickly that Honour can be gained, or lost, much like a military rank. This is the most fundamental aspect of an honour culture for it regulates how relationships are to be managed by providing a basis for authority and co-operation. This also suggests that an honour culture is a meritocracy. As people display their talents they rise within the social hierarchy or, if they show a level of incompetence, they fall. This is an important point for a dynamic meritocracy provides the best mechanism to maintain group strength and therefore success.

Question 5.9

> a. In your own life how have you risen up, or fallen back down, a social hierarchy? This might have been within your extended family, at work, or in other community contexts.
>
> b. How do the organisations to which you belong demonstrate meritocracy?
>
> c. What sorts of workplace legislation, policies and procedures may cause a dampening of meritocracy? What has been the effect of these on your organisation?

But who is considered the best, and therefore rises up the social hierarchy, is not always obvious. It is never so simple as to say that only high achievers receive positional honour. While we might think of high achievers as 'the great', there are other prominent people in any organisation/community who we refer to as 'the good'. These people are recognised for their exemplary character, wisdom or selflessness. They too will be accorded positional honour. But, strangely enough, we also tend to bestow positional honour on another group of people for what may be described as biological reasons.[11, 12] For instance, have you ever noticed that men, especially those who are taller, and more muscular, are often given positions of authority? There appears to be some underlying biological assumption that bigger people should be in authority because they are physically strong. The same applies to the elderly in a different way. Having lived long lives and experienced much we, rightly or wrongly, expect them to have Wisdom and so accord them positions of honour. Therefore, although high achievers do rise quickly within any organisation there are other ways to achieve positional honour that might be more in keeping with who you are as a person. To this end, never underestimate the value of a good character, or even of personal appearance.

Question 5.10

a. Physical beauty is also a biological marker which assists some people to climb a hierarchy quicker than others. What may beauty be 'signalling' that makes it so powerful?

b. Think about the 2016 US Presidential election. What biological features did Donald Trump use to his advantage to gain the ultimate in positional honour?

Having now received positional honour there are only two ways to go: stay where you are; or get demoted. What is interesting is that meritocracies seem to break their own rules from time to time to keep a person in a position of authority when their performance would suggest a demotion. Therefore face-saving is a counterintuitive phenomenon within honour cultures.

Found across the world, 'face' is all about maintaining the appearance of Honour in spite of reputational failures. But, surprisingly enough, face also has a number of very important functions within an honour culture. For example, face allows small, and private, matters to be ignored and thus maintains cohesiveness between community members. In the case of a faith community this allows a level of premarital sex to go unnoticed and thus for brides to wear virginal white on their wedding day. If the concept of face was not invoked by implicit agreement amongst community members then good young couples would be shamed, families angered and the community potentially thrown into disarray. In this way saving face maintains cohesion.

However, a need to maintain group cohesion can be taken too far. When saving face is applied to serious, if not criminal matters, then Honour is lost. The end result being that in a vain attempt to maintain cohesion the organisation will fracture, or even blow itself apart. In spite of its granite-hard appearance this has even been the experience of the Roman Catholic Church following its international child sex scandal. Not only is there now dissent from within the clergy on a variety of matters, but it is likely that the scandal has turned some young men off from training for the priesthood, while also contributing to declining parish numbers.[13, 14]

The second purpose of maintaining face can best be seen when an employee is still valued in their workplace in spite of poor performance. This is both an act of Kindness (see Chapter 7) and a calculated gamble on the part of their manager. For if the person's performance soon picks up then the cost to the organisation has been minimal when compared to the burden of performance management, or ending their employment and re-hiring. But if the employee remains a poor performer over a longer timespan then saving face will not pay off. Nevertheless, by managers taking a longer-term view of each person's productivity, especially in light of past good performance, saving face is a useful way to minimise cost and maximise social cohesion.

Question 5.11

> How have you seen 'face' used in either your workplace or in another organisation you are involved with? Was it a help or a hindrance?

If face is about staying put within a hierarchy then shame is about being demoted. In moving to discuss shame we also shift our focus from private, trivial or transitory problems to serious matters in which demotion within the social hierarchy becomes a necessity to preserve overall group fitness. Shame is therefore central to that aspect of Honour to do with a person's social value.[15]

That shame is a very strong negative emotion means that it affects individuals deeply. At a fundamental level an honourable person fears being shamed and therefore demotion. This not only motivates them to do their duty but also tempers any galloping excursions into folly they may otherwise entertain (see Chapter 4). However, if failure occurs shame also has a corrective effect for honourable people. In being shamed one reviews past actions and what should have occurred.[4] In this way shame teaches an honourable person what to do next time. Surprisingly enough, this process also prepares the person for their eventual rehabilitation into the social hierarchy. The trick, however, is to apply shame in small quantities and with cleverness — if not Wisdom. In this way it will only affect that part of Honour concerned with a person's external value, not their core self.

Question 5.12

> Society has moved away from shaming people. But, given what we have said above, is there still a place for shame in our community?

Having discussed what shame does for an individual let's now turn to what it does for the group, be they a family, an organisation, or a community. At the broadest level, by judging success vs. failure reputation and shame are accorded each person. Through this process order is brought to the group by defining who can have what functions and responsibilities based upon their relative value. In this way people of greater regard ascend to positions of authority while those suffering shame take lesser positions. The outcome of which is to maximise capacity if, and when, the group is faced with an external threat.

More specifically, by considering acts of shaming we see that they are often public. This is true for courts of law even today. The underlying reason for public trials and media access is not to ensure due process so much as to have people witness shaming and so have it act as a deterrent for anyone wavering on the brink of carelessness. In this way shaming becomes both a powerful method to induce conformity, albeit to the lowest standards of acceptable behaviour, and a way to motivate others to achieve beyond these minimal expectations.

At an even more basic level, shaming allows for the control of people who do not care for the opinions of others. This sort of 'house cleaning' is a necessary function of any organisation or community if it is to be cohesive and mission-focused. In this way shame is used to render harmless untrustworthy and unpredictable people who could present a genuine risk to all.[4] Is this not what performance management, 'sectioning' of the mentally ill or the sex offenders registry are all about?

Question 5.13

    a. When have you seen shame in operation? What happened? What effect did it have on the person being shamed, those around them and the group generally?

    b. As a social force shame can easily become a 'hard task master' leading to anxiety and cover-ups. What positive social forces may be needed to counterbalance shame in an honour culture?

While we have stated that shame can be used as an effective corrective tool we have not yet discussed how this occurs. In brief, the idea it to make it public; time-limited; proportional; and conducted within the context of the community so that the person is being supported while being shamed. To describe what we mean let's turn to the Medieval Crime Museum in the delightful German town of Rothenburg ob der Tauber. In amongst the pillory and the stocks used to hold people to ridicule in the town square are some of the most inventive methods of shaming yet devised. For instance, there are fanciful metal helmets with long tongues forcibly worn by women who were known to be gossips. The long tongue protruding from the helmet being a visible sign of their shame. But our favourite — and we say this with a little trepidation — is the 'double violin'. When neighbours were sick of hearing arguments from next door the angry couple would be put into this device which resembled a double collar. Unable to get away from each other the couple were now forced to calm down. More to the point, husband and wife had to wear this contraption around town as a sign of their shame and so incur the guffawing of friends and neighbours alike. As such, shame was felt as a social pressure from community and so acted as a corrective to bad behaviour.

Question 5.14

> Given that a shamed person still remains a member of their community does shaming have a place in cities where people feel little care for one another or are only loosely connected?

Bringing shaming into the present day The Bridgewater Associates were rated as the '… world's largest macro hedge fund …' in 2011 and one of their keys to success appeared to be an Honour-based corporate culture including the capacity for shame.[16, 17] Not only does The Bridgewater Associates maintain a culture of transparency and continuous improvement (see Chapter 3 — Diligence) but employees are also required to report their failings and work to correct them which is, in turn, rewarded by Management. And the result — they are the stand-out industry performers. Needless to say, those employees who cannot cope with regular shamings soon leave the firm, but, as the wheat is sorted from the chaff, the organisation grows from strength to strength.

Question 5.15

> How could your workplace lever-off ideas of shaming, as did The Bridgewater Associates, and so increase its competitive advantage?

So, if you remember nothing else about honour cultures remember this — the one thing which marks them out is their *commitment to meritocracy*. People expect to rise and fall in comparison to their peers as a consequence of their successes and failures. From sports clubs to business (and even the Mafia), it is the best way for an organisation to survive and thrive in a competitive environment.

Dishonour

The last dynamic of an honour culture that needs to be discussed is what it means to be 'dishonoured'. The term may sound strange to our ears but is fundamental to the success of groups confronted by threats *from within*. Gilmore cleverly disambiguated dishonour from shame by noting that shame refers to demotion but the maintenance of group membership, whereas dishonour has a person lose their group identity entirely.[4, 15] Therefore, dishonour represents such a significant failing as to cause a person to be ejected from their group. Oprisko clarifies this by commenting that while shame relates to when people fail in what is expected of them, dishonour represents a deliberate transgression of a group ideal or taboo.[4] In this way dishonour is catastrophic; so much so that the transgressor must be considered fundamentally untrustworthy and cast out.

But what does dishonouring look like? In simple terms it is to be: expelled from school for rampant bullying; sacked from a job for being lazy; laicised from the priesthood for hurting children; or even to be handed down a life sentence for murder.

 Question 5.16

> From your own experience think of a group which could broadly be termed an honour culture. It may be your family, your workplace or an organisation you are part of. Name those values or taboos which, if broken, could cause a person to be dishonoured.

But it is one thing to talk about the value of dishonouring bad people, it's another thing to do it. Because of the dread dishonour should invoke elaborate ceremonies have been placed around it over the centuries. Historically some very inventive dishonouring ceremonies have occurred, known formally as 'ceremonies of degradation'.

Using a 16th century text, Trigg (2006) described one such ceremony for a dishonoured knight.

> Having brought the knight forward for public scrutiny the ceremony commenced with the hushed prayers for the dead.
> They took off his Helmet as that which defended his traitorous eyes, then his Gauntlet on the right side ... then the Gauntlet of the left hand ... And so by piecemeal despoiled him of all his Arms ... which one after another were thrown to the ground: and [all] ... cried aloud, saying 'This is the Helmet of a disloyal and miscreant Knight'.[18] (spelling modernised for the convenience of the reader)

Warm water was then thrown over the dishonoured knight's face as if to reverse his baptism and then, in one loud voice, he was declared: 'Traitor!'. In variants of this solemn piece of theatre the knight's sword, being the very object of his honour, might also be broken above his head, or the spurs signifying his rank be cut from his ankles.

Surprisingly, this type of ceremony existed in modified form until at least World War I when military officers could be cashiered by being similarly degraded of all rank before their comrades. Even at the end of World War II the French collaborator, Marshal Petain, was stripped of rank and honours following his trial. And today, our courts still hold onto elements of these ceremonies when, for example, a defendant stands in the dock to hear 'Guilty!' and then is 'taken down' to begin his sentence.

Question 5.17

> What ceremonies of degradation can you think of? Have you ever witnessed one? What happened? How did it make you feel? In answering this last question what then is the value of such ceremonies being held in public?

Activity 5.3

> Honour cultures are very effective. At one level they provide resilience to all members through mutual bonds while also organising the group in such a way as to meet external challenges most effectively. However honour cultures can be of two sorts, benevolent or cruel. Identify some examples of both benevolent and cruel honour cultures from the media and/or history. Then list the features of both so as to distinguish a benevolent honour culture

from a cruel one. What you will likely find is not that the dynamics are different, so much as they way they are applied.

Growing in Honour

Consistent with past chapters the last aspect of Honour we'll discuss is how to develop it in your own life. To do this we must remember that Honour affects people and their group. As such, we will divide this section in half to talk about both personal honour and group honour. In this way you will see how both come together.

Personal honour

Personal honour is about being honourable. In many respects it is about having integrity. But both of these terms are, unfortunately, not often used in the psychological literature. For this reason we have to shift sideways and look at terms such as self-respect instead. And this is not a bad thing for people with honour demonstrate self-respect before all else. They dress the part, are on time to meetings, honour agreements and always give of their best. By contrast, people who show little in the way of personal honour, or self-respect, tend to have a great deal of conceit and, not surprisingly, a slack attitude.

But even self-respect is not a common psychological term. Instead, the psychological literature prefers to discuss related words including self-esteem, self-image, self-efficacy and self-concept. To understand the difference between these words Logan and King have provided some assistance.[19] For example, a simple description of one's self has to do with self-image. Whereas one's knowledge that a task will be completed invokes self-efficacy. Or, if we want to know about the totality of a person (i.e., 'Who are you deep down?') we need to ask about self-concept. It is only when we want to know how a person values themselves should we ever talk about self-esteem.

We can also begin to develop an understanding of self-respect by comparing and contrasting it to self-esteem. For example,

> Although at times 'self-respect' and 'self-esteem' are used interchangeably, self-respect and self-esteem are not identical. Thus if you complain that someone is lacking in self-respect you may not be deploring any lack of self-esteem … It is not unheard-of for persons to esteem themselves highly and for others who are fully aware of that fact to complain of them that they are notably deficient in self-respect.[20]

Finally, to draw out a clear understanding of self-respect, and therefore of personal honour, let us simply remark that to grow in self-respect is to deepen your self-concept, improve your self-efficacy, realise a positive self-image and ultimately develop a healthy self-esteem.

Question 5.18

a. To help you grapple with the terms above describe (a) aspects of your self-image; (b) whether you have good self-efficacy or not; (c) those things which contribute to your self-concept; and (d) your level of self-esteem.

b. Self-esteem is a very big idea in developmental psychology and education. Do you think it has been used well? In what ways has it been used poorly?

c. What are the dangers of developing self-esteem without supporting it with a strong self-concept, self-efficacy or self-image?

The process of building self-respect relies on both values and actions. One's value system must be stated before all else. Cultural, religious, national, community, organisational and family values must be sifted before personal values can be named and held with any gravitas. This is good work to do.

But in the end a person's developing value system must be tested if self-respect is to be found. By experiencing challenge, and ultimately success, a person comes to value themselves and find self-respect.

Cos, alerted me to the importance of challenge and success when discussing his two daughters:

> My wife and I agreed long ago that the girls would be raised to be independent, adventurous, wise and compassionate [with the hope that this would translate into self-respect].
>
> [By way of challenges our younger daughter], age 11, ... is a fearsome netball player who dominates the goal keeper's area ... [She] plays hard, plays to win and plays with her heart. Even after breaking her foot [last season] she pushed to get back on the court as soon as she could ... [And, at the end of the season her] beaming smile at awards night said it all, she had earned her glory and recognition. She's already plotting and scheming to be part of a division winning team in the new year.
>
> [Our oldest daughter] is a qualified lifesaver, holding her Surf Rescue Certificate, [and] works with the Nippers program. She's [also] been School

> House Captain, as well as School Captain; an impressive list [of accolades] for a 13 year old.
> Glory, self-efficacy, self-esteem and self-respect are all related ... [We have to] trust that we are raising capable children.

Cos then took the conversation further. In particular, he emphasised the value of challenges which were neither entirely safe nor where everyone got a participant ribbon. In this way the sorts of challenges he referred to were very different from those designed to simply boost self-esteem. He also noted that every challenge his girls were involved in was team-based. In this way the values which underpin personal honour are always fed back into the demands of group honour. Finally, he put forward one warning, 'choose appropriate challenges ...'. Parents and teachers must always set the right difficulty of challenge for the young person to whom it is directed. You do nothing for a child's self-respect if the challenge is either too hard or, for that matter, too easy.

Question 5.19

a. In what way(s) is personal honour and Courage related?

b. Specifically, how might personal honour and moral courage overlap?

Activity 5.4

a. Charles Colson was a person who transitioned from being honourable in the eyes of the world, to being dishonourable and then found a true sense of honour while in a very dark place. Read his story (https://en.wikipedia.org/wiki/Charles_Colson).

b If you are a psychologist, counsellor or social worker think of an adolescent you know who may need to grow in self-respect. Consider how you might work with them to help them identify their values and to challenge their abilities.

Group honour

Yet, to discuss personal honour is only half the story. Group honour considers the concept of personal honour but then supersizes it within the context of a family, club, workplace or other organisation. As such, it takes individuals and makes them a team. But group honour does more than this. It put the team together in a special way to maximise performance. This is the secret to any great organisation be it the SAS or Real Madrid football club. How this happens is a secret we are now going to share.

 Question 5.20

a. Given that corporations are always facing challenges do you think that they could benefit more than most organisations from using group honour?

b. What specific impediments might there be for a business/organisation to introduce an honour culture?

What we are talking about is developing an honour culture in your organisation. The first step in doing this is to identify your group, be it a sports team, a department you manage or even a school class. The trick, however, is not to make your group too large. Honour cultures work best at the scale of families, tribes and villages. In many respects their vigour is maintained through the personal relationships between all members. To this end, if you are in charge of a large organisation consider creating a number of teams, each of which will become its own honour culture within the larger organisation.

Now bring the members of the group together and get them to define both group values *and what taboos the group holds*. These will not just represent what the group aspires to, but how it actually measures excellence. It will also determine what the group sees as unconscionable (i.e., dishonourable) behaviour. In this regard a sporting club may value regular training, showing Courage on match day and ultimately measure success by aiming to win the premiership at the end of the season. On the flip-side the same club may hold taboos around laziness, cowardice or even drug taking. Ultimately, it is through these discussions that group members develop a strong sense of 'buy in', become a cohesive team and purpose-driven.

However, in doing this preparatory work it is important not to confuse naming group values and taboos with statements about organisational values or mission. The differences could not be more stark. In an honour culture all full members have equal respect and so everyone should participate. As such, this is not a Management, or HR-driven, exercise. In addition, the values espoused by an honour culture are deliberately purpose-driven and specific. So often organisational values remain vague. Finally, an honour culture names its taboos. What corporation would dare be so blunt?

 **Activity 5.5**

a. For a group that you lead develop it into an honour culture. As such:
   (1) Who will the members be?
   (2) What does the group define as its purpose-driven values?
   (3) What does the group define as its taboos?

b. For a business, or organisation, you are involved in look at its values and mission statement. Analyse these in accordance with Honour principles.
   (1) How are they similar?
   (2) How are they different?

Having done the 'big picture' work around group identity it is now necessary to make your burgeoning honour culture function like a well-oiled machine. The easiest way to do this is by designing an honour code. At its simplest, an honour code acknowledges group values. But it also describes normative behaviour while acting as a mechanism to regulate the relationship between members.[4] In this way it takes group values and grounds them in the day to day of group life. Furthermore, an honour code outlines the principles by which positional honour can be achieved, authority used and shame meted out. Therefore an honour code is a like the driver's manual you find in the glovebox of your new sports car. Best to read it before you hit the accelerator.

However, beyond this simple description Associate Professor Shannon French, who has taught at the US Naval Academy, takes a more sophisticated view of honour codes.[21] In the first instance militaries the world over use honour codes to exclude unfit, or untrustworthy, people from their ranks. In doing so any combat unit will ultimately be filled with motivated and capable personnel able to come together in a cohesive way. It is for this reason that military honour codes typically: (1) identify the ideal soldier, setting a standard of behaviour far higher than expected by a civilian; and (2) extend to apparently arcane matters of dress and etiquette. The reasoning being that such statements should deter the fearful from recruitment while identifying the sloppy during basic training who can then be removed without jeopardising a mission.

In addition, military honour codes also identify those behaviours expected of a soldier under extreme threat and in this way Honour and Courage are typically partnered. As once remarked by US general Norman Schwarzkopf, 'As young West Point cadets, our motto [or code] was 'duty, honor, country.' But it was in ... the rice paddies of Southeast Asia to the sands of the Middle East, [that I saw] ... gallant young Americans ... die, for 'duty, honor, and their country'.[22]

Nor are military honour codes always so formally stated. In fact what is honourable is often simply hinted at in a variety of ways. For instance, the expectations of an unwritten honour code may be found in pithy mottos such as the SAS's 'Who dares wins'. They may be idealised in concepts such as 'mateship' or the 'glorious dead'. The expectations of being an honourable soldier may also be implied in the stories of veterans. We even find the values inherent in unwritten honour codes amongst the general corpus of war literature dating right back to the *Iliad*.

To show you how this all fits together let's look briefly at the French Foreign Legion which is known for its distinct identity and fearlessness. Helpfully, the honour code of The Legion is actually written down (see Table 5.1). As you read it notice how it describes the ideal soldier and the virtues to be displayed in battle. In just about every way it conforms to what we have been discussing above.

But the French Foreign Legion goes further. Realising that a written statement of their ideals and expectations is not enough they ingrain their honour code through story and song. For example, the central narrative of the French Foreign Legion surrounds the Battle of Camerone back in 1863. All recruits learn of the heroic valour of a group of about 60 legionaries who fought to the death against 2,000 Mexican soldiers. Not only are the basic details of this story impressive, but when only five legionnaires remained they still refused to surrender, fixed bayonets and charged the Mexican army![24] And if this is not enough to set the expectations for new recruits they also must learn the slow mournful song of The Legion, *Le Boudin*, of which the first verse begins,

> We are crafty.
> We are rogues.
> We are no ordinary guys.
> We've often got our black moods,
> For we are Legionnaires ...[25]

What a way to inculcate the virtue of Honour!

 **Activity 5.6**

a. For your workplace read the HR documents which pertain to corporate culture and mission. Do they reflect an honour culture, let alone a code of honour?

b. Use what you have learnt earlier in the chapter to facilitate the designing of an honour code for a team that you lead either in the workplace or in the community.

c. Now take all that you have learnt in this chapter and transform your team into an honour culture. In doing so, consider the value of the following elements in creating your honour culture:

(1) A small and stable team membership

(2) A uniform

(3) A strong team name

(4) A team motto

(5) Regular times spent together such as training

(6) An annual awards night

(7) The value of memorabilia, trophies from past successes.

Table 5.1
The Honour Code of the French Foreign Legion[23]

Legionnaire, you are a volunteer serving France with honour and fidelity.

Each legionnaire is your brother in arms whatever his nationality, his race or his religion might be. You show him the same close solidarity that links the members of the same family.

Respect for traditions, devotion to your leaders, discipline and comradeship are your strengths, courage and loyalty your virtues.

Proud of your status as legionnaire, you display this in your always impeccable uniform, your always dignified but modest behaviour, and your clean living quarters.

An elite soldier, you train rigorously, you maintain your weapon as your most precious possession, and you take constant care of your physical form.

The mission is sacred, you carry it out until the end and, if necessary in the field, at the risk of your life.

In combat, you act without passion and without hate, you respect defeated enemies, and you never abandon your dead, your wounded, or your arms.

Chapter 5 Honour

As we move on …

Honour is not just the preserve of military officers or medieval knights. Nor is it about referring to a judge as 'Your Honour …'. Honour is about knowing that 'I am capable' and standing with others to be a team player. With these twin pillars Honour becomes the virtue of everyone who aspires to be better. Or, to put it another way, a person with honour has a heart as big as lion. They'll give of their best no matter the circumstance.

The Freedom of Virtue: Navigating excellence in the art of living amongst a world of instant gratification

Chapter 6

Justice

> Peace is not merely the absence of tension: it is the presence of justice
>
> — Martin Luther King Jr

Justice holds back chaos

While Honour may be the larger concept by which communities have traditionally been organised Justice has nevertheless always had a very important role to play. For without Justice disputes are not settled and restitution never comes. The result being that recrimination escalates and communities break apart. While true of Northern Ireland in the past we need only look to Israel and the Gaza Strip today to see the effects of injustice.

Yet to mention conflicts as only headlines fails to capture the pain of injustice. For that we must draw closer. Moving to a different conflict zone let's touch upon the struggles of the people who eke out a living in the Amazon jungle. Of their plight Scott Wallace wrote,

> [H]undreds of people have died in land wars; countless others endure fear and uncertainty, their lives threatened by those who profit from the theft of timber and land. In this Wild West frontier of guns, chain saws, and bull-

dozers, government agents are often corrupt and ineffective — or ill-equipped and outmatched.

He goes on,

> [This is a world of] squatters, speculators, ranchers, farmers, and, invariably, hired gunmen. The land sharks follow the roads deep into previously impenetrable forest, then destroy tracts to make it look as if they own them. Land thievery is committed through corruption, strong-arm tactics, and fraudulent titles and is so widespread that Brazilians have a name for it: *grilagem* ...[1]

The rest of Wallace's article is the sorry tale of rampant economic inequality which has even led to fire-bombings and the murder of a nun, Sister Dorothy Stang.

Put simply, injustice is synonymous with 'might is right' and leads only to barbarism. Or, inversely, the foundational virtue of Justice is the only strong bulwark we have against chaos. It is a virtue of great worth.

But what is just?

To ask 'What is just?' has great potency today as old certainties are being pushed aside so quickly. Legislators and ordinary citizens alike are now confronted with justice-based questions such as:

- Is it just for only heterosexual adults to marry?
- Is easy access to abortion just?
- Is euthanasia of the elderly a just response to their pain and despair?
- Is it just to allow a child to transition from one gender to another?
- Are gender-based workplace quotas just?
- Is it just to consider a person privileged just because of their skin colour and gender?

These and many other questions go to the heart of our discussion, and each holds a truth about human nature tied-up in a riddle.

That Justice is a riddle should come as no surprise. Plato, via Socrates, demonstrated this two and a half millennia ago. In a famous example from *The Republic* Socrates asks old Cephalus about aging and his approaching death.[2] Not afraid of death, Cephalus replies that he has lived a good life having always spoken truthfully and paid his debts. But here is when Socrates gets that naughty glint in his eye and begins to prod about living a just life. He says,

> For example, [what] if we had been given weapons by a friend when he was of sound mind, and he went mad and reclaimed them [as is his right], it would surely be universally admitted that it would not be right to give them back[?] Anyone who did so ... would not be just.[3]

So Plato, through Socrates, upsets the apple cart of Justice from the outset showing us that even the simplest issues have an inherent riddle inside. Given this, we cannot charge forth into a discussion of Justice without help. To assist, we'll make much use of Tom Campbell's excellent book, titled *Justice*, to help.[4] In this way, we can hopefully pick our way through the brambles with only a few scratches and finish a whole lot wiser about this fascinating virtue.

A just society

One of the most persuasive, and widely used, approaches to Justice is that of the 'utilitarians'. These people seek to calculate what will bring the greatest happiness to the most people and call this just. For example, when a government is deciding whether to subsidise a new medication they often make decisions based on utility given that there are only limited public funds available. For this reason a new antibiotic will more likely get a subsidy than a sophisticated cancer drug because antibiotics are more widely needed.

Utility can be a really good way to ensure Justice. It is a common sense approach being both easy to explain and rational. Utility also looks to the best interest of the majority of people and thus fits well with our democratic ideals. It also provides a solid framework to guide decisions in so much as they are about happiness. For these reasons utilitarianism is beloved of politicians and bureaucrats.

However, utility has a number of significant flaws when we peel back the surface. For example, an important test for any theory of Justice is how it understands fairness. In political terms this is typically shown by how a government treats minority groups. Utilitarians have no answer to this challenge. Returning momentarily to our example of the cancer drug above, a strict utilitarian approach would let a few cancer patients die to fund lots of antibiotics. Shame if you are the one with cancer! The theory also assumes some rather mechanical qualities about people. For instance, humans are always considered to be self-interested, motivated, ever rational and respond only to pleasure or pain. Yet as a species we are so much more interesting than that! Alarmingly, strict utilitarians cannot understand care and empathy. They look on bemused by a mum who refuses to abort a baby with Down's syndrome, and get confused by people who see dignity in an elderly relative with dementia. Indeed a strict utilitarian simply wonders 'How can these situations increase the general happiness?'.

But the problems with utilitarianism go further. How do we calculate general happiness with any accuracy? Furthermore, humans are not so shallow as to only be interested in happiness. More often than not people want to know their lives count for something, that their children will grow up healthy and that they will leave good memories for others when they die. These notions are so unutilitarian. Finally, utility's greatest flaw is that by having no interest in the individual, nor rights to protect them, situations of great injustice can actually come from the logical application of utilitarian Justice. Therefore, while utility has its place in telling bureaucrats where to build airports and schools it has a sting in its tail for you and me.

Question 6.1

    a. When have you had to make a utilitarian decision either at work or at home? Describe whether the outcome was:

    (1) appropriate,

    (2) good, or

    (3) satisfying.

    b. Have you ever been harmed by a utilitarian decision of someone else? What was it like for you to be in the disregarded minority?

Justice for people

Although utility is very useful to government it is not equipped to be a theory of Justice for each of us as individuals. To counter this problem academics such as John Rawls and Robert Nozick have devised other options based on personal rights.

From the early 1970's John Rawls' reputation as the pre-eminent scholar of Justice has grown alongside the increasing impact of his views on social-democratic governments around the world. In particular his 'difference principle' is enticing to welfare states who struggle to explain why *legitimately* accumulated wealth should be redistributed to people who *cannot* demonstrate why they should receive this boon. For without a good reason taxation as wealth redistribution simply becomes a form of government sanctioned theft.

In brief, Rawls argued that once basic rights were distributed to all people within a society then an unequal distribution of the remaining social goods, such as wealth, was just so long as it advantaged the worst-off. In this way his difference principle came to be associated with notions of Justice as fairness. Not only did this have intuitive appeal for governments facing election, but it also had considerable academic rigour to support it.

Nevertheless, Rawls probably over-reached. His starting point was to revive the almost dead political idea of the 'social contract' and then, through various acrobatics, argue how a just society would emerge all bright and shiny. For instance, he assumed all people entering into the social contract were (a) free to act in their own self-interest; (b) disinterested in the needs of all others; and (c) possessed an equal ability to negotiate their needs with all others present. He also added in the dual assumptions that people would be completely rational in their negotiations and that procedural fairness would somehow emerge to guide the way to a fair society. Does any of this sound like any school committee, local council or national government ever devised? Not one bit. Even if intended as a 'thought experiment' the mechanism by which Rawls' just society comes into existence appears extraordinary.

Even when it came to his all-important difference principle Rawls left several vital questions hanging. Redistributing social goods, such as wealth, to the worst-off might sound fair but who are the worst-off? And, more troubling still, why are the worst-off more morally worthy than the rest of us to receive this redistribution of wealth? Therefore, although Rawls' work has much to recommend it the prominence it has received around the Western world may have been a little overstated.

In response to Rawls' work another scholar of the 1970's, Robert Nozick, also took a rights-based approach to Justice but drove it in a very different direction. In fact his logic leads straight to a neo-conservative utopia familiar to people who remember the Reagan and Thatcher years of the 1980's. Soon enough we might also realise that Nozick's ideas have much to teach us about Trump's America.

Nozick began with the idea that rights were unassailable. They cannot be dispensed with by government *fiat* — even for the greater good. They are, in effect, sacrosanct. This is useful as it provides Nozick's version of Justice with a strong foundation. Moreover, that ordinary rights, such as to *not* be accosted by the police, can also be written down is valuable for what is just can now be clearly stated. Better yet, courts now become a mechanism for dispensing Justice, thus turning a philosophical idea into a practical reality for every citizen. That rights can be upheld, transferred or waived through legal means provides a simple and effective approach to Justice.

However, there are also some significant disadvantages to a rights approach to Justice, and to Nozick's approach in particular. For instance, if one's rights are foundational to a just society then we should have clearly recognised them a long time ago. Yet we see human rights emerge from time to time as the need arises. Be they in the Geneva Conventions, the *Universal Declaration of Human Rights* or UNICEF's *Convention on the Rights of the Child*, that new rights emerge undermines their foundational quality.

 Question 6.2

> From time to time we have differentiated between situational virtues and foundational virtues. While foundational virtues hold true all of the time, situational virtues are more specific and often context-dependent. Could this approach also work for human rights? What would be its implications?

The second challenge to Nozick's rights-based view of Justice is to ask how these foundational rights interact with personal morality. In many ways Nozick returns us to Socrates' dilemma. Within a rights-based view of Justice the suicidal man's right to his property, i.e., a sword, must be enforced in law. But morally, to return the sword is unconscionable given the harm that will result. To gain some control over this problem Nozick invested people with only three rights: (1) to property; (2) to life; and (3) to liberty. But in doing so produced outcomes which many of us would not find acceptable. For example, without a right to a subsistence wage people would be forced to seek charity and, if not forthcoming, may have to resort to theft or prostitution to survive. In effect Nozick would have us return to the crowded streets of Georgian London and leave some of us stranded in Gin Lane. In this way he produced a theory of Justice which could perpetuate innumerable acts of injustice.

Taken together, Rawls and Nozick were two great scholars of Justice. There is no doubt about that. And to be fair, a theory can only ever be a pale imitation of life with all its inherent complexities. Therefore we should not be too harsh on either of them, or on people who prefer a rights-based view of Justice. For Rawls aimed to produce fairness through his difference principle and Nozick identified a clear means through which Justice could be articulated and actioned. Theirs' was a good attempt to understand what is just, albeit flawed.

> **Question 6.3**
>
> If you had to design a theory of Justice based in unassailable rights what rights would you include, or not include, and why?

What if merit defined Justice?

Associating Justice and merit is a very old idea and intuitively appealing. It was thought so important that the Emperor Justinian (6th century) began his codification of Roman law with the axiom 'Justice is the … wish to render everyone his due'.[5] A concept that most people would happily support even today.

Rather than focusing on the anonymous majority, as utilitarians do, a merit-based approach to Justice is all about the individual. That is, you and me. In this way a merit-based approach to Justice has a sense of fairness about it that is both personal and intuitively correct. In terms of economic justice, if not social justice, a merit-based approach may also be a missing link in Rawls' difference principle. In fact it is what makes the difference principle work. For here now is a way to assess who are the worst-off in society and thus worthy of assistance.

But how do we assess merit? In the first instance we have to realise that although we can more or less accurately assess the merit of family and friends, whom we know well, it is much harder to do so for other members of our community. Indeed the less we know about a person the more vague our calculation of their merit becomes. Moreover, in assessing merit we have to consider two component parts: (1) a person's contribution to society; and (2) their personal character. And the devil is always in the detail. For example, if we take a person's contribution to society as a key indicator of merit then we must assume everyone has an equal chance in life. But this is so wrong. Except for the most virtuous, or lucky, amongst us our opportunities to contribute to society often come down to the vagaries of good genes, a loving family and an excellent education. Therefore this criterion as a measure of merit is flawed from the outset. As for measuring a person's character, being the second criterion to determine merit, this is a 'fool's errand' except in the most obvious of circumstances given that we all have character flaws.

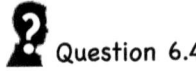 Question 6.4

> In what way are notions of good character culturally biased, changeable over time and influenced by gender? How might these ideas confuse any measurement of a person's character?

Taken together, a merit-based approach to Justice has immediate appeal. We love to see strugglers get ahead in life and the lazy to get what they deserve. But that is also the world of make-believe. For the most part, life is too complicated to make simple statements of causality, or to assign prestige or blame. Therefore, and in sum, merit is a lovely idea but like all theories of Justice it remains incomplete.

 Question 6.5

> When have you applied a merit-based approach to Justice in: (a) parenting; and (b) in the workplace?

Bringing all our discussions together, any good theory of Justice must (a) separate what is just from unjust; (b) explain why people can be considered of equal worth while providing a legitimate reason to differentiate between them; and (c) provide a mechanism through which Justice can be meted-out fairly.[4] Utilitarians speak to the first point most clearly. For them, that which is just is whatever gives the greatest happiness to the most people. By corollary something is unjust if it either decreases general happiness or if the needs of individuals are placed above the group. As to the second point, a merit-based approach to Justice does provide legitimate reasons to differentiate between people; but ultimately fails in its application when it comes to issues of wealth redistribution because people are not equally free to pick-and-choose how they live their lives. Finally, a rights-based approach to Justice speaks best to the third point. Moreover a rights-based approach, and especially that of Nozick, demonstrates clearly how Justice can be sought and dispensed. For him, people have rights which can be articulated, defended and upheld.

Therefore no one theory of justice has all the answers — or is entirely virtuous. In fact all theories of justice have their vices and some dramatically so. It is as if we have to pick and choose amongst the various perspectives on Justice depending upon our need. And maybe that's ok. But, as we close this section, we have to raise one last question: 'So where, then, amongst all these perspectives lies the virtue of Justice?'. After all this is our key question! But the answer is a disappointing one. No theory of Justice is virtuous in, and of, itself. Virtue lies with people and thus the application of Justice. In the end this means that although we can 'set the scene' with theories of Justice we have to look elsewhere to find the virtue in Justice. For this reason we will now turn to the psychology of Justice and so place people, not theory, centre stage.

The psychology of Justice

That we intuitively know what is just, and feel the sting of injustice, makes it worthy of psychological study. In fact, because of the intimate way in which we experience Justice the discipline of Psychology will probably get us closer to its heart than Philosophy ever could. Luckily, much work has been done on the psychology of Justice over the last half century, even if it has been confused with morality from time to time. To get a handle on this important topic let's turn immediately to the work of Lawrence Kohlberg (1927–1987).

Kohlberg was as much an adventurer as a psychologist. As a young man he helped smuggle Jewish refugees into Palestine, was captured by the British, promptly hatched an escape and found himself present at the birth of Israel in 1948. Long story short, he then returned to the USA and decided to get a degree. But, true to style, young Lawrence did not take three years to complete his studies, passing all exams within a single year! Needless to say a PhD was to follow and ultimately a teaching position at Harvard.

Based on the earlier work of Piaget, and with deference to John Rawls, Kohlberg's work has been decisive in our understanding of what it is to reason morally and, by corollary, justly. His approach was to assess the subtlety of people's reasoning about moral problems and, in particular, the number of perspectives they could take in formulating a solution.[6]

For example, his most famous fictional moral dilemma involved a poor man called Heinz whose wife was dying of cancer. Heinz knew the local pharmacist was selling the cure, but that he could never afford to buy it. What should Heinz do? Obey the law and let his wife die? Or steal the cure and have her live? Typically younger children reply that stealing is wrong. But older children, and most other people, are able to see the problem from multiple perspectives. They recognise that the law is not infallible and, at best, also realise the underlying principle that life is more important than property. Therefore most people respond that Heinz should just steal the medicine, save his wife's life and any legal penalty, by comparison, would be a small burden. Ultimately by assessing the differences in the complexity of responses

Kohlberg was able to sort people across three levels of moral development, each with two stages.

To summarise Kohlberg's levels of moral development the most basic is called the Pre-conventional Level and includes Stages 1 and 2.[6] Typical of children, although sometimes used by adults, moral reasoning begins as self-centred and understood only in terms of 'good' and 'bad'. Rewards for good behaviour and punishments for bad behaviour feature prominently in the child's thinking. Yet as a child grows older they become aware of simple notions of reciprocity given that their care is now structured around the principle of *quid pro quo* in which one good turn deserves another. In this way their thinking about Justice begins to mature.

Next comes the Conventional Level and it includes Stages 3 and 4. This is often considered an adolescent way of understanding morality, but works quite well for most adults. At this level the intentionality of acts begins to factor in a person's reasoning. At first this is about pleasing others, such as parents, teachers or pastors, and has the effect of reinforcing cultural and family values. But then this shifts as the adolescent become aware of situational virtues such as duty, loyalty and respect for authority. As a consequence they then become interested in upholding the social order.

Finally, there is the Post-conventional Level (i.e., Stages 5 and 6). Not all people reach this level and when they do it commonly occurs in adulthood. What characterises this highest level of moral reasoning is that a person can differentiate between what is 'good' vs. what is 'right'. In this way moral contradictions can be wisely entertained. People at this level also realise that others rightly hold different views to themselves necessitating a democratic means of maintaining society. In addition, it is recognised by these people that society is not always just and they reflect upon this sad fact. Ultimately, those who reason at the highest moral stage develop their own coherent set of moral principles, appeal to 'human dignity' as a basis for Justice and act on conscience.

Question 6.6

    a. Looking at Kohlberg's levels of moral reasoning what level do you most often operate in?

    b. Do you want to move up a level in Kohlberg's hierarchy? What do you need to get there?

However Kohlberg's work has been criticised on a number of fronts. For example, it focused on moral reasoning, when it is moral action that changes lives. While Blasi did review 75 studies and concluded that there was a correlation between moral thought and moral action it is interesting that Kohlberg chose not to make moral action a focus of his research.[7]

Nevertheless, and to his credit, Kohlberg did engage the idea of moral 'Type', or orientation, as a way to link moral reasoning and moral action. What's interesting is that moral Type works irrespective of the moral stage a person operates in. As such, moral Type is about a way of engaging the world as opposed to how sophisticated one's thinking is.

Usefully, there are only two moral types (i.e., Type A and Type B) and they can be contrasted based on a number of criteria (see Table 6.1). But for our purposes we need only note that it is those people with a Type B orientation who are more likely to act morally and therefore justly.

TABLE 6.1

Kohlberg's moral types (adapted from Snarey and Samuelson, 2014)[8]

Attribute	Type A	Type B
Understanding of hierarchy	Pragmatic.	Prefers/values hierarchy.
Instrinsicality	Instrumental view of persons.	Respects personal autonomy and human dignity.
Prescriptivity	Moral duty is hypothetical.	Moral duty as moral obligation.
Universality	Judgements assumed to be held by all. Based on self-interest.	Nuanced according to context.
Freedom	External authority is important.	External authority, or tradition, is devalued.
Mutual respect	Obedience focused.	Cooperation focused.
Reversibility	Singular perspective on a moral situation.	Individual engages other people's perspectives and reciprocity.
Constructivism	Rules/laws are rigid.	Rules/laws are adaptable.
Choice	Fairness/justice is down-played in determining outcomes to moral dilemmas.	Outcomes to moral dilemmas are generally considered fair/just.

Even so, the relationship between moral reasoning and moral action appears more complex than just considering a person's moral Type. From our perspective, only when the virtue of Courage is paired with the virtue of Justice can moral thought be translated into moral action.

Activity 6.1

a. Name a time when you acted morally. Describe your thinking which led to the moral action and also the motivator which spurred you into action. In identifying these two parts to moral action how might they help you to act morally more often in the future?

b. Looking at Table 6.1 what attributes of a Type B orientation are you strong/weak in? For those attributes that you need to develop how might you go about doing this?

Kohlberg's work has also been challenged for its gender bias. This criticism has been championed by Gilligan.[9] To understand her concerns read these following two extracts taken from an 11 year old boy and an 11 year old girl trying to solve the moral dilemma of Heinz, described earlier.

> *Jake* (resolute in his answer): For one thing, a human life is worth more than money, and if the druggist only makes $1000, he is still going to live, but if Heinz doesn't steal the drug, his wife is going to die ... [P]eople are all different, and so you couldn't get Heinz's wife again.[10]
>
> *Amy*: Well, I don't think so. I think there might be other ways besides stealing it ... [If he steals the medicine] he might save his wife then, but if he did, he might have to go to jail, and then his wife might get sicker again, and he couldn't get more of the drug, and it might not be good. So, they should really just talk it out and find some other way to make the money.[11]

For Gilligan, Jake's response was a logical attempt to solve the dilemma whereas Amy preferred to reason in terms of relationships and conflict resolution. In this simple way she showed how male and female reasoning about Justice appeared to differ and thus in what ways Kohlberg's work may be limited.

However, in reply to Gilligan's concerns Snarey noted that in 17 studies across 15 countries, 14 showed no significant differences in how males and females reasoned morally.[12] More recently Skoe has also suggested that both males and females engage logic *and* care when solving moral dilemmas.[13] Therefore, in spite of a feminist critique of Kohlberg's work his theory does appear to apply well across the board.

Question 6.7

From your experience do girls reason-out moral problems differently from boys?

Finally, much of the work surrounding Kohlberg's theory has been to demonstrate its universal applicability. To this end his stages of moral development have been investigated in cross-cultural studies, between rural vs. city dwellers and by comparing people of different social classes. Indeed as early as 1985 over 40 studies across 26 different cultural areas broadly demonstrated the universality of his work.[12]

However there has also been some unexpected findings as well. Vasudev, for instance, found that while Kohlberg's ways of reasoning were found in India, not all Indian ways of reasoning about moral dilemmas were found in Kohlberg's work.[12] Therefore moral reasoning may be much broader than Kohlberg could have imagined working with an urban US population.

In addition, if Kohlberg was correct then people should proceed through his stages of moral reasoning in a fairly orderly fashion. However Snarey reported that while Stages 2 and 4 appeared almost universal Stages 1 and 5 occurred only two thirds of the time.[12] Most interestingly, post-conventional reasoning (i.e., Stage 5) appeared to be limited to middle class adults who lived in urban centres. While tribal/village cultures did not appear use post-conventional reasoning at all! Given that tribal/village people are obviously no less intelligent than city dwellers this suggests that post-conventional reasoning may be an aberration of place and class. It is, in effect a 'city thing'. The striking implication of this finding is that the heart of Justice lies not with the agendas of inner-city elites but with simpler notions of equity, reciprocity and the need to uphold social conventions. Something that is entirely consistent with our previous chapter on Honour.

To drive this point home let's briefly consider two examples. Ernesto 'Che' Guevara and Mohandas Ghandi both fought for Justice, of this there is no doubt. What is interesting, however, is that both men were elites within their society by upbringing and profession, city dwellers and post-conventional thinkers. They also dramatically departed, at times, from any semblance of virtue as it might ordinarily be applied to Justice.

For instance, Che Guevara turned from being a respected medico to a South American revolutionary guided by Communist post-conventional thinking. That, in the end, he became a lost soul is summed up best in his own words when describing an execution he performed during the Cuban revolution, 'The situation was uncomfortable ... so I ended the problem giving him a shot with a .32 pistol in the right side of the brain ....'.[14] Was this an act of Justice, or something else?

As for Ghandi, his highly developed post-conventional thinking on Justice was articulated in his twin philosophies of *satyagraha* (i.e., 'holding firmly to the truth') and *ahimsa* (i.e., non-violence). While these guided him, and his followers, through many decades of struggle in both South Africa and India they also perpetuated moments of great injustice. Quite simply, his moral reasoning was dreadfully askew when in a letter to Lord Linlithgow, dated May 1940, he described Hitler as '... not a bad man ....'.[15] In addition, at the height of the war he also publically asked the British people to,

> [Lay] down the arms you have as being useless for saving you or humanity. You will invite Herr Hitler and Signor Mussolini to take what they want ... Let them take possession of your beautiful island, with your many beautiful buildings. You will give all these but neither your souls, nor your minds.[16]

Therefore, and in sum, the heart of Justice may lie with conventional, not post-conventional, reasoning. And this is not a poverty-stricken approach. Reciprocity is fair; understanding the intentionality of others requires insight; and upholding the values of your family and community maintains relationship. In fact, all these ideas about Justice are entirely virtuous and in keeping with Chapters 2 to 5.

 Question 6.8

> From what you have read above have your views on Justice shifted?

A specialised topic: Forgiveness

Justice can be hollow, cold or even cruel. When two women petitioned King Solomon, both claiming to be the mother of an infant, he threatened to cut the baby in half and give each woman one portion. Needless to say the real mother broke down in tears and was given the child unharmed. Whether this was Solomon's gambit to uncover the real mother, or his actual intent, does not matter for our purposes. What is important to realise is that Justice must be tempered lest it become its own form of injustice. For this reason mercy becomes one of Justice's most important attributes. However, mercy and compassion are so closely related that we will hold-off our discussion until Chapter

7. But, in the meantime, we can still detail one beautiful expression of mercy being the act of forgiveness.

Although not always given the prominence it deserves in the literature forgiveness is a virtuous act like no other.[17, 18] For those who have been hurt, offering forgiveness is cathartic, while for an offender both receiving forgiveness, and forgiving oneself, can be truly life changing. As such, any discussion of the virtue of Justice without acknowledging forgiveness remains shallow.

Question 6.9

    a. At some time in the past you have probably had to forgive another person? What was this experience like? What came of it?

    b. Have you ever had to be forgiven? Again, what was this like and what occurred as a result?

To demonstrate the beauty of forgiveness let's briefly turn to the experience of Eric Lomax as both a victim and a survivor. In his words:

> If you are a victim of torture you never totally recover. You may cope with the physical damage, but the psychological damage stays with you forever.
>
> In 1945 I returned to Edinburgh to a life of uncertainty, following three and half years of fear, interrogation and torture as a POW in the Far East. I had no self-worth, no trust in people, and lived in a world of my own. The privacy of the torture victim is more impregnable than any island fortress. People thought I was coping, but inside I was falling apart. I became impossible to live with; it was as if the sins my captors had sown in me were being harvested in my family. I also had intense hatred for the Japanese, and was always looking for ways and means to do them down. In my mind I often thought of my hateful interrogator. I wanted to drown him, cage him and beat him — as he had done to me.
>
> After my retirement in 1982, I started searching for information about what had happened in Siam [Thailand]. The need to know is powerful. In the course of my search I learnt that Nagase Takashi — my interrogator and torturer — had offered to help others with information. I learnt that he was still alive, active in charitable works, and that he had built a Buddhist temple. I was sceptical. I couldn't believe in the notion of Japanese repentance.

I strongly suspected that if I were to meet him I'd put my hands round his neck and do him in.

My turning point came in 1987 when I came across The Medical Foundation for Victims of Torture. For the first time I was able to unload the hate that had become my prison. Seeing the change in me, my wife wrote to Nagase. The letter he wrote back was full of compassion, and I think at that moment I lost whatever hard armour I had wrapped around me and began to think the unthinkable.

The meeting took place in 1998 in Kanburi, Thailand. When we met Nagase greeted me with a formal bow. I took his hand and said in Japanese, 'Good Morning Mr Nagase, how are you?' He was trembling and crying, and he said over and over again: 'I am so sorry, so very sorry.' I had come with no sympathy for this man, and yet Nagase, through his complete humility, turned this around. In the days that followed we spent a lot of time together, talking and laughing. It transpired that we had much in common. We promised to keep in touch and have remained friends ever since.[19]

 Activity 6.2

In Eric Lomax's story identify the essential elements that led to forgiveness. In doing so consider the individual contributions of Eric Lomax and Nagase Takashi to the process of forgiveness.

However, forgiveness is a complicated business. For example, when is forgiveness to occur? If it happens too quickly it runs the risk of being incomplete, or even inauthentic. In the case of violent crime a period of mourning is especially important for the victim needs time to process who they thought they were, who they were becoming and who they are now as a consequence of the harm inflicted.[20]

More complicated still is to ask who needs to be forgiven and by whom? While it is obvious that the perpetrator of a crime is the one in need of forgiveness from their victim this view is too narrow. For example, a victim's family typically suffers their own pain following a violent crime. At worse their loved one is dead, at best their loved one is traumatised and requires assistance with rehabilitation. As such, an entire family becomes touched by the harm done and so may benefit from entering into a process of forgiveness with their loved one's perpetrator.[21] Perhaps, surprisingly, the perpetrator has also to forgive themself. This is especially true of acts of violence fuelled by alcohol, rage or hurt where in a moment two lives are changed forever. Most interestingly, however, the victim of a violent crime may also have to embark on a similar process of self-forgiveness. Although not often acknowledged this occurs most often when a victim has put themselves in danger, or failed to act as bravely as they though they should. Therefore, as you can see, forgiveness is not one thing, but a web of possibilities in which many people have to play their part.

Academics have also noted that forgiveness can begin with different people. For example, a Christian theological view of forgiveness has the victim initiate the process. Yet other approaches to forgiveness would have the offender begin. While the way in which forgiveness is done also differs according to one's perspective. The theological model of forgiveness, for example, would have a victim approach their perpetrator in an open-handed manner which is in obvious contrast to a perpetrator seeking forgiveness only after they have shown remorse and a degree of repentance.[18]

Even whether forgiveness can be, or should be, considered unconditional is a hotly debated topic. Fiddes, for example, would say from a Christian worldview that forgiveness must be unconditional.[18] But Shapland makes the important point that forgiveness may exist on a continuum stretched between conditional and unconditional depending upon the amount of harm done.[21] From this perspective a slight can be forgiven unconditionally but grave crimes of violence may reasonably limit the forgiveness possible.

Finally, the process of forgiveness itself is also contested in the literature. Blyth notes that some consider forgiveness to be about 'letting go' which is self-focused, if not selfish.[22] Others, like Eric Lomax, discuss forgiveness as a transformative experience in which the relationship between victim and perpetrator is fundamentally altered. If we consider forgiveness from this perspective then it becomes a journey towards reconciliation; even if reconciliation is a somewhat separate issue. While we will explore both of these perspectives below let's take the last one first.

Forgiveness as a walk towards reconciliation is best seen from a theological perspective which comes out of a Christian worldview. The process begins when the victim offers forgiveness to the one who has harmed them. As such, this grace-filled — and virtuous — approach to forgiveness has the victim play the role of the wounded Christ. In doing so it is believed that something is touched deep within the perpetrator who is compelled to respond out of a genuine sense of shared humanity. But this is only the beginning. For now both people share in a journey towards a deeper understanding of their mutual suffering. However, only when this journey is completed can forgiveness be given.[18]

Nevertheless this theological model has real limitations. For example, in many instances a victim and their perpetrator have no pre-existing relationship prior to the harm that was inflicted, nor want any ongoing relationship. In addition, the forgiveness offered must also be unconditional and therefore Christ-like. As we learnt above, whether this is even possible is debatable. Nevertheless, to the extent that unconditionality can be a part of the forgiveness offered it most likely represents the one necessary and sufficient element for transformation. But perhaps the most challenging aspect of this approach to forgiveness is that it offends our sense of Justice and care for the victim. For in the journey of forgiveness the victim becomes vulnerable once more to the perpetrator's anger, silence, blame or manipulations.[18]

By contrast, a psychological approach to forgiveness is often more measured. Notions of whole-scale transformation are not necessarily considered and virtue is found in the small hard-won victories of daily life. What's more, a psychological approach is often based in understanding a client's thinking which McCollough and his colleagues have boiled down to two questions: (1) 'What if I forgive?', and (2) 'What about revenge?'.[23] Yet while forgiveness may be a cognitive process, we inhabit a social world full of emotions. And so we *feel* hurt, rather than *think* hurt. To this end any therapeutic process which utilises forgiveness must engage both cognitive and emotional elements.[24, 25] For this reason therapists seek to shift feelings of bitterness towards a perpetrator and have them give way to positive emotions.[26, 27] Ultimately McCollough's two questions and the pragmatics of therapy find their outlet in developing healthy displays of anger and also in building empathy towards the perpetrator. This, then, brings about psychological forgiveness.

Although numerous ways to forgiveness have been put forward let's focus on the Forgiveness Process Model as the approach which has received the most support.[25, 26, 28] This four stage therapeutic method follows a standard Cognitive Behavioural approach by having a client 'think' and 'do' differently. But differs in so far as emotions such as anger are considered with depth and respect.[29, 30]

In brief, Stage 1 has the client uncover the painful events which triggered their distress and note how they were changed as a result of the harm done to them. This can be painful, if not angry, work full of anxiety and shame. Stage 2 asks the client to *choose* forgiveness as a way to improve personal functioning through better coping. That forgiveness is a decision is important because it empowers the client, perhaps for the first time since the harm occurred. Stage

3 is all about seeing the offender from multiple perspectives and thus developing empathy for them. Finally, Stage 4 concludes the process of forgiveness by seeking to consolidate the gains made and motivate for additional forgiveness over time.[26, 31] Ultimately it is hoped that forgiveness translates into action. In this way a victim becomes a survivor before taking on the mantle of being considered virtuous.

Question 6.10

    a. Given that virtues provide a person an evolutionary advantage what may be the advantage implicit in forgiveness?

    b. Forgiveness is often described as a choice. In what ways does emotion also play a part in choosing whether to forgive or not?

    c. People are more than their thoughts and feelings. In what way is the activity of forgiveness:

       (1) creative

       (2) intuitive

       (3) relational.

    d. How could you apply what you have now learnt about the process of forgiveness in your own life?

    e. If you are a psychologist or counsellor what has been your experience of bringing forgiveness into therapy?

    f. If you work in restorative justice, perhaps in the community or in a school, what have you learnt about fulsome forgiveness?

Activity 6.3

Think about a time in your life when you were hurt by somebody. Perhaps choose a small hurt rather than a big one. See if you can use Stages 1 through 4 of the Forgiveness Process model to assist yourself to forgive that person.

How to grow in Justice

For each of us to grow in Justice can only improve our lives and make the world, little by little, a better place. Usefully, psychologists have had a lot to say about growing in Justice over recent decades and have therefore touched on the virtuous qualities of Justice.

Beginning with young children, Augustine and Stifter noted the value of certain parenting styles in teaching Justice.[32] For them, parent–child interactions should always be mutually warm and engaging for this develops respect for authority and acknowledges the value of reciprocity as the basis for fairness. In addition, discipline which is firm but fair is more likely to develop moral reasoning than harsh discipline designed only to assert control.[33, 34]

However, these broad comments must be adapted in light of each child's temperament. For example an introverted, or sensitive, child may see punishment as more threatening than other children. Therefore the discipline shown these children needs to be adjusted so as not to be perceived as harsh.[35, 36] In fact because sensitive children already often have excellent self-control good parenting around Justice is often about getting them 'to do' rather than 'Don't you dare...!'. The opposite, of course, applies to rambunctious children. Finally, the beneficial effects of this style of discipline are further enhanced when the parent explains their reasoning to the child. In this way they kickstart, or model, moral reasoning for the youngster.[32]

Question 6.11

    a. While Augustine and Stifter discussed young children, how can their ideas about parenting be adapted to older children and adolescents?

    b. How might schools manage the competing demands to be child-focused while also showing equality in the dispensing of discipline (i.e., Justice)?

Activity 6.4

    If you are a parent describe the temperament of each of your children. Are they introverted or extraverted? Now consider how you parent them. Are your parenting methods likely to improve their moral reasoning, and thus their sense of Justice, or not?

As children grow parents inevitably hand over some of the responsibility for maturing their sons or daughters to the local school. This was an early consideration for Kohlberg and he had much to say on the topic. However, as a headline statement keep in mind that children grow in Justice, or morality for that matter, only when they have the opportunity to engage '… rich experiences in the social–moral realm.'.[37]

Kohlberg promoted this rich form of engagement in three ways. First, children need to become aware of moral exemplars and learn from these people. For teachers, simply having students work through classroom case studies detailing how contemporary and historical figures dealt with moral issues is a simple and effective way to begin to develop moral reasoning in their pupils. But it is often not enough. Moral exemplars also need to be 'real'. As such, children should be encouraged to find, and interact with, moral exemplars in their own lives. This might be a parent, relative, sports coach or some other worthy figure. In doing so the dusty pages of history give way to all the nuances inherent in living a moral, or just, life. Moreover, the child's real-life exemplar is able to encourage them in living a moral life in ways that a history book could never do. As an extension to this Kohlberg also placed a significant burden on teachers to be moral exemplars in the life of their students. In this way students become held within an environment that will enliven and promote their moral/Justice development.[8]

Question 6.12

    a. What can you do to be a moral exemplar to a child whom you know?

    b. If you are a teacher, how important is it to teach history from a positive, if not virtuous, perspective and so engage students with past moral exemplars?

Activity 6.5

    For a child you know well, develop a list of moral exemplars and identify some books which highlight the actions of these people.

Next comes the use of moral dilemmas for growing a sense of Justice in children and Kohlberg had much to say about this,

> What can teachers and schools do to stimulate moral development? The teacher must help the student to consider genuine moral conflicts, think

about the reasoning he uses in solving such conflicts, see inconsistencies and inadequacies in his way of thinking and find ways of resolving them.[38]

By engaging students in moral dilemmas teachers do many useful things. At one level they assist their students to become nuanced thinkers. At another they build empathy, especially when moral dilemmas are Justice-focussed. But most importantly teachers help their students to develop a Type B moral orientation (see Table 6.1) thus beginning the transformation of moral reasoning into moral action.

In demonstrating how to conduct a discussion around a moral dilemma we have the following account from a sixth grade class:

> [The instructor] presented moral dilemmas which engaged the classes in a good deal of heated debate. He tried to leave much of the discussion to the children themselves, stepping in only to summarise, clarify, and sometimes present a view himself. He encouraged arguments that were one stage above those of most of the class.[39]

As to the outcome of presenting moral dilemmas, the researchers were surprised to find that these children improved their moral reasoning by an entire stage in only weeks thus demonstrating the effectiveness of this form of learning.

However, there is subtlety in how a moral, or Justice-based, dilemma needs to be constructed and presented to a class if it is going to be effective in boosting students' moral reasoning. For example, 'The most powerful interventions for stimulating moral stage change are those that involve discussions of real … problems and situations … [and] in which all participants are empowered to have a say in the discussion'.[8] Therefore moral dilemmas need to be real and the discussions peer-based. In fact, the best outcomes occur when children engage peers who sit somewhere between a 1/3 and 2 stages above themselves in moral reasoning.[8]

Although the discussion of moral dilemmas should be peer-to-peer teachers are always an important variable in determining outcomes. However, difficulties arise when a teacher is not practiced in moderating, or facilitating, a Socratic conversation. In particular, teachers have to be careful to not become participants by peppering the discussion with their own values lest they stifle debate. Rather, teachers produce maximum change in their students when they '… restat[e] the child's reasoning, ask … for an opinion, ask … questions of clarification, and check … for understanding'.[40] In this way it is the teacher's job to develop each child's reasoning and self-insight (i.e., Wisdom; see Chapter 4), not to guide the discussion to a pre-ordained conclusion.

Question 6.13

> If you are a parent or teacher do you find that political agendas placed within a curriculum enhance or detract from a student's capacity to grow in Justice thinking?

The last important consideration for teachers in presenting a moral dilemma to their class is the duration of the experience. Although dilemmas are a reasonably quick way of eliciting growth in Justice they are not brief interventions either. One's ability to grow students in moral reasoning will be reduced if the dilemma is not fully worked through. In fact, teachers should probably revisit the dilemma with their class more than six times for a fulsome discussion to be had and moral development to really take hold.[8]

 Question 6.14

> a. Given that fairness, reciprocity and upholding social conventions are the hallmarks of Justice, how might a classroom conversation about Justice differ from a conversation about moral reasoning more generally?
>
> b. Although often focused on classroom activities, and therefore teachers, how might a school chaplain, counsellor etc. also contribute to students' ability to reason justly?

Activity 6.6

> If you are a teacher write a Justice-based dilemma for your students in accordance with what we have discussed above. If you are a parent how might you craft such a discussion around the dinner table this evening?

The final aspect of Kohlberg's approach to moral (i.e., Justice) education was to recognise the importance of a school's moral atmosphere. Of this he wrote,

> [C]lassroom discussion[s] ... should be part of a broader, more enduring involvement of students in the social and moral functioning of the school ... [Teachers] should challenge students with the moral issues faced by the school community ... One must create a 'just community.'[41]

To achieve this broader aim Kohlberg began by giving the same basic rights to all members of the school community, be they student or teacher. However, he balanced these rights against mutual responsibility and focused them on the promotion of human dignity. Not only did this have people consider, on a daily basis, higher forms of moral reasoning/action but, interestingly enough, paid deference to a much older tradition given that personal dignity is the basis of Honour (see Chapter 5).

Kohlberg also saw advantage in promoting democracy within a school community rather than persist with rigid hierarchies that stifle moral choice. However … One suspects that Kohlberg's notions of democracy were not the egalitarian forms that we have becomes familiar with today. For example, at his Cluster School there was a once-a-week 'Town Meeting' in which students and teachers came together to discuss important matters and vote on what should happen. This, for him, was the epitome of a democratic institution. Yet, inherent in this democratic decision-making were obvious power imbalances. Although students and teachers all had one vote the teachers were physically bigger, older, more articulate and held greater implicit authority. In many ways these Town Meetings were, perhaps, more like a Viking *Thing* (i.e., feudal parliament) than an exercise in egalitarianism. As such, his notions of democracy were contained within the strong bonds of group honour (see Chapter 5) especially given that '[t]he general aim was for students to achieve a sense of community solidarity …'[42]

So, taken together, growing children in Justice is not a quick, or simple, task. However there are deliberate initiatives that parents and teachers can use to effect positive change. Bound within relationships of emotional warmth and mutual respect parents and teachers should act as moral exemplars while also pointing out others who could fulfil this role. Both parents and teachers can also engage children in reasoning through moral dilemmas rather than just stating an opinion or an expectation. In this way they grow children into moral maturity. Finally, although we all value democracy, it is only a *benevolent* honour culture that necessitates the dignity of all members and has within it an obligation for fairness. Therefore, parents and teachers should consider this sort of family dynamic, or school culture, as the best context for children to know and experience Justice.

 Activity 6.7

> a. If you are a parent or teacher get hold of your school's policies and procedures. Consider also how your school's culture is prac-

ticed. In what way is dignity a prime concern as opposed to simpler values such as respect?

b. If you are part of a school community what initiatives can you put forward to make your school a just one in accordance with Kohlberg's work?

c. Reflecting on this chapter and the ideas put forward in Chapter 5 on Honour, how might you construct a benevolent honour culture in your family, school or other organisation you are involved with?

A final word

Justice is about fairness, of that we can have no doubt. But just reasoning is never enough. Good intentions count for very little. In this way the virtue of Justice comes about when just reasoning is translated into just action. But to do this requires that one enemy, more than any other, be overcome — fear.

Think about it for a moment. Fearful people do not share, they do not forgive. They are loathed to take up another's burden. They hold back what is owed and take more than they need. Fearful people are unjust people. And they are as unjust to themselves as much as to everybody else. But there is a way forward. Overcome fear with Courage and so walk justly in this world.

The Freedom of Virtue: Navigating excellence in the art of living amongst a world of instant gratification

Chapter 7

Kindness

> Kindness can accomplish much. As the sun makes ice melt, kindness causes misunderstanding, mistrust, and hostility to evaporate
> — Albert Schweitzer

Kindness is life at its best

Kindness has been shown to improve general wellbeing, increase happiness, decrease depression, boost our immune systems and improve our daily work.[1,2,3,4] It is, in every way, good medicine.

But beyond its immediate benefits Kindness is also profound. For only Kindness has the power to redeem the lost and restore them to community. In fact Kindness even has the power to renew entire communities by entirely peaceful means. So while some may consider it gentle, or even trivial, it is the most powerful virtue of all.

 **Activity 7.1**

Think of a person who displays a lot of kindness. List their personal qualities which contribute to them being so kind. Is this person happy and healthy?

What does it mean to be kind?

Kindness goes by many names, be it generosity, *ren*, mercy, benevolence, *caritas*, compassion, *agape*, *chesed*, grace, *metta*, *karuna* etc. For this reason it is difficult to pin down. So to introduce Kindness it is much more satisfying to present a story than persist with dry old academic discussions. In this way you'll come to see the heart of Kindness without distraction.

However, what story do we tell for every culture has its cherished fables of Kindness? Be it *The Collared Crow* from Southern Africa, *The Banyan Deer* from Asia, *How the Kangaroo got its Pouch* from Australia or *A Calabash of Poi* from Hawaii there is no shortage.[5] Without wanting to appear banal perhaps one of the greatest stories of Kindness is one which many of us grew up with, namely *The Prodigal Son*. Let's read,

> There was a man who had two sons. The younger one said to his father, 'Father, give me my share of the estate'. So he divided his property between them. Not long after that, the younger son got together all he had, set off for a distant country and there squandered his wealth in wild living.
>
> After he had spent everything, there was a severe famine in that whole country, and he began to be in need. So he went and hired himself out to a citizen of that country, who sent him to his fields to feed pigs. He longed to fill his stomach with the pods that the pigs were eating, but no one gave him anything.
>
> When he came to his senses, he said, 'How many of my father's hired servants have food to spare, and here I am starving to death! I will set out and go back to my father and say to him: Father, I have sinned against heaven and against you. I am no longer worthy to be called your son; make me like one of your hired servants.'
>
> So he got up and went to his father. But while he was still a long way off, his father saw him and was filled with compassion for

him; he ran to his son, threw his arms around him and kissed him. The son said to him, 'Father, I have sinned against heaven and against you. I am no longer worthy to be called your son.' But the father said to his servants, 'Quick! Bring the best robe and put it on him. Put a ring on his finger and sandals on his feet. Bring the fattened calf and kill it. Let's have a feast and celebrate. For this son of mine was dead and is alive again; he was lost and is found.'. So they began to celebrate.

Meanwhile, the older son was in the field. When he came near the house, he heard music and dancing. So he called one of the servants and asked him what was going on. 'Your brother has come,' he replied, 'and your father has killed the fattened calf because he has him back safe and sound.' The older brother became angry and refused to go in. So his father went out and pleaded with him. But he answered his father, 'Look! All these years I've been slaving for you and never disobeyed your orders. Yet you never gave me even a young goat so I could celebrate with my friends. But when this son of yours who has squandered your property with prostitutes comes home, you kill the fattened calf for him!'. 'My son,' the father said, 'you are always with me, and everything I have is yours. But we had to celebrate and be glad, because this brother of yours was dead and is alive again; he was lost and is found.' *(paragraphing inserted to help the reader)*[6]

Now where in this story do we find Kindness? Except for the older brother's response the entire parable is all about this one beautiful virtue. Not only did the father lavish the greatest Kindness on his wayward son but also treated the indignation of his older son with tenderness.

In fact this story of Kindness is useful in a number of ways. Not only does it demonstrate Kindness in many forms but also allows us to ask an important question. What act of Kindness within the story was the greatest? In answering this question we inevitably draw close to the heart of Kindness and thus begin to address it by its proper name.

The mistake that most people make in thinking about Kindness is to assume that it is always commensurate with abundant generosity. In this way most people answer that the greatest kindness shown in the story of the Prodigal Son was in the exuberant manner by which the boy was welcomed home. After all, his father ran to him, had him adorned with jewellery, held a mighty big party and killed the fatted calf in celebration. Yet, if we think a little deeper we might discover something else.

More than likely the father's greatest act of Kindness was at the start of the story when he handed over considerable wealth to his son, wished him well, sent him off in style and knew all along that the boy was a fool and would probably squander the lot. But how could this be Kindness, let alone the greatest Kindness? After all it resulted in a good Jewish boy ending up looking after pigs! Nevertheless, the father's actions were most kind for the fact that they pre-empted the boy learning humility and a little Wisdom. The father was not gifting him money so much as the opportunity to grow up. And in doing so the father must also have been stricken by grief. How could a good father not worry over a son he knew would get into trouble? To let his son go, and hope for his safe return, must have been the hardest thing that father ever did. In fact it would have wrenched at his very soul.

So, as you read on don't confuse Kindness for simple giving. Don't assume virtue where there may be little. Look for actions in which virtue begets virtue and where compassion is evident. Here is where you will find the heart of Kindness.

Ordinary Kindness: Good deeds and altruism

Everyone loves a giver. Children love their grandparents when they give them a $5 note to spend at the local shops. And who doesn't think well of people known to give generously to good causes. It makes us feel all warm inside to know that good people are in the world. Nor is there anything wrong with this. But don't confuse that sort of giving with virtue. Being generous is, in actual fact, only the doorway to Kindness. Be generous, of course, but realise that virtue asks so much more.

Having now played the cynic let's explore why generosity is only the threshold to Kindness. Psychologists have investigated all sorts of pro-social behaviours such as charity, benevolence, generosity and even altruism. Yet for all their efforts it is clear that each serves the same function. Be it generosity shown to family and neighbours, or charity towards the community at large, the simple function of giving is to maintain our web of relationships through economic means. Or, put another way, generosity was the missing link for Rawls when he tried to justify his difference principle as we learnt about in Chapter 6.

In this way we can define giving as an *ordinary* form of Kindness. Moreover, that it is dedicated to holding relationships together means that it is motivated by a complex set of personal needs, social expectations and evolutionary necessity. At the risk of dipping into cynicism once more it is as Jamal said in the movie *Slumdog Millionaire*, 'Blind singers earns double. You know that!'.[7]

So let's investigate the pragmatics of ordinary kindness. In this way we are asking what motivates charitable behaviour? In a tangential way we are also asking if altruism actually exists? By doing so we will ultimately come to see what is truly virtuous about Kindness.

To start with the obvious, people love to give when they can be seen to be doing so. This can occur in subtle, and not so subtle, ways. For example, just recently my wife and I (i.e., Tom) listened to a wonderful busker in one of the main train stations in Sydney, Australia. Here was a talented young man playing his violin with tremendous gusto. The quality of his performance alone meant that he would elicit some giving from passers-by but, in watching how this giving occurred, we saw something very interesting. We noticed that as people came forward to drop a few coins in his hat they made eye contact with him. Their giving also prompted others to do likewise. While it could be argued that this collective giving behaviour was an example of modelling it is also reasonable to suggest that people gave because they knew others were looking on. In this regard people give when they can be seen to be doing so.

Another example of what we are trying to describe is the cringeworthy display of some people at charity dinners. Not only will these people host a table, and hold court all evening, but as the raffle tickets are passed around they buy a bundle. After dinner, and probably a little liquored-up, such people are also the ones to make the inflated bids on items to be auctioned. But would they have behaved the same way if nobody was about? Probably not. In fact this sort of giver implicitly recognises one important pay off for generosity. That is, winning the esteem of others. They may even have an inkling of a second, and more subtle, pay off for being generous which is to plaster over the cracks of a fragile ego. Even if just for a while.

Question 7.1

a. Have you ever witnessed acts of charity or benevolence which appeared designed to advertise the generosity of the giver? What did you feel as you saw it happening?

b. Compare that feeling to how you have felt when you have discovered acts of charity being done quietly, if not privately.

c. What does the difference in these feelings tell you about the virtue inherent in Kindness?

Yet charity is not always so mercenary. Oftentimes giving is simply an immediate response to an unexpected situation of need. Therefore, some acts of charity may be true acts of Kindness. But, in so much as the giver and recipient enter into a fleeting relationship so social forces come to bear on the situation. This, in turn, acts to undermine any sense of altruism. For example, we have all been charitable when a weedy looking homeless person comes up to us on a street corner. And this is, at one level, a response to obvious need. But in so much as we feel a mix of fear and guilt in their approach we give to shoo them away as much as to be kind.

More insidious is that the best panhandlers know how to manipulate us into being altruistic. One such story concerned my (i.e., Tom) father-in-law who was down from the country. Eating lunch alone in an inner-city pub he was approached by a cute blonde backpacker who struck up a conversation and, after a little innocent flirting on her part (i.e., manipulation #1), casually mentioned that her funds were running low (i.e., manipulation #2). You can guess what happened next, all because my father-in-law 'felt sorry for her' as he told us that evening. So, in sum, while being charitable is kind it may not always be virtuous given that it serves the purpose of the giver, the receiver, or both.

 Question 7.2

    a. In what way do advertising campaigns emotionally trigger people into donating money to large charities?

    b. More generally, have you ever felt obligated, or manipulated, into giving to some cause? What happened?

 Activity 7.2

    In thinking about your response to Question 7.2b, analyse the factors that caused you to give against your better judgement.

Psychologically, if not evolutionarily, Konnikova discussed generosity in blunt terms by suggesting it to be nothing more than the redistribution of excess resources within a group by pre-defined rules.[8] To demonstrate this point we can turn to the work of Stevens who looked to uncover the rules of sharing as the basis for all other forms of giving. Working with monkeys, Stevens centred his research around the ability of a 'wealthy' monkey to defend its food and the ability of a 'beggar' monkey to harass. In every case increased harassment from the beggar monkey produced increased food sharing. In this way both monkeys got what they wanted, the beggar monkey got some food, while the wealthy monkey got some peace and quiet.[9] The immediate implication being that sharing (i.e., giving) represented the outcome of a simple cost/benefit analysis on the part of the wealthy monkey. However, at a broader level, sharing also served the survival needs of the community in so much as both monkeys now had enough food.

While the above scenario may appear to have a comical element to it we nevertheless learn a fundamental truth about sharing as summed up by the Latin phrase, *quid pro quo*. That is, sharing is not so much about being selfless, or altruistic, as trading something for something. More remarkable still, it appears that primates may even keep score suggesting an economics of generosity.[10, 11, 12]

In human terms what the above studies tell us is that perhaps many of our motivations towards generosity are fuelled by self-interest. For to give coins to a homeless person is to avoid further harassment, to give roses to a date is to hope for sex and to be accommodating at work means that you can call-in a favour in time. If this sounds too cynical Komter backs it up when she writes:

> Empirical research shows that human generosity is selective: kin and close relatives are favoured over others. Moreover, generosity generates its own rewards and is therefore again selective: the more you give, the more you receive.[13]

While still being a social good, giving really isn't very virtuous. Charity, benevolence and generosity are coded for in our genes and wired into our brains. We also tend to give out of our wealth, not our poverty. Therefore, so long as giving remains transactional we have to look elsewhere for the virtue of Kindness.

Question 7.3

    a. Do you agree with the research that acts of giving are inherently pragmatic, if not selfish?

    b. Can you think of examples in your own life when this was, and was not, the case?

Activity 7.3

Compare and contrast acts of generosity in the workplace with acts of generosity in the home. Are there any differences, perhaps in intent? Is the nature, or amount, of the generosity different? Is the outcome different? If there are differences reflect on the nature of generosity between unrelated people and those with a strong genetic tie.

Extraordinary Kindness: Compassion is the key

In so much as ordinary Kindness has its own rewards it is good but not virtuous. However extraordinary Kindness is something altogether more special for it is the wilful giving of one's self and often without reward. Indeed this sort of giving can become so heavy to bear that it comes at considerable cost. It is for this reason that acts of extraordinary Kindness are so prized.

When we think of acts of extraordinary Kindness we tend to focus on remarkable people such as Mother Theresa or Nelson Mandela. But extraordinary Kindness is within the grasp of us all. For instance, mentoring a junior colleague can be an act of extraordinary Kindness for the burden of this relationship is born entirely by the mentor. Similarly, people who renounce wealth to live modestly also demonstrate extraordinary Kindness. Not only might they privately give of their wealth, but by avoiding excess they refuse to take more than their fair share of natural resources thus showing great kindness to the planet. Foster carers are also a great example of people showing extraordinary Kindness by welcoming children into their home who are in desperate need. Even social activists can be proponents of extraordinary Kindness for they set aside time to be involved in community renewal, or to help people whom they don't know through organisations like Amnesty International. So don't think that extraordinary Kindness is unattainable. Look for opportunities, you will find them.

 Question 7.4

a. Taking the notion of 'virtue is as virtue does' think about your own life. What acts of extraordinary Kindness have you performed?

b. What acts of extraordinary Kindness can you perform?

Compassion eclipses empathy

Compassion, *not* empathy, fuels extraordinary Kindness. While empathy is not a bad thing, it is not the best thing either. Although this is perhaps a surprising differentiation to make think of it this way. A teacher, therapist or pastor, for example, can have lots of empathy but little compassion. When a person seeks their help they do get a fair hearing and perhaps some good advice. But inevitably the person comes away still suffering. Their burdens have not been lifted nor the humanity of their situation honoured. In this way compassion works at a much deeper level than empathy ever could.

In fact, compassion also works in a quite specific way. While empathy is about matching another's emotions, good or bad, compassion is felt when one is moved to help carry another's burdens.[14] Compassion, therefore, is about suffering. Even more precisely, it is about your willingness to enter into another person's suffering. As such, compassion (a) is about feeling the suffering of another; (b) wills us to act to alleviate that suffering; and (c) has us 'join' with the suffering person.[15]

Therefore compassion is empathy's big brother. In borrowing some terms from Dietrich Bonhoeffer: empathy is 'cheap'; compassion is 'expensive'. While empathy may help the person to whom it is directed, compassion will actually change the quality of the suffering which is being experienced.

Question 7.5

> Can you think of a time when you have been (a) empathetic; and (b) another time when you were compassionate? What was similar about each situation? What was different? Did the outcomes differ?

Nor does compassion stand alone for it can be linked to at least three other foundational virtues. For example, Joan Halifax writes about compassion in the context of working with the dying. In doing so she comes close to naming the first of these related foundational virtues,

> Over the years people have asked me questions like 'How can you touch someone whose body is covered in lesions?' 'Isn't it difficult to be around so much pain and suffering?' ...
> In the beginning it wasn't easy. It did not come naturally or instinctively. Working so closely with death often scared me; I was afraid ... [But when] I recognised, however, that I already have what dying people have — mortality — I stopped being afraid ...

Recognising this very interconnectedness is the ground of giving no fear, and the beginning of compassion.[16]

From this short excerpt we can thus surmise that compassion requires Courage. It has a fearlessness about it. This also explains why empathy is easy. It does not, fundamentally, require anything of the empathetic person. But nor does empathy have the ability to shake the foundations of one's life. Compassion will.

Question 7.6

In what ways does fear hold you back from living a life of compassion?

As for the second foundational virtue to which compassion is linked we need to consider how Buddhists understand compassion. Buddha once wrote, 'Hatred is ... never appeased by hatred ... It is appeased only by loving-kindness'.[17] In this way Buddhists consider compassion to be the highest form of Wisdom.[18] But, as you no doubt realise, this is a very particular form of Wisdom. It is not Aristotelian or legalistic, but existential. This sort of Wisdom recognises that we are all born into the world alone, share happiness and suffering in equal measure and soon enough die. Such Wisdom takes the absurdity of life and makes it beautiful by giving meaning to every minute we have.

Question 7.7

What works of literature, and characters within, also speak of this sort of existential Wisdom?

Finally, compassion must also be linked with the foundational virtue of Justice and, in particular, restorative justice. However, this linkage is not a simple one for compassion is never given out equally.[15] We look for the blameless victim on whom to bestow compassion, or an offender who is worthy of compassion given their remorse. Williams even confounds our notions of deserved compassion when he quotes Amir by saying, 'the 'virtuous' victim is not always the innocent and passive party' and, by corollary, offenders are not without their merits if only we take the time to look.[19] As such, compassion and Justice are linked in complex and nuanced ways.

Chapter 7 Kindness

> **Question 7.8**
>
> Can you remember a time when you chose to withhold compassion given that you considered 'the victim' to have contributed to their misfortune? What was it about the situation or person that made you feel this way?

So, in sum, compassion is extraordinary and thus the hallmark of Kindness. It is greater in depth than empathy and so very virtuous.

The purpose of compassion

Although we have established the purpose of charity it is more difficult to understand the purpose of compassion given that it is so costly. Nevertheless compassion is evolutionarily rooted, but now favours the community, not the individual. As such compassion has a purpose, even more than one. For example, without compassion Justice would become inherently punitive, if not cruel. Essentially, good people could find themselves severely punished for small misdemeanors. By extension their punishments could exclude them from community, or even from the gene pool, and thus weaken the community in time. By way of a fictional example of this we need look no further than Victor Hugo's heroic character Jean Valjean in *Les Miserables*. Here was a good, if not virtuous, man locked up for 20 years for stealing a loaf of bread.

In a not dissimilar way Goetz and colleagues also noted that compassion provides a strong basis for social cooperation.[20] But whereas sharing was between two people a compassionate attitude replicated across a community has the effect of creating a space in which everyone feels safe to live and love. In this way compassion provides a stable base for a community to flourish. In fact, if we did not have compassion then it is likely that our communities would descend into Orwellian dystopias and 'flame-out' all too quickly.

> **Question 7.9**
>
> Can you think of an historical example(s) of societies which lacked compassion and came to an abrupt end?

More intriguing, however, was when Goetz's research group focused their attention on the formation of strong families. Unexpectedly they first found that there was great value in finding a romantic partner who was compassionate. In fact Kindness was amongst the highest ranked attributes when young people were surveyed on what they found attractive in another person. But compassion was not an end in itself. Compassionate partners were thought more likely to be faithful, recognise the needs of their spouse and assist in the care of children. In other words, compassionate partners make sure their family flourishes.[20]

Even in the workplace, which is a community of sorts, compassion has been shown to curb anxiety and burn-out, reduce bad behaviour between employees, improve job performance and, over time, likely save employers significant costs associated with staff turn over.[21]

Question 7.10

    a. Can you think of any other reasons why compassion is necessary for family and community?

    b. In our discussion earlier we talked about the importance of compassionate communities. If you are a social worker or community psychologist what compassion interventions, or activities, have you participated in with respect to your community?

    c. What might the dangers of too much compassion be? What virtue(s) are needed to balance compassion?

While compassion may be considered virtuous given the cost inflicted, and because it benefits the community rather than the person, there are nevertheless individual benefits to being compassionate which we cannot ignore. For example, it is not unreasonable to suggest that some people derive a certain satisfaction from being seen to be compassionate. However the cost involved, or their visible inauthenticity, soon curtails their efforts. If anything, to understand any individual pay-off for being compassionate we need to approach this topic from a different perspective. In doing so we read,

> Research indicates that individuals who are self-compassionate demonstrate better psychological health than those who lack self-compassion. For instance, greater self-compassion has consistently been found to predict lower levels of anxiety and depression ... Greater self-compassion is also linked with less rumination, perfectionism, and fear of failure ... At the same time, self-compassionate people are less likely to suppress unwanted thoughts and are more willing to acknowledge their negative emotions as valid and important ...
>
> Self-compassion is associated with positive psychological strengths such as happiness, optimism, wisdom, curiosity and exploration, personal initiative,

and emotional intelligence ... Another strength of being self-compassionate is the ability to cope effectively with life stressors ... [including] chronic pain. Self-compassionate individuals have been found to have improved relationship functioning ... Self-compassion also promotes health-related behaviors such as sticking to one's diet ..., reducing smoking ..., seeking medical treatment ..., and exercising...[22]

In other words, self-compassionate people are happy people.[23] So, while a significant cost is born in being compassionate to others, self-compassion pays a handsome dividend.

Taken together, while generosity and compassion both have evolutionary origins they are very different. Indeed compassion for others is even different to self-compassion. But whatever the differences may be our ultimate objective is to grow in Kindness.

How do we grow in Kindness?

The last section of our chapter will now be devoted to growing in Kindness. In doing so we will make some general remarks about generosity before delving into the more important topic of compassion.

Developing generous people

Parents are very good at developing generosity in their children when they:

- praise cooperative behaviour with siblings/friends,
- sit with youngsters and teach them how to share toys and ask for their safe return,
- develop trusting relationships through shared activities such as listening to their child's daily dramas and reading a bedtime story,
- have older children do chores on behalf of the family *without* the expectation of pocket money, and
- always provide a general sense of safety and emotional warmth in the home.

In these ways children come to hold two opposing ideas in tension from which emerges generosity: 'I am important' and 'others are important too'.

At school generosity can also be encouraged by collaborative work within a high-support high-expectation environment. Whatever the context, be it in the classroom, in the school orchestra, or on the sports field, when students learn to compromise and look out for each other they are training in generosity.

However, there is also a warning implicit within these statements. School/family ethos is important. If the ethos is, 'Who cares?', or 'It's ok to be good enough', then generosity will not be encouraged. Such middling expectations simply have the effect of devolving responsibility onto other people. Generosity is not a spectator sport! At the other end of the continuum an ethos focused only on high achievement similarly kills off generosity. For now life is a race that *I* must win!

More formally, we can also look to Psychology to help grow young people in generosity and so make targeted interventions. For example, Ashton and colleagues investigated the personality traits associated with various forms of giving (i.e., kin altruism vs. reciprocal altruism) and highlighted the specific importance of a trait called Agreeableness.[24] We may therefore conclude from their study that not only is this the trait that marks out generous people but also, when in deficit, says something about stinginess. What is interesting is that the personality trait of Agreeableness is all about working well with others, if not also trusting them.

However the personality trait of Agreeableness is only one part of the puzzle. In discussing generosity Sommerfeld also noted the importance of Agreeableness but went further by pairing this trait with two others.[25] Specifically, high levels of Conscientiousness were found to be important for generosity as well as low levels of Neuroticism (see Chapters 2 and 3). And as for how Neuroticism thwarted generosity Sommerfeld found that all six facets of this negative personality trait were involved![25] Together, we can therefore conclude that generous people show a pro-social demeanour through the personality trait of Agreeableness. They are motivated to act on their pro-social disposition via the trait of Conscientiousness. And because these people have low levels of Neuroticism they also do not fear being generous or feel an unwarranted burden for being so. The upshot being that any psychological intervention designed to grow generosity should target these three personality traits.

Question 7.11

a. In what ways has fear prevented you from performing acts of kindness?

b. If you are a psychologist or counsellor what ways do you know of to boost a client's sense of Agreeableness and Conscientiousness? How would you go about reducing their levels of Neuroticism?

 Activity 7.4

> Go online and look up the personality trait of Neuroticism. Do you recognise any part of yourself in what you read? What might you do about it?

We can also develop generosity in ourselves and other adults in simple ways. In the first instance we should expect ourselves, and others around us, to be generous. For example, we should want to help a neighbour, look after an elderly parent, or volunteer our time within the community. After all, if we are not responsible for our neighbourhoods who is? Generosity is therefore not a state of mind but an action.

 Question 7.12

> In what ways has the widespread provision of government services decreased our capacity for generosity?

In the workplace it is also possible to suggest generosity interventions in keeping with the three personality traits mentioned above. For instance, it is easy enough to promote Agreeableness by having people work in teams and be customer focused. In this way compromise and negotiation is fostered. What's more, team-based KPI's also promote a level of generosity because people now rise or fall together. As for Conscientiousness we have already shown in Chapter 3 how a workplace culture of continuous improvement is the way to go. For this reason we'll say no more. Lastly, decreasing Neuroticism in the workplace is no small task. Customers complain, deadlines are often tight and quarterly reviews deliberately put employees under pressure. In fact workplaces may even be designed to be neurotic so as to squeeze out the last dregs of productivity from staff. So how do we reverse this trend? We do this by avoiding punitive Justice-based outcomes and turn our attention instead to Honour. Put simply, by having employee's personal integrity guide outcomes a level of control is fostered and workplace Neuroticism drops.

Taken together, growing people in generosity must occur by both direct and indirect means. We must expect children to do family chores, for students to help each other with learning and for adults to both volunteer in the community and create healthy workspaces. But we can go further. We must also promote a society which values the bonds of community, upholds personal responsibility (i.e., Honour) and which refuses to buy into media fear-mongering.

 Activity 7.5

> In your own family, or workplace, consider ways to promote people's sense of generosity. To help you, describe these interventions in terms of boosting Agreeableness and Conscientiousness while lowering Neuroticism.

Developing compassionate people

In so many ways the development of compassion makes for a worthy end to our chapter. What is surprising is that there already exists several recognised ways to do this. While some of these methods are highly technical, and others quite laborious, we would be remiss not to review them briefly. For in doing so we will see key ingredients in the development of compassion which can be adapted and employed in our own lives.

One way to develop compassion is to get involved in a deliberate training programme. For instance, psychologists have found that even brief training in cultivating compassion can be effective. Indeed one study showed an average improvement of ≥ 20% in self-compassion and a whopping 40% improvement in the feeling of compassion for others after only 9 weeks of training![26] While a fantastic outcome the process by which these results were achieved was not a simple one. For example, facilitators had participants focus on four aspects of compassion being,

> (1) an *awareness* of suffering (cognitive/empathic awareness), (2) *sympathetic* concern related to being emotionally moved by suffering (affective component), (3) a *wish* to see the relief of that suffering (intention), and (4) a *responsiveness* or readiness to help relieve that suffering (motivational).[27]

In addition, these four aspects of compassion were placed within a six step curriculum and grounded using a variety of time consuming techniques including,

> (a) pedagogical instruction with active group discussion, (b) a guided group meditation, (c) interactive practical exercises related to the specific step of the week..., and (d) exercises designed to prime feelings of open-heartedness or connection to others, either through reading poetry or through reflecting on inspiring stories. Participants are [also] encouraged and instructed to engage in daily informal and formal home meditation practice for at least 15 min (building up to 30 min) using pre-recorded guided meditations.[28]

The process of developing compassion becomes even more complicated when we turn our attention to compassion-focused therapy which has the laudable goal of replacing automatic fear responses with both a sense of wellbeing and self-valuing.[29] Although useful in the treatment of eating disorders, and generally in school-based settings, compassion-focused therapy is best undertaken by those with considerable training.[30, 31]

The reason for this is not just scope of practice. Schools, for instance, are places of competing interests which have to be negotiated, if not navigated by welfare staff. While welfare staff may see the need for a high-achieving student to develop self-compassion their teachers are probably positively reinforcing those same perfectionistic tendencies given that excellent grades will follow. In addition it is a curious fact that offering compassion to students in need, as a way to inculcate self-compassion, may backfire. Showing compassion too soon to self-critical students, or those from harsh backgrounds, may cause them to retreat or result in the bursting of a dam wall with a flood of uncontrolled emotion. Either way good intentions from an inexperienced practitioner might make a student's situation worse.[31]

In spite of these difficulties, let's capture the basics of what compassion-focused therapy hopes to achieve for its insights are valuable in our own lives. Essentially, compassion-focused therapy asks people to make compassion, not the expectations of others, the standard by which life is lived. Questions like, 'What sort of situations could present a problem for you in being self-compassionate?' are considered. Participants are also encouraged to place themselves in a self-compassionate mindset and think about how to cope, if not self-soothe, in such situations. As such, compassion-focused therapy makes self-compassion a critical ingredient both in coping and in a life well lived.[30, 31]

Question 7.13

- a. If you are a psychologist or counsellor what have been your experiences of making compassion the focus of therapy?

- b. In what ways have you been positively reinforced that have compromised your capacity for self-compassion? How might you address this problem?

 **Activity 7.6**

If you are a parent or teacher consider ways to balance compassionate schooling with the need for a child to succeed scholastically.

Another recognised approach to developing compassion comes from the Buddhist tradition and is known as *metta* (i.e., loving-kindness) meditation. However, let's not confuse this with mindfulness meditation which is something altogether different; even if it too has been shown to help bringing about compassion.[23, 26, 32, 33, 34] Specifically, the difference between these two forms of meditation is that while mindfulness meditation would have us hold our attention on a fixed point (e.g., our breath) to calm the mind, *metta* meditation can deliberately use painful emotions and traumatic memories as a way to grow in loving-kindness.[35]

In reviewing this valuable approach to compassion let's begin with the Buddhist worldview for it frames the entire practice of *metta* meditation. Put simply:

- that to live is to suffer (i.e., *dukkha*),
- that life is about escape from suffering,
- that we are self-centred by nature, and
- that the reality we perceive is wrong in so much as nothing is permanent.[18]

Given this worldview without loving-kindness the world becomes intolerable.

For Buddhists the way to manifest loving-kindness is through meditation which has destructive emotions such as anger, fear and resentment fall away. In doing so the meditation practitioner comes to experience self-compassion and then compassion for others and ultimately for all creation.

However, the process of *metta* meditation is not a simple one. Especially for the fact that the goal of compassion cannot be got at first, or in isolation, given that it sits amongst the 'four immeasurable attitudes'.[18] To get to compassion practitioners must first learn forgiveness and then loving-kindness. What is interesting for psychologists and scholars of restorative justice (see Chapter 6) is that forgiveness is placed before compassion in the Buddhist tradition and not considered a result of it.

As to the practice of *metta* meditation devotees learn to harness the value of several mantras (see Table 7.1). Through repetitive practice it is believed that the intention of each mantra seeps down into a person, becoming meaningful to them and ultimately being felt as a real experience of love. When this occurs the meditative practice takes a different turn in so much as one can now send out one's *metta* to other people and feel compassion for the world.

Ultimately, the transition from loving-kindness (i.e., *metta*) to compassion (i.e., *karuna*) is described by Makransky in the following way, 'Sensing all beings as dear through the practice of love, and reflecting on the sufferings they undergo, compassion for them naturally arises ... [W]ith immeasurable love, the mind of compassion is extended to all beings everywhere ....'[36]

However this is not the end of the story ... *metta* (i.e., loving-kindness) and *karuna* (i.e., compassion) also link to sympathetic joy (i.e., *mudita*) and equanimity (i.e. *upekkha*). This is important because it is equanimity that sustains compassion. Moreover, Wisdom and compassion now become fused in so

TABLE 7.1
***Metta* meditation mantras**[35]

Forgiveness mantras

'In many ways, I have caused harm and suffering to other beings, I forgive myself. May they be free from their suffering.'

'In many ways, I have caused harm and suffering to myself, I forgive myself. May I be free from my suffering.'

'In many ways, others have caused harm and suffering to me, I forgive them. May we all be free from our suffering. They are suffering, I am suffering, may we all be free from our suffering.'

Loving-kindness (i.e., metta) mantras for self

'May I be free from enmity and danger.'

'May I be free from mental suffering.'

'May I be free from physical suffering.'

'May I take care of myself happily.'

Loving-kindness (i.e., metta) mantras for others

'May you be free from enmity and danger.'

'May you be free from mental suffering.'

'May you be free from physical suffering.'

'May you take care of yourself happily.'

much as a compassionate response to all people becomes the wisest way to live.[18] In this way *metta* meditation is a virtuous practice of the highest order.

Even so, *metta* meditation and other formalised ways of growing compassion take time, effort, training and even money. For our purposes what can we learn today and apply tomorrow? To answer this question is not as difficult as it may seem; especially if we analyse one group of very compassionate people and simply copy their way of being.

Foster carers are compassionate on a daily basis and therefore represent a particularly virtuous group of people worth learning from. Not only do these people open their homes and lives to strangers' children. They do so often in the dead of night without regard for adequate recompense or recognition. To show how extraordinary this compassion can be I (i.e., Tom) recently read a story of a burly Muslim man in Los Angeles who only fosters dying children. I can't even begin to imagine how he does this without being broken in the attempt.

To help us identify what makes foster carers so compassionate let's consider two valuable studies. First, Ciarrochi and colleagues used a large sample of men and women who were interested in becoming foster carers.[37] What they noted was that these people already had high levels of social support, had large amounts of empathy, demonstrated the virtue of hope and were good problem-solvers.

But in observing actual foster carers Sinclair, as reported by Luke and Sebba, also identified a set of core competencies.[38] Not surprisingly, foster carers who demonstrated emotional coldness towards their foster child, intolerance, or apathy were likely to struggle with placements. Interestingly, the authors attributed these negative feelings to the carer's inability to manage their own sense of rejection. By contrast, foster carers who focused on the emotional needs of the child in their care were the ones likely to have successful placements. Beyond this, successful foster carers also demonstrated emotional resilience and, again, hope.

If we generalise these finding what we learn is that compassionate people appear to:

- manage their emotional needs well and so have the space to focus on the needs of others,
- are supported within a broader network of family and friends,
- are good problem solvers, and
- possibly because of these factors, possess a resilient, if not hopeful, disposition.

Therefore, if you want to grow in compassion do likewise. Focus on yourself before trying to focus on the needs of others. In this way you will not only be self-compassionate but never be accused of meddling in someone else's business. As part of this, if you have unresolved childhood hurts, or struggle to contain strong emotion, go and get help. This is only wise. Once these emotional waters have been calmed you will find you have the space to take care of others in the way that *they need* and this is truly compassionate. But to sustain compassion, be sensible. Develop your support network, problem solve your way through life and, as your energies flag, seek rest. Finally, in disagreement with a Buddhist worldview we would argue that the world *is* beautiful, people want to be good and there is much to be thankful for. So, in whatever way you can, have hope!

 Question 7.14

> Many people in the helping professions suffer compassion fatigue. But what exactly is it, what are its effects and how can it be avoided?

 Activity 7.7

> Reflect on what you have read above regarding the attributes of foster carers as emblematic of compassionate people. Amongst these qualities list what may be your strengths and weaknesses. Now determine practical ways to capitalise on your strengths and overcome your weaknesses and so grow in compassion.

Finally, be a blessing to others

Rather than providing a conclusion to this chapter let us simply hold for a moment and focus on compassion. For talking about compassion is not as important as feeling compassion. And feeling compassion is not as important as acting it out. But in the end, sharing compassion with others is the best of all.

> *Let no one ever come to you without coming away better and happier.* (Mother Theresa)

The Freedom of Virtue: Navigating excellence in the art of living amongst a world of instant gratification

Chapter 8

In the pursuit of excellence: Using multiple virtues

> Individuality is only possible if it unfolds from wholeness
>
> — David Bohm

A brief recap

In Chapter 2 through to Chapter 7 we dealt with each of the six foundational virtues in turn and learnt that:

- Courage was the ability to manage fear over time,
- Diligence was often about being conscientious and sometimes about being precise,
- Wisdom often had one manage ambiguity but was underscored by insight,

- Honour was complicated because it was divided two ways. Personal honour engaged notions of self-respect, while group honour described a way to organise people that maximised their collective potential,

- Justice was all about fairness and forgiveness, and

- Kindness touched on generosity, but lept over empathy to be epitomised by compassion.

Although it was necessary to silo each foundational virtue in those earlier chapters so as to provide you with a detailed understanding of each this approach was nevertheless unrealistic when we consider daily life. For on any given day we may need a dose of Courage, a little Wisdom or, perhaps, have to speak a kind word. In truth, all six foundational virtues work together to form the fabric of our lives. For this reason let's now bring together all that we have learnt to create a dynamic, and integrated, system of foundational virtues. In this way you'll come to see the true potential of the foundational virtues in creating excellence.

In developing our argument we will first examine situations of only limited integration amongst the foundational virtues. Even so, we'll suggest that you only need to master two foundational virtues to have a strong chance of being a success in life! We'll also provide a number of examples to prove this point. But what happens if a person aims for an even greater level of integration amongst the foundational virtues? By mastering three or more foundational virtues remarkable things begin to happen. It is now that success turns to excellence. To demonstrate this we'll take a look at Churchill in his middle years and describe the personal growth of Nelson Mandela from an arrogant young man to a statesman of world renown.

Having done this we will go on to develop an integrated model of the foundational virtues. Importantly, this model has been developed with considerable rigour and from it all sorts of implications flow. While we only have time to touch upon the most important of these you'll nevertheless see how the six foundational virtues can be used to change lives. Our hope is that you will be enthused by all the possibilities. Finally, as we say good bye we'll leave you with a couple of practical steps you can take on your journey towards excellence in the art of living. Although simple steps they are important and we recommend them to you.

Chapter 8 In the pursuit of excellence: Using multiple virtues

 Question 8.1

Think about an average day. How do you use each of the six foundational virtues? Do you rely on some foundational virtues more than others?

When virtues come together we find excellence

No person is virtueless — not even one! Indeed the average person has all six foundational virtues working well enough most of the time. The trick, if anything, is to turn average into excellence and thus achieve a virtuosity in life. To put it another way there is an inherent potentiality in our approach. In fact the analogy we like to use is that working to grow the foundational virtues is like going to a gym. While a person may enter a gym for the first time a little unsure of what they are doing, if not also a little flabby, in time hard work breeds confidence as muscles grow and fitness improves. Growing in virtue is no different.

 Activity 8.1

Use the checklist in Table 8.1 to determine which three foundational virtues you are strongest in. This will be something worth reflecting on as you move through Chapter 8. For in knowing this you'll come to realise which life situations you'll thrive in and where also to put in effort for change.

To complete the checklist, rate all 12 items as either 1, 2 or 3. A score of 1 recognises your belief that you struggle to meet the expectation put forward in the item; a score of 2 suggests you meet this expectation; while a score of 3 suggests you exceed this expectation.

Given that each foundational virtue comprises two items add both item scores together to receive a compound virtue score. This compound score can be used to compare and contrast the various foundational virtues and so identify your virtue strengths and weaknesses.

Ultimately we suggest naming the three foundational virtues, represented by the three highest compound scores, as your virtue strengths. The remaining three foundational virtues thus become acknowledged weaknesses. Nevertheless if one or more of your three virtue strengths scored below 3 out of 6 then hold this strength(s) provisionally. If, however, some/all of your virtue weak-

195

nesses scored greater than 3 out of 6 then perhaps think of them as weaknesses only in a relative sense.

Career success: Maximising just two foundational virtues

While it is obvious that the more foundational virtues you cultivate the greater is your chance of life success, it is perhaps surprising to realise the level of renown people can achieve by maximising only two of six foundational virtues. By being only one step ahead of most other people the virtuous find promotion, position and reward for their labour. Moreover, it does not seem to matter which two foundational virtues are cultivated so long as they match one's professional context. For example, Einstein had both Wisdom and Courage; the Wisdom to see into the underlying structure of the universe and the Courage to publish his highly controversial findings. But had he cultivated Kindness instead of Courage he'd have probably made a far better funeral director. To this end, Table 8.2 provides 10 examples of people who achieved in life by maximising just two foundational virtues. The trick being that they maximised the right ones for what they wanted to achieve.

TABLE 8.1
Your virtue checklist

Foundational virtue	Item	Item score (out of 3)	Compound virtue score (out of 6)
Courage	I can handle fear.		
	I am not prone to impulsive risk-taking.		
Diligence	I complete the tasks I set for myself.		
	I like accountability.		
Wisdom	I am good at problem solving.		
	I can hold my emotions in check.		
Honour	I respect myself.		
	I work well within a team.		
Justice	I am a fair person.		
	I have acted for Justice in the past.		
Kindness	I am a 'people person'.		
	I can handle the weight of being compassionate.		

TABLE 8.2

People who exemplify two foundational virtues, matched well to their abilities and professional choices, and who have found renown

Example	Virtues exemplified
Anna Meares An Olympic cyclist who in January 2008 fractured her neck seven months before the Olympics but fought back against the odds to claim the silver medal in Beijing. She won gold at London in 2012.	Courage and Diligence
Lord Nelson The naval commander who defeated Napoleon's fleet at Trafalgar by the use of daring and unorthodox tactics. Although he lost his life in that battle, England gained a naval supremacy which would not be challenged for 100 years.	Courage and Wisdom
Queen Boudica (1st century AD) The Queen of the Iceni who faced-off against the Roman legions after the rape of her daughters and the annexation of her kingdom.	Courage and Honour
Father Damien A Roman Catholic priest who chose to minister to the lepers on Molokai Island in the 19th century knowing that he too would probably become infected. He did contract leprosy and suffered with his parishioners, eventually dying of the disease.	Courage and Kindness
Mohandas Ghandi An activist and inspirational leader who fought for human rights in South Africa and then for Indian independence advocating nonviolent civil disobedience to achieve political ends.	Diligence and Justice
Mother Teresa A nun and missionary who, for over half a century, worked for the poor and dying, first in India and then internationally.	Diligence and Kindness
Muhammad Ali Lauded as a boxer of unparalleled brilliance. Ali also fought against racism and for human rights.	Courage and Justice
General George Marshall A soldier who was instrumental in World War II, but is rightly remembered for the Marshall Plan which rebuilt a devastated West Germany thus preventing both an expansion of Soviet influence and a third world war.	Wisdom and Honour

The Freedom of Virtue: Navigating excellence in the art of living amongst a world of instant gratification

Hammurabi (18th century BC) A king of Babylon who was responsible for its extensive legal code. The code was published, judges appointed and notions of jurisprudence established.	Wisdom and Justice
Betty Williams and Mairead Corrigan Two women who brought together Protestants and Roman Catholics in Northern Ireland to protest the sectarian violence of the 'Troubles' and for which they won the Nobel Peace Prize.	Justice and Kindness

Question 8.2

a. What other examples can you think of whereby people have achieved in life by harnessing two foundational virtues?

b. In thinking about your own life what two virtues should you concentrate on to achieve career success? Are they amongst your virtue strengths? If not, what should you do about it?

Achieving excellence in the art of living: Maximising three or more foundational virtues

But what if more than two foundational virtues are cultivated? These people often become 'the greats', are inducted into 'halls of fame', or are referred to only by their surname. They are, if anything, the virtuous ones amongst us.

While examples of such people are rarer two stand out: Winston Churchill in his middle years; and Nelson Mandela later in his life. Specifically, Churchill epitomised the foundational virtues of Courage, Diligence and Wisdom while Mandela coupled Wisdom and personal honour with Justice and Kindness. To study their example is to see clearly how the foundational virtues work together to produce excellence.

But examples such as these also reveal the prickliness of virtue which cannot be ignored. For the virtuous are not always the most moral, easiest to get along with or necessarily have the best mental health. They can even be infuriating as Clementine Churchill well knew. Yet, the respect accorded these people transcends their personal eccentricities and this is often the hallmark of a virtuous person.

Winston Churchill's life reads like an adventure story. Born into one of the great aristocratic families of England, just when the Empire was achieving its furthest reach, the young Winston cut his teeth as a dashing cavalry officer and then as a war correspondent. From the North-West Frontier of Pakistan to the Sudan, and eventually to South Africa, Churchill appeared to look for danger — and often found it. Amongst these exploits he even escaped from a prisoner of war camp during the Second Boer War and with his tales of 'derring-do' came to national prominence. Given family connections, and media attention, politics beckoned and, as they say, 'the rest was history'.

Yet to discuss Churchill as virtuous is extremely difficult for we have to try to pull apart the man from the myth and, in some way, give account for a life of 90 years. However, to the extent that his own words have been recorded, and first-hand accounts documented, we might just have a hope of capturing something of the essence of Churchill in his middle years which spanned the rise of Nazi Germany through to the commencement of the Cold War.

Although Churchill exemplified Courage and Diligence let's begin with Wisdom, for it showed itself first. While many in England were applauding Hitler's economic achievements during the 1930's Churchill took the counter-position. Having a genius for foresight he saw through the charade and the naivety of his own countrymen.[1] In this way Churchill's wisdom was of a particular sort and akin to that of a prophet.

As war broke over the continent, and as the Chamberlain government faltered, Churchill seized his opportunity to take the Prime Ministership. No sooner had he done this than his zeal transformed into an extreme form of Diligence which was then imposed upon generals and public servants alike,

> The effects of Churchill's zeal was ... felt immediately in Whitehall ... respectable civil servants were actually to be seen running along the corridors. No delays were condoned; telephone switchboards quadrupled their efficiency; the Chiefs of Staff and the Joint Planning Staff [including Churchill] were in almost constant session; regular office hours ceased to exist and weekends disappeared with them. (*from Best (2005) quoted in Churchill: Leader and Statesman*)[2]

As for Churchill's physical courage this was already legendary from his days as a young soldier and war correspondent. But it took on a new quality during the Blitz for not only did he choose to stay in London, but on some evenings Churchill could even be found on city rooftops as Nazi bombers swarmed overhead. Nor was he afraid to go and visit bombed-out streets the next day and chat with locals. Even so Churchill's visceral courage was exemplified best by, '[His] own opposition to all forms of defeatism ... [which] established the nature and pattern of his war leadership' (from Keegan (1989) quoted in *Churchill: Leader and Statesman*).[2] So, while European nations fell one-by-one,

Churchill and the British people remained defiant. He, and they, held their courage often only by sheer bloody mindedness.

That Churchill is honoured so many decades later is a testament to his greatness. From our perspective we would argue that this is a direct consequence of (a) him excelling in at least three foundational virtues; (b) understanding how to use his virtues in concert; and (c) being able to focus their power towards solving the problems he faced. Given this there is more to the foundational virtues than simple cultivation, you must add to this application.

But despite his legacy, Churchill was not a perfect man and this raises two interesting points about being virtuous. First, virtues can, and do, sit alongside small vices. Take, for example, the virtue of humility. No one would have ever accused Churchill of being humble. Especially given remarks like, 'We are all worms, but I do believe I am a glow worm'. Or, what about the virtues of thriftiness and moderation? Not only did Churchill spend more than he could afford, but chain smoked and drank his way through the war. Yet in the scheme of things these were small vices by comparison and connected only to situational, not foundational, virtues.

Second, Churchill suffered with a debilitating form of depression. In this regard virtue can sit alongside poor mental health. As an extension of this idea we may very well wonder if living with mental health problems can, for some people, even increase their capacity for virtue through suffering? For instance, in my own (i.e., Tom) practice those clients who struggle most with their mental health are often the most courageous, the most just and/or the most kind. In this way the foundational virtues represent an important part of a person's identity which often appears independent of mental health problems. What opportunities this provides for those in the helping professions!

Taken together, what we learn about Churchill, and virtuous people in general, is that they are complicated. The mistake we all fall into when looking at professional success, excellence in life, and even good health, is to align them with a slender set of qualities which are labelled 'good'. The world is just more complicated than that.

 Question 8.3

    a. Psychologically, how does an understanding of virtue change our perspective on identity?

    b. If virtuous people have small vices, what vices then separate the virtuous from the unvirtuous and even from those people we might label as bad?

c. If you are a psychologist or counsellor what options do virtues open for you when working with a client?

 Activity 8.2

Compare and contrast two people whom you know. The first should be a person of strong intellect and who has achieved in life. If possible the second person should be someone you know who struggles with a mental health problem. Who is the more virtuous? In what ways do these two people show (or not show) depth of character?

Moving to our second example of what can be achieved when a person cultivates multiple foundational virtues let's review the life of Nelson Mandela, for his 'long walk to freedom' represents a well-documented account of trial and transformation. While enthusiasts might ascribe all the foundational virtues to Mandela, and there is evidence for each, let's just focus on Wisdom, personal honour, Justice and Kindness. For these were the foundational virtues he used to transition South Africa to a multi-ethnic state.

Although born into a privileged family within black society the young Nelson was not born for greatness.[3, 4] In fact it is rather remarkable that he didn't 'go off the rails' as a teen for, by his own admission, he was headstrong, lacked a studious nature and was arrogant.[3, 5]

These decidedly unvirtuous character traits were, however, no barrier to a budding politician. Through his friendship with Walter Sisulu, Mandela was introduced to the African National Congress (ANC) and quickly rose through its ranks as both a political organiser and an orator of some note. However his nature remained so petulant that by the early 1960s he had embraced radical politics leading to the formation of the ANC's terrorist wing known as 'MK' (i.e., 'spear of the nation'). So now Mandela, a man of mature years, dangerously combined zeal, a born to rule mentality and violence.[6]

However, fate stepped in. While the South African government would ultimately allege that MK committed over 200 acts of sabotage Mandela was arrested before a guerrilla war could be unleashed which saved his public image.[7] Moreover, as trials go Mandela got lucky in that Justice de Wet was an honourable man. Rather than presiding over a sham trial Justice de Wet rendered the following, unusual, sentence for a terrorist leader,

> The crime of which the accused have been convicted ... is in essence one of high treason ... [Yet the] State has decided not to charge the crime in this form.

> Bearing this in mind, and giving the matter very serious consideration I have decided not to impose the supreme penalty, which in a case like this would usually be the penalty for such a crime. But consistent with my duty, that is the only leniency which I can show. The sentence in the case of all the accused will be one of life imprisonment. (*Justice de Wet quoted in Linder, 2010*)[8]

So Mandela's life was spared to be replaced by the drudgery of Robben Is.. Yet Robben Is. was the making of Mandela. In so many ways he matured, not just in years, but as a person. While early days on the island were marked by confrontation this ultimately gave way to a more nuanced, or wise, approach to prison life summed up by his acknowledgement, '[that the] best way to effect change on Robben Island was to influence officials privately rather than publically'.[9] While he also learnt to be '... decent to the warders in my section; [as] hostility was usually self-defeating'.[10] In other words Mandela was learning the power of virtue.

Ultimately Mandela would languish in jail for 27 years and, in this time, grow well into middle age. On the outside these decades became increasingly hard ones for the South African people as international boycotts affected everything from sport to shopping. The anti-apartheid struggle had also become increasingly militant — as was the government's response to it. As such, by the late 1980's those in power were starting to confront the idea of a failed state. It was these tensions, and not goodwill, that made the government of the day free Mandela and publically negotiate with the ANC.

However power sharing between ethnic groups, let alone a transition to black-majority rule, was no easy thing to conceive. Apartheid had been legislated since 1950 and so by 1990, the year of Mandela's release, had been part of South African society for 40 years. It was also the source of white privilege, and black anger. Would the white minority (i.e., less than 10% of the population) just simply handover both privilege and power? The rise of political movements such as the Afrikaner Resistance Movement suggested not. Even if the white minority did choose to handover the keys of government there were reasonable fears that they might do so by simply emigrating. This, in turn, would have left South Africa broken, if not beyond repair. Finally, a transition to black-majority rule was also a complex question for black South Africans who comprised different ethnic groups (e.g., Zulu & Xhosa), each with its own claim on power. In many respects what faced Mandela and the other negotiators in the early 1990's was, at best, a Gordian knot. Bluntly stated, any betting person would have placed odds on Mandela failing and the nation ripping itself apart in civil strife.

Yet this did not happen. Even in spite of the Boipatong and Bisho Massacres, and the assassination of Chris Hani, Mandela kept his calm and kept focused.[11] He understood that authority came from a sense of personal honour and this was best shown by a clear resolve. A style of virtuous behaviour first refined on Robben Is. when he refused to forgo his dignity.

Coupled with the Wisdom he'd learnt over 27 years living cheek to jowl with other activists Mandela began to see the way forward. But his genius lay not in a technocratic solution to South Africa's woes, but in coupling Wisdom to the dual virtues of Justice and Kindness. In this way he spoke to his nation's heart, not its head. Specifically, Justice for black South Africans could not occur without an attitude of gracious magnanimity towards the white minority. By refuting any notion of victor's justice Mandela argued for both democratic power-sharing and a commission in which his nation could grieve and heal. While economic inequality would persist, and AIDS burn a hole in South African society, black and white citizens now felt able to approach each other in both hurt and in hope.

So, to conclude, we yet again see the remarkable accomplishments of a man who cultivated multiple virtues. But beyond this we also learn two truths about virtue. First, nobody is born to virtue and even those who we'd hold out little hope for may, in time, become the most virtuous of all. Second, and more importantly, virtue is often born of suffering. It took 27 years in jail for Mandela to learn the lessons he would need to guide South Africa. So don't shy away from trouble, embrace it, learn from it, and be patient with it. Virtue often defies what is comfortable in life and sometimes sits beyond common notions of good and evil.

Question 8.4

a. How have you developed in virtue over your life? What has brought this growth about?

b. In thinking about Nelson Mandela, do some foundational virtues have to wait for middle age to develop?

c. Given that Mandela was, in the first part of his life, a man of arrogance and of violence, what does this say about rehabilitating prisoners today? What might an understanding of the foundational virtues give to prison staff as they seek to rehabilitate offenders?

However, before we close off this section there is one last important question to ask. So far we have made the assertion that excelling in multiple virtues leads to both professional success and an excellence in the art of living. We have even demonstrated this point through various examples and case studies. But while these examples have been useful they have also related to specific situations. In this way they appear bound to time, place and circumstance. Therefore we also need to ask about the general characteristics of people who may be considered virtuous. In this way we free ourselves of restrictions to see a deeper truth. In practical terms this is important for three reasons. First, it guides our progress in the virtues if we know what, in general terms, the end-goal looks like. Second, if we are helping another person to grow in virtue we can measure their progress. Third, to know the general characteristics of virtuous people allows us to sniff out imposters. This is, if nothing else, a wise thing to do.

Virtuous people seem to display four qualities irrespective of circumstance. In the first instance they are socially minded. Virtuous people are both interesting and interested in the lives of others. They may even be committed to a cause or some form of the common good. Be it Socrates and Plato wrestling with the nature of good government, or Franklin D. Roosevelt pushing his New Deal, those who demonstrate virtue think beyond themselves. Second, virtuous people have the ability to hold opposites in tension and thus embrace strain-and-stress as a creative opportunity. As such, they have the habit of infuriating lesser people who'd define arguments in terms of simple 'right and wrong'; more so for the fact that they will resist peer pressure in doing so. Nevertheless they don't opt-out of problems either, but look for a 'third way' that speaks well into the lives of all. Third, virtuous people show a unique approach to the world characterised by honesty. Gone will be socially appropriate, or simplistically moral, ways of behaving. In their place one sees joy when it is fundamentally correct to be joyful or, for that matter, anger when it is right to be angry. Fourth, and finally, virtuous people have hope. In Mandela's own words we read,

> I never seriously considered the possibility that I would not emerge from prison one day. I never thought that a life sentence truly meant life and that I would die behind bars. Perhaps I was denying this prospect because it was too unpleasant to contemplate. But I always knew that someday I would once again feel the grass under my feet and walk in the sunshine as a free man.
>
> I am fundamentally an optimist. Whether that comes from nature of nurture, I cannot say. Part of being optimistic is keeping one's head pointed towards the sun, one's feet moving forward. There were many dark moments when my faith in humanity was sorely tested, but I would not and could not give myself up to despair. That way lay defeat and death.[12]

Nor is this the hope of the wishful thinker. The hope of a virtuous person is rougher, tougher, than that. It is a defiant hope which must be practiced daily in full knowledge that the alternative is no alternative at all.

Question 8.5

a. Can you think of examples of famous, and likely virtuous, people who exemplified each of the four points above?

b. What are the fundamental characteristics of vice-addled people?

The foundational virtues as an integrated system

Given the power of the foundational virtues to change lives it stands to reason that we should want to harness as many as possible. Yet strengthening virtue is not easy. Only if you are serious about sticking to the plan will change happen. And what is that change? Virtue is not about superficial happiness but a life well lived, a life guided by deep purpose and a life in which you will find respect. If that is what you want then read on.

Question 8.6

What is your purpose in life? What do you want to be remembered for?

Activity 8.3

If you were having trouble with the question above then try this simple, but confronting, activity. If you were to die tomorrow what do you want written on your gravestone? Now repeat the exercise having lived a long life. Consider both gravestones, what is common about the inscriptions? This must be important. What also is unique about the epitaph written for your elderly self? Does it give you more insight into what you hold dear?

As stated, harnessing the foundational virtues is no small task. Courage is quite different from Kindness and Wisdom seems to be needed to make all the other foundational virtues function well. Therefore we need some sort of picture, or model, of how the six foundational virtues fit together if we are going to build lots of 'virtue muscle'.

While virtue models are not new (e.g., Aristotle, Confucius and recently Seligman all give their interpretations) we have tried to construct ours with a degree of pragmatism so that virtue is seen to be achievable. But what shape, or picture, should represent this new model? Naturally, six foundational virtues could be represented as the six sides of a cube. But this model fails for the arrangement of virtues around the sides of a cube implies properties that we just don't observe. For example, a cube has faces which join along edges and faces which are positioned in opposition. There is, in the end, no adequate way to pair and oppose the six foundational virtues to have them fit around a cube. Better is to simply recognise that each foundational virtue can act alone, or in concert with other foundational virtues all under the guidance of Wisdom. From this we conjecture that the best model of the foundational virtues is interlaced, star-shaped and has Wisdom at the centre (see Figure 8.1).

Question 8.7

Do you agree with this arrangement of the six foundational virtues as shown in Figure 8.1? If not, how would you arrange them differently?

Activity 8.4

Wisdom is necessary for the correct expression of all other foundational virtues. To demonstrate this point complete the following sentences:

(a) Courage without Wisdom can become = H_ _ _ _ _s.

(b) Diligence without Wisdom may lead to = B_ _ _-o_ _ or p_ _ _ _ _ _ _ _ _ _ _.

(c) Personal honour without Wisdom becomes = Arro_ _ _ _e.

(d) Group honour without Wisdom will end in = Cat_ _ _ _ _ _ _y.

(e) Justice without Wisdom can end in = Cr_ _ _ _y.

(f) Kindness without Wisdom leads to = Gul_ _ _ _ _ _ _y.

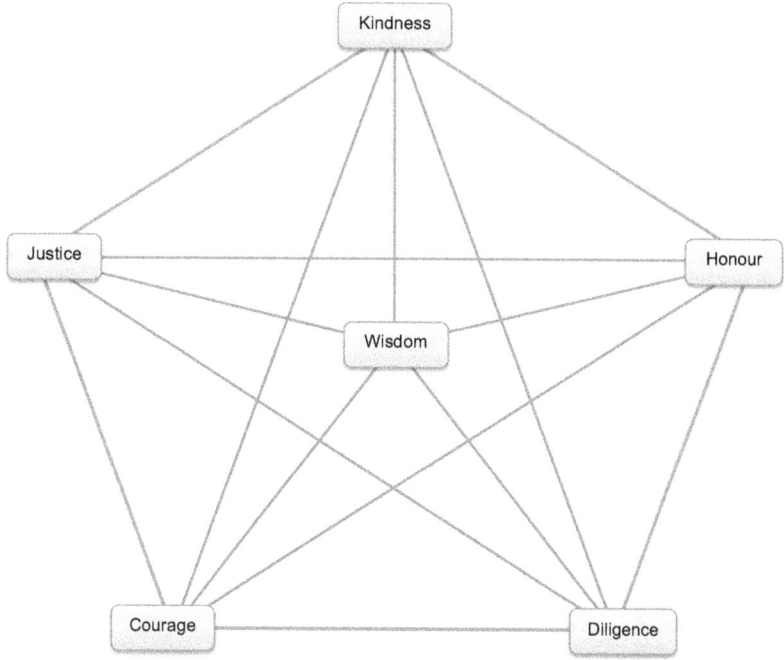

FIGURE 8.1

A visual representation of our integrative model of the foundational virtues. Wisdom sits at the centre of the five-point star because of its general utility even although all foundational virtues are linked. This arrangement allows for multiple virtues to be used together to solve complex life problems. Hence the model works as a coherent whole or can create virtue sub-systems as required.

This star-shaped model has a number of advantages. For example, although the neurology of virtue is still being established the integrated nature of the model mimics the integration seen in large virtue-capable brain circuits such as those found in the prefrontal cortex, the Mirror Neuron System and the Default Mode Network. As such we can bring together a real-world understanding of virtue, place it within an evolutionary framework and suggest a corresponding neurology. In addition, by placing Wisdom at the centre of the model we acknowledge its role as 'the first amongst equals' and because of this remain consistent with older virtue traditions. That the model is interlaced also allows for virtue sub-systems to be created thus acknowledging individual differences in virtue strengths and weaknesses — let alone the different virtues needed to succeed in different jobs etc. The model also suggests how other virtues come into existence from only six foundational virtues. For either these situational virtues are solitary aspects of one foundational virtue, or develop out of multiple foundational virtues within a particular social context. For instance, the situational virtue of *rei* (i.e., courtesy) is an element of group honour for it structures relationships; while the situational virtue of truthfulness is nothing more than personal honour + Justice.[13] Finally, the model has therapeutic advantages for it shows clearly how to use virtue to help others. In particular, the model allows for an individual foundational virtue to be strengthened directly, for a foundational virtue to be strengthened through reinforcement of the remaining five foundational virtues, or even that a virtue weakness can be overcome by targeting a virtue strength. As such, the model has something for everyone. For academics there is a wealth of research possible. For clinicians 'virtues work' now becomes a real possibility. For teachers here is an effective way to integrate virtue into a curriculum. While, for parents, these virtues are the qualities to instil in your children to see them grow into capable adults who will make a difference in the world.

Question 8.8

    a. If you are a psychologist or counsellor how could you use the six foundational virtues, if not the model, to effect real change in a person's life?

    b. Within the model are clusters of foundational virtues called 'sub-systems'. In fact, one of the things that makes us all different is that we excel in some foundational virtues over others. Therefore we each have a preference for a different sub-system. What is your sub-system?

Activity 8.5

Looking at Figure 8.1 how many sub-systems can you find and in what circumstances might these smaller clusters of virtues be useful?

Future dreaming

Virtue is powerful stuff! So powerful in fact that as we draw this chapter, and book, to a close we feel as if we have only told half the story. Nevertheless to give you a taste of how to go deeper with virtue consider the delicious ideas below.

We posit that the six foundational virtues represent the primary ways in which people look at, organise, and engage the world. Furthermore, given that we understand our world through story this must mean that the foundational virtues have something very important to teach us about narratives and how they are constructed — whether it is in the context of literature or Narrative Therapy. Be it 10th century Norse sagas, Georgian novels including *Pride and Prejudice*, or contemporary fiction from the post-colonial world, embedded within each are strong themes of Courage, Diligence, Wisdom, Honour, Justice and Kindness. As for Narrative Therapy don't clinicians listen for the 'absent but implicit' within a client's story and so highlight some unrecognised strength — or virtue?

Not only do we argue that the six foundational virtues shape narratives to form identity but also to communicate 'truth'. Take, for example, Donald Trump's surprise win in the 2016 US Presidential Election. How did he do it? From our perspective the 'truth' he spoke was to Courage, Honour and Justice while Hillary Clinton was virtue-vague. By being a Washington outsider, yet daring to seek the highest office in the land, Trump showed a swaggering degree of Courage to the American people. Moreover, he played on Justice time-and-again when he spoke to the disaffected while middle class outside major cities. As for Honour this was Trump's trump card. Like him or loath him, it doesn't really matter, for he had won his glory in redefining the New York skyline. In addition, he demonstrated time-and-again that he was the boss, or 'headman', on his TV show *The Apprentice*. While he also played perfectly to the nation's sense of Honour as summed up in his campaign slogan, 'Make America great again'. As you can see, the implications of crafting a message by using virtue are enormous and have relevance not just for politicians but also for lawyers arguing a case, for teachers communicating an idea and even for the advertising industry. If you want people to take note, speak the language of virtue.

Finally, what do the six foundational virtues have to teach us about who we are? The answer is a great deal. It's not just that we create narratives according to the foundational virtues but that the foundational virtues sit in that gap between our mindless instincts, such as attachment and agency, and who our memories say we are. In so many ways the six foundational virtues shape our identity and give purpose to our lives. They are, in another way, what separates humans from artificial intelligence. In saying this we now have a way to understand identity much more clearly. We also have a way to shift identity as needed. Be it helping a child to develop a strong sense of identity; assisting a traumatised client to re-establish identity; or even in working with prisoners to develop a new sense of identity; the six foundational virtues represent a solid way forward. Even with the toughest of the tough, such as convicted terrorists, the six foundational virtues can initiate healthy change. Where once jihadi recruiters worked to subvert new recruits' sense of Wisdom by appeals to authority, over-inflated Justice by magnifying the grievances of the *Ummah* (i.e., Muslim community) against the West, and by dangerously replacing Honour with glory, we now have a way to shape otherwise *ad hoc* deradicalisation programmes. That is, stabilise a convicted terrorist's identity for it is often fragile, unstable or lopsided.[14] Moreover, do this by renormalising their sense of Wisdom, Justice and Honour.

Taken together, we humans are a remarkable bunch. We are often lost, and sometimes we break, but thanks to the six foundational virtues we also have a compass which orientates us to a better tomorrow.

Question 8.9

> a. Psychologists love to talk about self-actualised people. Is this consistent with excelling in all six foundational virtues?
>
> b. What would such a person be like?

Activity 8.6

> a. To demonstrate the pervasive nature of the six foundational virtues simply sit down and watch an iconic movie. How do the six foundational virtues feature in this story, or narrative?
>
> b. If you are a community worker consider one social problem. Construct a virtues-rich solution. If you can, test the effectiveness of your solution.

Five stepping-stones to virtue

Before we say goodbye we have one last job to do. It's all well and good to demonstrate that growing in multiple virtues is a ticket to a life well lived, if not also excellence in the art of living, but what are the first steps we need to take on this journey? While Chapters 2 to 7 showed you how to grow in each foundational virtue what can we do to grow in multiple virtues at once? Picking up on common themes across these chapters we come to the realisation that there are five stepping-stones to virtue. They are:

Know what you value

This sounds simple for we all value something. Whether it is an old car we've worked on and restored, our position in the workplace or the lovely garden we keep we all attribute value to the things around us. Typically, we also attribute greater value to family and friends. But all of these, even family, are transitory and external to our very nature. Therefore when we ask, 'What do you value?', we are asking a very personal question and not an obvious one at that.

To get closer to the mark we could ask, 'What is it about … that makes you value it/them so much?'. In answering this question people tend to shift their attention from the object, or outcome, to some deeper connection with it. By exploring these connections we bet you'll be able to recognise a few key words that describe very deep aspects of yourself from which virtue will flow. Moreover, in knowing those deep things of value you stand on rock when all about is shifting sand.

From a virtues perspective knowing what you truly value gives you a reason to be courageous. It helps you identify meaningful goals to achieve and so Diligence simply emerges. Finding what you value is also a deep form of self-Wisdom. As for Honour, it is difficult to be honourable if you lack a strong value system. While Justice and Kindness are entirely dependent upon moving past valuing objects, even people as objects, to value what lies beneath.

Avoid black and white thinking

To talk about thinking focuses our attention on Wisdom and that's ok, for Wisdom helps optimise the remaining five foundational virtues. As to the specifics, black and white thinking is a psychological term for a cheap type of thinking that we all give way to from time to time but nevertheless causes problems, for very few things in life are either totally right or totally wrong.

So our encouragement is to learn to accept and use nuance in dealing with people. To leave fear behind and step into that place of unknowing. But we are not asking you to accept that the world operates in various shades of grey. As a senior colleague once said to me (i.e., Tom), 'What colour sits between black and white?'. Answer: 'All the colours of the rainbow!'. By stepping-out of simplicity and braving nuance we embrace all the colours of the world with all their wonderful possibilities.

Live beyond yourself

'I am because you are' is a famous headline from philosophy. And it is true. In the end it's not about me, or about you, but about us. Virtue writ large recognises this point. Moral courage acts for another's best, Honour underpins culture, while Justice and Kindness are explicitly held between people. To grow in virtue is to step-out and join with others in this great messy thing called humanity.

What's lovely about this point is that there are so many ways to do this. Be it team learning, team sports, volunteer work, or whatever else you can think of. The idea is simply to get involved in community life. But how you get involved is important. Don't come in as the expert, come alongside people instead.

Be not afraid

Fear is the great enemy of virtue for it neuters Courage, prevents one from setting out to diligently pursue worthy goals and holds back Wisdom. Fear also marks the dishonourable, the unjust and the stingy. It is, in every way, unvirtuous. In fact it is a sad truism of life that people often prefer to live with fear as their dark companion rather than risk happiness. Why? We do not know. It is its own special form of insanity.

Yet we also acknowledge that to break from fear is one of the hardest things anyone can do and, to this end, many ways have been devised. Although aphorisms are useful to remind us that '… the only thing we have to fear is fear itself' that is all they tend to do.[15] While mastery exercises (see Chapter 2) do help us to manage fear can they rid us of it? Not really. To this end the graded desensitisation protocols beloved of psychologists offer more hope, for now action is taken to engage that which is feared and to reduce its effects. But even these protocols do not fully grasp what we all truly fear. To this end we must consider existential fear which is the realisation of our smallness; our fragility; the inconsequential nature of all that we do; and our impending deaths. Only when we grasp the brokenness of our condition do we learn not to fear. But, be warned. To come to this realisation often involves searing loss. While the fearless one who emerges on the other side is the most dangerous person of all.

Act with integrity

This stepping-stone towards virtue is given last for it relies on all that we have just discussed and so is often the hardest to do. To act with integrity is to be honourable. When people around you are behaving badly it can also be a supreme act of Courage. In a different way acting with integrity can be troubling because it requires the Wisdom to do what is deeply right, not just what is expected or proper. Given this, acting with integrity can, at times, be unethical, or even illegal, but never unjust.

So how do we begin to act with integrity? At the simplest level when a deadline is set, meet it. No excuses. When you strike a bargain, fulfil it. Plain and simple. But that's the easy stuff. How do you act with integrity when your job is on the line? Or when you're suffering in a bad marriage year after year? Or what about when a little nudge to the rules will give you a big win? In each case, go back to the first three stepping-stones. Know what you value deeply and hold to it. Next, hold back from obvious black and white decisions until you understand the nuances that may be swirling about. In this way when you do choose to act with integrity your actions will be well considered. Third, don't just vaguely consider what other people will think of any action you may, or may not, take. Ask, 'What will the most vulnerable people think?'. In doing so you'll be able to measure the real consequences of your actions. Armed now with these three pieces of knowledge go and do what is right.

So, that's your start. Growing in virtue takes time, especially if you want to develop more than one. Take the time you need, be patient, but also be attentive. Exercise that virtue muscle regularly and you'll see results.

Final thoughts

Virtue lies not in the extraordinary, but in the ordinariness of life done beautifully. Vincent Van Gogh once remarked that a normal life '... is a paved road: It's comfortable to walk, but no flowers grow on it'. In closing, Cos and I would wish you the satisfaction found along the byways of life where Van Gogh's little flowers can be found. We put it to you that six of the brightest are Courage, Diligence, Wisdom, Honour, Justice and Kindness and these, in turn, grow amongst hope, respect, dignity and many others. Life is good — live it.

The Freedom of Virtue: Navigating excellence in the art of living amongst a world of instant gratification

Endnotes

Chapter 1

1. Hagstrom, R.G. (2013). *The Warren Buffett Way*. New Jersey: John Wiley & Sons. Quote taken from p. 4. In at least one other edition this quote appears on p. 22.
2. Arthur, J. (2014). Traditional approaches to character education in Britain and America. In L. Nucci, D. Narvaez, & T. Krettenauer (Eds.), *Handbook of Modal and Character Development* (pp. 43–60). New York: Routledge.
3. Gier, N.F. (2009). *Dharma* morality as virtue ethics. In P. Bilimoria and J. Prabuhu (Eds.), *Indian Ethics*. New York: Springer. Retrieved from the University of Idaho website
   http://www.webpages.uidaho.edu/ngier/hinduVE.htm
4. Lao-Tzu. (1963). *Tao Te Ching* (D.C. Lau Trans.). London: Penguin Books. (original work published approx. 5th century BC). Quote taken from Book 1, Chapter XXI.
5. Ibid. Quote taken from Book 2, Chapter XXXVIII.
6. Plato. (1971). *The Republic* (A.D. Lindsay, Trans.). London: Heron Books. (Original work published 4th century BC). See Book 4, 420.
7. Aristotle. (1934). *Nicomachean Ethics* (H. Rackham, Trans.). Retrieved from the Tufts University website
   http://www.perseus.tufts.edu/hopper/text?doc=Perseus%3atext%3a1999.01.0054. See Book 2, Chapter 6, Section 15.
8. Hill, T.E. (2012). In *Kantian Virtue and 'Virtue Ethics'*. Oxford: Oxford University Press.
9. Pegis, A.C. (Ed.). (1948). *Introduction to Saint Thomas Aquinas*. New York: Random House. See *Summa Theologica*, Question 55, Article 4.
10. Nietzsche, F. (1989). *Beyond Good & Evil* (W. Kaufman, Trans.). New York: Vintage Books. (Original work published 1886). See aphorism 219.
11. Willige, A. (2017, February, 23). *Which are the world's strongest democracies?*. Retrieved from https://www.weforum.org/agenda/2017/02/which-are-the-worlds-strongest-democracies/

12 Gray, A. (2017, March, 9). *The world's 10 biggest economies in 2017.* Retrieved from https://www.weforum.org/agenda/2017/03/worlds-biggest-economies-in-2017/

13 List of countries and dependencies by population. (n.d.). In Wikipedia. Retrieved from https://en.wikipedia.org/wiki/List_of_countries_and_dependencies_by_population

14 Conway, T. (2015, February 4). Cross-Cultural Dialogue on the Virtues: The Contribution of Fethullah Gulen. Retrieved from http://rumiforum.org/cross-cultural-dialogue-on-the-virtues-the-contribution-of-fethullah-gulen/

15 Seligman, M.E.P. (2002). *Authentic Happiness: Using the New Positive Psychology to Realize Your Potential for Lasting Fulfilment.* Sydney: Random House Australia.

16 Lloyd, G.E.R. (2005). *The Delusions of Invulnerability: Wisdom and Morality in Ancient Greece, China and Today.* London: Duckworth.

17 Pérez-Álvarez, M. (2016). The Science of Happiness: As Felicitous as It Is Fallacious. *Journal of Theoretical and Philosophical Psychology, 36*(1), 1–19. doi:10.1037/teo0000030. Quote taken from p. 1.

18 Martin, M.W. (2007). Happiness and Virtue in Positive Psychology. *Journal for the Theory of Social Behaviour, 37*(1), 89–103. doi:10.1111/j.1468-5914.2007.00322.x. Quote taken from p. 101.

19 Peterson, C., & Seligman, M.E.P. (2004). *Character strengths and virtues: A handbook and classification.* New York: Oxford University Press. Quote taken from p. 30.

20 Seligman, M.E.P. (2002). *Authentic Happiness: Using the New Positive Psychology to Realize Your Potential for Lasting Fulfilment.* Sydney: Random House Australia. Quote taken from p. 133.

21 Kristjánsson, K. (2010). Positive Psychology, Happiness, and Virtue: The Troublesome Conceptual Issues. *Review of General Psychology 14*(4), 296–310. doi:10.1037/a0020781

22 Held, B.S. (2005). The 'Virtues' of Positive Psychology. *Journal of Theoretical and Philosophical Psychology, 25*(1), 1–34.

23 Maat. (n.d.). In Wikipedia. Retrieved from https://en.wikipedia.org/wiki/Maat. Although from Wikipedia this provides an accessible introduction for interested readers.

24 Warner, R. (1983). *Encyclopedia of World Mythology.* London: Peerage Books.

25 Prince, J. D. (1904). The Code of Hammurabi. *The American Journal of Theology, 8*(3), 601–609.

26 Gunn, B.G. (1909). *The instruction of Ptah-hotep and the instruction of Ke'gemni: The oldest books in the world*. London: John Murray. Retrieved from http://www.gutenberg.org/files/30508/30508-h/30508-h.htm. Quote taken from statement 21.

27 Diogenes. (2012). *Anecdotes of the Cynics* (Trans. Dobbin, R.). London: Penguin. (original work published 4th century BC). Quote taken from p. 31.

28 Plato. (1971). *The Republic* (A.D. Lindsay, Trans.). London: Heron Books. (Original work published 4th century BC).

29 Prudence. (n.d.). In *New Advent*. Retrieved from http://www.newadvent.org/cathen/12517b.htm. A simple introduction for the interested reader.

30 Aristotle. (1934). *Nicomachean Ethics* (H. Rackham, Trans.). Retrieved from http://www.perseus.tufts.edu/hopper/text?doc=Perseus%3atext%3a1999.01.0054

31 Aristotle. (1926). *Rhetoric*. (J.H. Freese, Trans.). Retrieved from the Tufts University website http://www.perseus.tufts.edu/hopper/text?doc=Perseus%3atext%3a1999.01.0060. See Book I, Chapter 9.

32 Aristotle. (1934). *Nicomachean Ethics* (H. Rackham, Trans.). Retrieved from the Tufts University website http://www.perseus.tufts.edu/hopper/text?doc=Perseus%3atext%3a1999.01.0054. Quote taken from Book 2, Chapter 6.

33 Flesher, P.V.M. (2015). UW Religion Today: The Triumph of Abrahamic Monotheism?. Retrieved from the University of Wyoming website http://www.uwyo.edu/uw/news/2015/08/uw-religion-today-the-triumph-of-abrahamic-monotheism.html

34 Posner, M. (n.d.). The Ten Commandments. (n.d.). In *Chabad.org*. Retrieved from http://www.chabad.org/library/article_cdo/aid/2896/jewish/The-Ten-Commandments.htm

35 *Shemot (Book of Exodus)* 20:1–14.

36 Isaacs, R.H. (n.d.). The Ten Commandments. In *My Jewish learning*. Retrieved from http://www.myjewishlearning.com/article/the-ten-commandments/

37 Aseret ha-Dibrot: The 'Ten Commandments'. (n.d.). In *Judaism 101*. Retrieved from http://www.jewfaq.org/10.htm

38 Sacks, J. (2014). *On Rosh Hashanah, A Breath of Life — Rabbi Sacks' message for Rosh Hashanah 5775*. Retrieved from http://rabbisacks.org/a-breath-of-life-rosh-hashanah-5775/

39 Kunkle, L. (2008). *Ethics and pro-social values in Judaism, Christianity and Islam.* Retrieved from http://abrahamicfamilyreunion.org/ethics-pro-social-values-in-judaism-christianity-and-islam/

40 *Matthew* 5:3–11.

41 *Luke* 10:25–27, NIV.

42 *1 John* 4:7–12.

43 Harris, J. (2015). *The Lost World of Byzantium.* New Haven, USA: Yale University Press.

44 Seward, D. (2000). *The Monks of War.* London: The Folio Society.

45 *Isaiah* 11:1–3.

46 *1 Corinthians* 12:7–11.

47 *Galatians* 5:22–23, NIV.

48 *Romans* 12:9–21, NIV.

49 Saint Thomas Aquinas. (2014). In *Stanford Encyclopedia of Philosophy.* Retrieved from the Stanford University website https://plato.stanford.edu/entries/aquinas/. A good introduction for the interested reader.

50 *1 Corinthians* 13:4–13, NIV.

51 Ramadan, T. (2017). *Islam: The Essentials.* UK: Pelican Books.

52 Escobedo, T., (2017). The world's fastest growing religion? Islam. Retrieved from http://edition.cnn.com/2017/03/16/world/islam-fastest-growing-religion-trnd/index.html

53 *Qur'an* 2:281. N.J. Dawood, Trans..

54 Ibid 5:38.

55 Ibid 45:18.

56 Islamic Virtues. (n.d.). In *Islamic Virtues.* Retrieved from http://www.islamondemand.com/islamic_virtues.html. A useful list of Qur'anic verses relating to virtue.

57 Haque, M. (2016, August 26). *Concept of virtue in Islam.* Retrieved from http://www.amda.us/index.php/khutba/289-concept-of-virtue-in-islam-part-1-august-26-2016

58 *Qur'an* 2:153–157.

59 Ibid 7:55–56.

60 Ibid 39:7.

61 Ramadan, T. (2017). *Islam: The Essentials*. UK: Pelican Books. Quote taken from p. 171.
62 *Qur'an* 5:45, N.J. Dawood, Trans..
63 Ibid 42:36–42.
64 Ibid 4:36.
65 Ibid 17:70.
66 Cairo Declaration on Human Rights. (1990). Retrieved from the University of Minnesota website http://hrlibrary.umn.edu/instree/cairodeclaration.html
67 Maximus, V. (2000). Memorable Deeds and Sayings: One Thousand Tales from Ancient Rome (D.R. Shackleton Bailey, Trans.). Cambridge, MA: Harvard University Press.
68 Sheridan, P. (2015, September 19). *Selected anecdotes by Valerius Maximus*. Retrieved from http://www.anecdotesfromantiquity.com/selected-anecdotes-by-valerius-maximus/
69 Lefkowitz, M.R., & Fant, M.B. (n.d.). *Women's life in Greece and Rome*. Retrieved from http://www.stoa.org/diotima/anthology/wlgr/wlgr-mensopinions53.shtml#mofn8
70 Smart, N. (1974). *The Religious Experience of Mankind*. New York: Charles Scribner's Sons.
71 *Yogasūtra* 2.29–2.39
72 *Śāṇḍilya Upaniṣad* 1.1–2.
73 *Hatha Yoga Pradipika* 1.17–18.
74 Dharma (Hinduism). (n.d.). In *Berkley Center for Religion, Peace & World Affairs*. Retrieved from the Georgetown University website https://berkleycenter.georgetown.edu/essays/dharma-hinduism
75 Mohapatra, A., & Mohapatra, B. (1993). *Hinduism: Analytical Study*. New Delhi: Mittal Publications.
76 *Dhammapada*, verse 183.
77 Harvey, P. (1998). *An Introduction to Buddhism: Teachings, History and Practices*. Cambridge: Cambridge University Press. Quote taken from p. 106.
78 Ibid, excluding above quote.
79 The Eight-Fold Path. (n.d.). In *Buddhist Studies*. Retrieved from http://www.buddhanet.net/e-learning/8foldpath.htm. A simple introduction for the interested reader.
80 Hewege, C. (Sept. 5th, 2017). Personal communication.

81 Khenchen Thrangu Rinpoche. (n.d.). *Buddhist Conduct: The Ten Virtuous Actions*. Retrieved from http://www.rinpoche.com/teachings/conduct.pdf

82 Confucius. (2009). *The Analects* (D.C. Lau, Trans.). London: The Folio Society. (Original work published 1st millennia BC). Quote taken from Book XII, number 22.

83 Havens, T. (2013). Confucianism as Humanism. *CLA Journal, 1*, 33–41.

84 Main concepts of Confucianism. (n.d.). In *Oriental philosophy*. Retrieved from the Lander University website
http://philosophy.lander.edu/oriental/main.html

85 Smart, N. (1974). *The Religious Experience of Mankind*. New York: Charles Scribner's Sons. Quote taken from p. 198.

86 Confucius. (n.d.). *The Analects*. Retrieved from the University of Southern California website http://china.usc.edu/confucius-analects-8. Quote taken from Book VIII number 2.

87 Confucius. (2009). *The Analects* (D.C. Lau, Trans.). London: The Folio Society. (Original work published 1st millennia BC). See Book XV, number 24.

88 Confucius and Aristotle. (n.d.) Retrieved from the Wabash Centre for Teaching and Learning in Theology and Religion website
http://www.wabashcenter.wabash.edu/syllabi/g/gier/308/conarist.htm

89 Yao, X. (2000). *An Introduction to Confucianism*. Cambridge: Cambridge University Press.

90 Schlosser, D. B. (2017). In *The Five Virtues of Confucius*. Retrieved from http://www.dbschlosser.com/five-virtues-of-confucius/. A simple introduction for the interested reader.

Chapter 2

1 King, M.L. (1968, April 3). *I've been to the mountaintop* [Audio podcast]. Retrieved from http://www.americanrhetoric.com/speeches/mlkivebeen-tothemountaintop.htm

2 Harrington, E. (2013, June 4). Climbing Morocco: A 24-Hour Big-Wall Adventure with Emily Harrington and Hazel Findlay [web log post]. Retrieved from
http://adventureblog.nationalgeographic.com/2013/06/04/climbing-morocco-a-24-hour-big-wall-adventure-with-emily-harrington-and-hazel-findlay/

3 A History of Firsts. (n.d.). In *The University of Adelaide*. Retrieved from https://www.adelaide.edu.au/seek-light/stories/douglas-mawson.html

4   Bickel, L. (1987). *This Accursed Land*. Melbourne: The MacMillan Company of Australia Pty. Ltd..

5   Turney, C. (2018, March 22). Douglas Mawson, Antarctic scientist and explorer. In *Adventure Journal*. Retrieved from https://www.adventure-journal.com/2018/03/historical-badass-douglas-mawson-antarctic-scientist-and-explorer-2/

6   Australasian Antarctic Expedition. (n.d.). In *Wikipedia*. Retrieved from http://en.wikipedia.org/wiki/Douglas_Mawson#Australasian_Antarctic_Expedition

7   Jacka, F., & Jacka, E. (Eds.). (1991). *Mawson's Antarctic Diaries*. Sydney: Allen & Unwin.

8   Bickel, L. (1987). *This Accursed Land*. Melbourne: The MacMillan Company of Australia Pty. Ltd.. Quote adapted from p. 185.

9   Goud, N. H. (2005). Courage: It's Nature and Development. *The Journal of Humanistic Counselling, Education and Development, 44*(1), 102–116. doi: 10.1002/j.2164-490X.2005.tb00060.x

10 A Conversation with Hazel Findlay. (2015). In *Warriors Way*. Retrieved from http://warriorsway.com/hazel-findlay_interview_2015-10/

11 Plato. (1955). *Laches* (W.R.M. Lamb Trans.). Retrieved from the Tufts University website http://www.perseus.tufts.edu/hopper/text?doc=Perseus%3atext%3a1999.01.0176%3atext%3dLach. (Original work published 4th century BC).

12 Aristotle. (1934). *Nicomachean Ethics* (H. Rackham, Trans.). Retrieved from the Tufts University website http://www.perseus.tufts.edu/hopper/text?doc=Perseus%3atext%3a1999.01.0054 (Original work published 4th century BC).

13 Aurelius, M. (2006). Meditations (M. Hammond, Trans.). London: Penguin Group. (Original work published 2nd century AD). Quote taken from Book 10, Section 11.

14 Putman, D. (2010). The philosophical roots of the concept of courage. In C.L.S. Pury & S.J. Lopez (Eds.), *The Psychology of Courage: Modern Research on an Ancient Virtue* (pp. 9–22). Washington, DC: American Psychological Association.

15 Rate, C. R. (2007). *What is courage? A search for meaning* (Doctoral thesis, Yale University, USA). Retrieved from http://gateway.proquest.com/openurl?url_ver=Z39.88-2004&res_dat=xri:pqdiss&rft_val_fmt=info:ofi/fmt:kev:mtx:dissertation&rft_dat=xri:pqdiss:3293368

16 Weinstein, H. (2012). *Beyond Courage: The Psychology of Heroism*. (Doctoral thesis, Yale University, USA). Retrieved from http://gateway.proquest.com/openurl?url_ver=Z39.88-2004&res_dat=xri:pqdiss&rft_val_fmt=info:ofi/fmt:kev:mtx:dissertation&rft_dat=xri:pqdiss:3591893

17 Pallone, N.J., & Hennessy, J. J. C. (1998). Counterfeit courage: Toward a process psychology paradigm for the 'Heroic rescue fantasy'. *Current Psychology, 17*(2), 197–209. doi:10.1007/s12144-998-1006-7

18 Hartley, D. H. (2011). Sun Tzu and Command Assessment: A Study on Commander's Courage. *International Journal of Leadership Studies, 6*(2), 263–273. Retrieved from the Regent University website http://www.regent.edu/acad/global/publications/ijls/new/vol6iss2/6_Hartley_pp263-274_jm.pdf. Quote taken from p. 271.

19 Pury, C. L. S., Kowalski, R., & Spearman, J. (2007a). Distinctions between general and personal courage. *The Journal of Positive Psychology, 2*(2), 99–114. doi:10.1080/17439760701237962

20 Pury, C.L.S., & Kowalski, R. (2007b). Human strengths, courageous actions, and general and personal courage. *The Journal of Positive Psychology, 2*(2), 120–128. doi:10.1080/17439760701228813. Quote taken from p. 120.

21 Pury, C.L.S., Starkey, C.B., Kulik, R.E., Skjerning, K.L., & Sullivan, E.A. (2015). Is courage always a virtue? Suicide, killing, and bad courage. *The Journal of Positive Psychology, 10*(5), 383–388. doi:10.1080/17439760.2015.1004552. Quote taken from p. 383.

22 Rate, C.R. (2010). Defining the features of courage: A search for meaning. In C.L.S. Pury & S.J. Lopez (Eds.), *The Psychology of Courage: Modern Research on an Ancient Virtue* (pp. 47–66). Washington DC: American Psychological Association.

23 Slezá ková, A., & Luká ová, F. (2011). *Relation between temperament dimension Harm Avoidance and character strengths Curiosity and Courage*. Second World Congress on Positive Psychology, Philadelphia, USA.

24 Norton, P. J., & Weiss B. J. (2009). The Role of Courage on Behavioral Approach in a Fear-Eliciting Situation: A Proof-of-Concept Pilot Study. *Journal of Anxiety Disorders, 23*(2), 212–217. doi:10.1016/j.janxdis.2008.07.002. Quote taken from p. 214.

25 Marshall, W.L., Bristol, D., & Barbaree, H.E. (1992). Cognitions and courage in the avoidance behavior of acrophobics. *Behaviour Research and Therapy, 30*(5), 463-470. doi: 10.1016/0005-7967(92)90030-K

26 Cox, D., Hallam, R., O'Connor, K., & Rachman, S. (1983). An experimental analysis of fearlessness and courage. *British Journal of Psychology, 74*(1), 107–117. doi:10.1111/j.2044-8295.1983.tb01847.x

27 Ibid. Quote taken from p. 107.
28 O'Connor, K., Hallam, R., & Rachman, S. (1985). Fearlessness and courage: A replication experiment. *British Journal of Psychology*, 76, 187–197. doi:10.1111/j.2044-8295.1985.tb01942.x
29 McMillan, T.M., & Rachman, S.J. (2011). Fearlessness and courage: A laboratory study of paratrooper veterans of the Falklands War. *British Journal of Psychology*, 78(3), 375–383. doi: 10.1111/j.2044-8295.1987.tb02255.x
30 Macmillan, T., & Rachman, S. (1988). Fearlessness and courage in paratroopers undergoing training. *Personality and Individual Differences*, 9, 373-378. doi:10.1016/0191-8869(88)90100-6
31 Rachman, S.J. (1984). Fear and Courage. *Behavior Therapy*, 15(1), 109–120. doi: 10.1016/S0005-7894(84)80045-3
32 Masten, A.S., & Reed, M.J. (2002). Resilience in development. In C.R. Snyder & S. Lopez (Eds.), *Handbook of Positive Psychology* (pp. 74–88). Oxford: Oxford University Press.
33 Edwards, T.M., & Jovanovski, A. (2016). Hope as a Therapeutic Target in Counselling — In General and in Relation to Christian Clients. *International Journal for the Advancement of Counselling*, 38(2), 77–88. doi:10.1007/s10447-016-9257-8
34 Putman, D. (1997). Psychological Courage. *Philosophy, Psychiatry, & Psychology*, 4(1), 1–11. doi:10.1353/ppp.1997.0008
35 Hawkins, S. F., & Morse, J. (2014). The praxis of courage as a foundation for care. *Journal of Nursing Scholarship*. 46(4), 263–270. doi:10.1111/jnu.12077
36 Moore, A. (1997). Commentary on' Psychological Courage'. *Philosophy, Psychiatry, & Psychology*, 4(1), 13–14. doi:10.1353/ppp.1997.0005
37 Asch, S.E. (1956). Studies of independence and conformity: I. A minority of one against a unanimous majority. *Psychological Monographs: General and Applied*, 70(9), 1-70. Retrieved from http://psyc604.stasson.org/Asch1956.pdf
38 Nemeth, C., & Chiles, C. (1988). Modelling courage: The role of dissent in fostering independence. *European Journal of Social Psychology*, 18(3), 275–280. doi:10.1002/ejsp.2420180306
39 Grady, C., Danis, M., Soeken, K. L., O'Donnell, P., Taylor, C., Farrar, A., & Ulrich, C. M. (2008). Does Ethics Education Influence the Moral Action of Practicing Nurses and Social Workers?. *The American Journal of Bioethics*, 8(4), 4–11. doi:10.1080/15265160802166017

40 Linn, R., & Gillian, C. (1990). One action, two moral orientations- The tension between justice and care voices in Israeli selective conscientious objectors. *New Ideas in Psychology, 8*(2), 189–203. doi:10.1016/0732-118X(90)90008-P

41 Osswald, S., Greitemeyer, T., Fischer, P., & Frey, D. (2010). What is moral courage? Definition, explication, and classification of a complex construct. In C.L.S. Pury & S.J. Lopez (Eds.), *The Psychology of Courage: Modern Research on an Ancient Virtue* (pp. 149–164). Washington, DC: American Psychological Association.

42 Batson, C. D., Lishner, D.A., Carpenter, A., Dulin, A., Harjusola-Webb, S., Stocks, E. L., ... Sampat, B. (2003). '... As you Would have Them Do Unto You': Does Imagining Yourself in the Other's Place Stimulate Moral Action?. *Personality and Socical Psychology Bulletin, 29*(9), 1190–1201. doi:10.1177/0146167203254600

43 Bronstein, P., Fox, B. J., Kamon, J. L., & Knolls, M. L. (2007). Parenting and Gender as Predictors of Moral Courage in Late Adolescence: A Longitudinal Study. *Sex Roles, 56*(9), 661-674. doi:10.1007/s11199-007-9182-8. Quote taken from p. 661.

44 Forced Sterilization. (n.d.). In *United States Holocaust Memorial Museum*. Retrieved from https://www.ushmm.org/learn/students/learning-materials-and-resources/mentally-and-physically-handicapped-victims-of-the-nazi-era/forced-sterilization

45 Aktion T4. (n.d.). In *Wikipedia*. Retrieved from https://en.wikipedia.org/wiki/Aktion_T4

46 Pury, C.L.S., & Starkey, C.B. (2010). Is courage an accolade or a process? A fundamental question for courage research. In C.L.S. Pury & S.J. Lopez (Eds.), *The Psychology of Courage: Modern Research on an Ancient Virtue* (pp. 67–88). Washington, DC: American Psychological Association.

47 Rachman, S.J. (2010). Courage: A psychological perspective. In C.L.S. Pury & S.J. Lopez (Eds.), *The Psychology of Courage: Modern Research on an Ancient Virtue* (pp. 91–108). Washington, DC: American Psychological Association. Quote taken from p. 95.

48 Ibid. Quote excepted.

49 Woodard, C. R. (2004). Hardiness and the Concept of Courage. *Consulting Psychology Journal: Practice and Research, 56*(3), 173–185. doi: 10.1037/1065-9293.56.3.173

50 Woodward, C. R., & Pury, C.L.S. (2007). The construct of courage: Categorization and measurement. *Consulting Psychology Journal: Practice and Research, 59*, 135–147. doi:10.1037/1065-9293.59.2.135

51 Do you know your 24 character strengths?. (n.d.). In *VIA Institute on Character*. Retrieved from https://www.viacharacter.org/www/Character-Strengths/VIA-Classification#nav

52 Hannah, S.T., Sweeney, P.J., & Lester, P.B. (2010). The courageous mind-set: A dynamic personality system approach to courage. In C.L.S. Pury & S.J. Lopez (Eds.), *The Psychology of Courage: Modern Research on an Ancient Virtue* (pp. 125–148). Washington, DC: American Psychological Association.

53 Rachman, S.J. (2010). Courage: A psychological perspective. In C.L.S. Pury & S.J. Lopez (Eds.), *The Psychology of Courage: Modern Research on an Ancient Virtue* (pp. 91–108). Washington, DC: American Psychological Association. Quote taken from p. 96.

54 Lopez, S.J., Rasmussen, H.N., Skorupski, W.P., Koetting, K., Petersen, S.E., & Yang, Y.-T. (2010). Folk conceptualizations of courage. In C.L.S. Pury & S.J. Lopez (Eds.), *The Psychology of Courage: Modern Research on an Ancient Virtue* (pp. 23–46). Washington, DC: American Psychological Association.

55 Lester, P.B., Vogelgesang, G.R., Hannah, S.T., & Kimmey, T. (2010). Developing courage in followers: Theoretical and applied perspectives. In C.L.S. Pury & S.J. Lopez (Eds.), *The Psychology of Courage: Modern Research on an Ancient Virtue* (pp. 187–208). Washington, DC: American Psychological Association.

56 Rachman, S.J. (2010). Courage: A psychological perspective. In C.L.S. Pury & S.J. Lopez (Eds.), *The Psychology of Courage: Modern Research on an Ancient Virtue* (pp. 91–108). Washington, DC: American Psychological Association. Quote taken from p. 97.

57 Matobo, T.A., Makatsa, M., & Obioha, E.E. (2009). Continuity in the traditional initiation practice of boys and girls in contemporary Southern Africa society. *Studies of Tribes and Tribals, 7*(2), 105–113. Retrieved from http://www.krepublishers.com/02-Journals/T%20&%20T/T%20&%20T-07-0-000-09-Web/T%20&%20T-07-2-000-09-Abst-PDF/T&T-07-2-105-09-172-Matobo-T-A/T&T-07-2-105-09-172-Matobo-T-A-Tt.pdf.

58 Whittington, A., & Mack, E. N. (2010). Inspiring Courage in Girls: An Evaluation of Practices and Outcomes. *Journal of Experiential Education, 33*(2), 166–180. doi: 10.5193/JEE33.2.166. Quote taken from p. 166.

Chapter 3

1 Bevis, M. (2015, April 1). *Laureus Awards 2015: Navratilova on 'diligent' Djokovic and Federer 'GOAT' debate*. Retrieved from http://www.thesportreview.com/tsr/2015/04/laureus-awards-2015-navratilova-on-diligent-djokovic-and-federer-goat-debate/

2   Novak Djokovic. (2015). In *ShortList*. Retrieved from http://www.shortlist.com/entertainment/sport/novak-djokovic

3   Marie Curie. (2017). In *Biography.com*. Retrieved from http://www.biography.com/people/marie-curie-9263538#synopsis

4   The discovery of radioactivity. (2000). Retrieved from the Lawrence Berkeley National Laboratory website http://www2.lbl.gov/abc/wallchart/chapters/03/4.html

5   Adolff, J.-P. (2011). A Short History of Polonium and Radium. In *Chemistry International*. Retrieved from the International Union of Pure and Applied Chemistry website https://www.iupac.org/publications/ci/2011/3301/5_adloff.html

6   Sklodowska Curie, M. (1904). Radio-active substances (Translator unknown; Doctoral thesis, University of Paris, France). In *Chemical News* reprinted from volume 88. Retrieved from https://archive.org/details/radioac-tivesubst00curi

7   Arthur, C.G. (2002). Student Diligence and Student Diligence Support: Predictors of Academic Success. Research report delivered to the *Annual Meeting of the Mid-South Educational Research Association* (Chattanooga, TN).

8   Arthur, C.G., Shepherd, L., & Sumo, M. (2006). The Role of Students' Diligence in Predicting Academic Performance. *Research in the Schools, 13*(2), 72-80. Quote taken from p. 72.

9   Doherty, E.M., & Nugent, E. (2011). Personality factors and medical training: a review of the literature. *Medical Education 45*(2), 132–140. doi: 10.1111/j.1365-2923.2010.03760.x. Quote taken from p. 132.

10 Brown, C., & Lilford, R.J. (2008). Selecting medical students. *British Medical Journal, 336*(7648), 786. doi: 10.1136/bmj.39517.679977.80. Quote taken from p. 786.

11 Barrick, M.R., & Mount, M.K. (1991). The Big Five personality dimensions and job performance: A meta-analysis. *Personnel Psychology, 44*, 1–26. doi: 10.1111/j.1744-6570.1991.tb00688.x

12 Kern, M. L., Friedman H.S., Martin, L.R., Reynolds, C.A., & Luong, G. (2009). Conscientiousness, Career Success, and Longevity: A Lifespan Analysis. *Annals of Behavioral Medicine, 37*, 154-163. doi:10.1007/s12160-009-9095-6

13 Kern, M. L., & Friedman H.S. (2008). Do conscientious individuals live longer? A quantitative review. *Health Psychology, 27*(5), 505–512. doi: 10.1037/0278-6133.27.5.505

14 *Proverbs* 22:6, NIV.

15 Hoff, E., Laursen B., & Tardif, T. (2002). Socioeconomic status and parenting. In Bornstein, M.H. (Ed.), *Handbook of parenting: Biology and ecology of parenting* (vol. 2, pp. 231–252). New Jersey: Lawrence Erlbaum Associates, Publishers.

16 Vinson, K.E. (2013). Hovering Too Close: The Ramifications of Helicopter Parenting in Higher Education. *Georgia State University Law Review, 29*, 423. doi: http://dx.doi.org/10.2139/ssrn.1982763

17 Heaven, P.C.L., & Ciarrochi, J. (2008). Parental Styles, Conscientiousness, and Academic Performance in High School: A Three-Wave Longitudinal Study. *Personality & Social Psychology Bulletin, 34*(4), 451–461. doi: 10.1177/0146167207311909

18 Walton, S. (2012). Types of Parenting Styles. In *The Positive Parenting Centre*. Retrieved from http://www.the-positive-parenting-centre.com/types_of_parenting_styles.html

19 Dombeck, M. (2014). The Long Term Effects of Bullying. In *The American Academy of Experts in Traumatic Stress*. Retrieved from http://www.aaets.org/article204.htm

20 Rozental, A., & Carlbring, P. (2014). Understanding and Treating Procrastination: A Review of a Common Self-Regulatory Failure. *Psychology, 5*(13), 1488–1502. doi:10.4236/psych.2014.513160

21 Burka, J.B., & Yuen, L.M. (2008). *Procrastination: Why You Do It, What to Do About It Now*. Boston: Da Capo Press.

22 Rozental, A., & Carlbring, P. (2014). Understanding and Treating Procrastination: A Review of a Common Self-Regulatory Failure. *Psychology, 5*(13), 1488–1502. doi: 10.4236/psych.2014.513160. Quote taken from p. 1491.

23 Freudenberger, H.J. (1977). Burn-out: The organisational menace. *Training and Development Journal*, July, 26-27. Quote taken from p. 26.

24 Robbins, M., Francis, L., & Powell, R. (2012). Work-related psychological health among clergywomen in Australia. *Mental Health, Religion & Culture, 15*(9), 933–944.

25 Prinz, P., Hertrich, K., Hirschfelder, U., & de Zwaan, M. (2012). Burnout, depression and depersonalisation – Psychological factors and coping strategies in dental and medical students. *GMS Zeitschrift für Medizinische Ausbildung, 29*(1), 1-14. doi: 10.3205/zma000780

26 Armon, G., Shirom, A., & Melamed, S. (2012). The Big Five Personality Factors as Predictors of Changes Across Time in Burnout and Its Facets. *Journal of Personality, 80*(2), 403-427. doi: 10.1111/j.1467-6494.2011.00731.x

27 Chung, M.C., & Harding, C. (2009). Investigating Burnout and Psychological Well-Being of Staff Working with People with Intellectual Disabilities and Challenging Behaviour: The Role of Personality. *Journal of Applied Research in Intellectual Disabilities, 22*, 549–560. doi: 10.1111/j.1468-3148.2009.00507.x

28 Armon, G., Shirom, A., & Melamed, S. (2012). The Big Five Personality Factors as Predictors of Changes Across Time in Burnout and Its Facets. *Journal of Personality, 80*(2), 403-427. doi: 10.1111/j.1467-6494.2011.00731.x. Quote taken from p. 407.

29 Henderson, J. M. (2016). Four Signs You're About To Burn Out. In *Forbes*. Retrieved from https://www.forbes.com/sites/jmaureenhenderson/2016/10/14/four-signs-youre-about-to-burn-out/#ebef12e69469

30 Edwards, T.M. (2017). Ideas for clergy in the prevention and management of burnout. *Pointers, 27*(2), 2–6.

31 Dunkley, D.M., Blankstein, K.R., & Berg, J.-L. (2012). Perfectionism Dimensions and the Five-Factor Model of Personality. *European Journal of Personality. 26*, 233–244. doi: 10.1002/per.829

32 Stoeber, J., Otto, K., & Dalbert, C. (2009). Perfectionism and the Big Five: Conscientiousness predicts longitudinal increases in self-oriented perfectionism. *Personality and Individual Differences. 47*(4), 363–368. doi: 10.1016/j.paid.2009.04.004

33 Margot, K.C., & Rinn, A. N. (2016). Perfectionism in Gifted Adolescents: A Replication and Extension. *Journal of Advanced Academics. 27*(3), 190–209. doi: 10.1177/1932202X16656452

34 Ibid. Quote taken from p. 202.

35 Ibid. Quote taken from p. 203

36 Antony, M.M. (2015). Cognitive-Behavioral Therapy for Perfectionism. Presentation to the *Anxiety and Depression Association of America*. Retrieved from https://www.adaa.org/sites/default/files/Antony_MasterClinician.pdf

37 Chokkalingam, S., Akhilesh, K.B., & Nagendra, H.R. (2015). Effect of Yoga on Conscientiousness and Performance of Employees: An Action Research Study. *Innovative Journal of Business and Management, 4*(3), 45–51. doi: 10.15520/ijbm.vol4.iss3.22

38 Della Porta, S.S. (2013). Increasing Conscientiousness to improve health behaviors: Findings from a self-regulation intervention (Doctoral thesis, University of California, Riverside). Retrieved from http://escholarship.org/uc/item/06b6s7vc#page-1

39 Hernández, J., & Mateo, R. (2012). Indications of virtues in Conscientiousness and its practice through continuous improvement. *Business Ethics: A European Review, 21*(2), 129–237. doi: 10.1111/j.1467-8608.2011.01650.x

40 Mateo, R., Hernández, J., & Neriz, L. (2016). Experimental evidence for the effects of a continuous improvement environment versus a mechanical environment on routines based on Conscientiousness. *Total Quality Management & Business Excellence. 27*(1–2), 157–168. doi: 10.1080/14783363.2014.968988

Chapter 4

1 Jessica Watson. (n.d.). In *Wikipedia*. Retrieved from https://en.wikipedia.org/wiki/Jessica_Watson

2 AAP. (2010, June 15). Jess Watson and tanker both to blame for collision. In *The Sydney Morning Herald*. Retrieved from http://www.smh.com.au/national/jess-watson-and-tanker-both-to-blame-for-collision-20100615-ybig.html

3 Harry Gordon Selfridge. (n.d.) In *Wikipedia*. Retrieved from https://en.wikipedia.org/wiki/Harry_Gordon_Selfridge

4 Alderman, L. et al. (2016, June 17). Explaining Greece's Debt Crisis. In *The New York Times*. Retrieved from http://www.nytimes.com/interactive/2015/business/international/greece-debt-crisis-euro.html?_r=0

5 Tax evasion and corruption in Greece (n.d.). In *Wikipedia*. Retrieved from https://en.wikipedia.org/wiki/Tax_evasion_and_corruption_in_Greece#cite_note-22

6 Phronesis. (n.d.). In *Wikipedia*. Retrieved from https://en.wikipedia.org/wiki/Phronesis. A simple introduction for readers.

7 Russo, M.S. (2001). *Plato in a Nutshell: A Beginner's Guide to the Philosophy of Plato*. Retrieved from https://www.northampton.edu/Documents/Subsites/HaroldWeiss/Intro%20to%20Philosophy/russo_plato1.pdf

8 Plato. (4th century BC/1966). *Apology* (H.N. Fowler, Trans.). Retrieved from the Tufts University website http://www.perseus.tufts.edu/hopper/text?doc=Perseus%3atext%3a1999.01.0170%3atext%3dApol.

9 Wisdom. (2013). In *Stanford Encyclopedia of Philosophy*. Retrieved from the Stanford University website https://plato.stanford.edu/entries/wisdom/. A comprehensive introduction for readers.

10 Aristotle. (1934). *Nicomachean Ethics* (H. Rackham, Trans.). Retrieved from the Tufts University website

http://www.perseus.tufts.edu/hopper/text?doc=Perseus%3atext%3a1999.01.0054

11   Aristotle's Ethics. (2014). In *Stanford Encyclopedia of Philosophy*. Retrieved from the Stanford University website https://plato.stanford.edu/entries/aristotle-ethics/. A comprehensive introduction for readers.

12   Pegis, A.C. (1948). *Introduction to Saint Thomas Aquinas*. New York: Random House.

13   Staudinger, U.M., & Gluck, J. (2011). Psychological wisdom research: Commonalities and differences in a growing field. *Annual Review of Psychology, 62*, 215-241. doi: 10.1146/annurev.psych.121208.131659

14   Yang, S.-Y. (2008). A process view of wisdom. *Journal of Adult Development, 15*, 62-75. doi: 10.1007/s10804-008-9037-8

15   Baltes, P., & Kunzmann, U. (2004). The Two Faces of Wisdom: Wisdom as a General Theory of Knowledge and Judgment about Excellence in Mind and Virtue vs. Wisdom as Everyday Realization in People and Products. *Human Development, 47*, 290–299. doi: 10.1159/000079156. Quote taken from pp. 294–295.

16   Baltes, P., & Smith, J. (2008). The Fascination of Wisdom: Its Nature, Ontogeny, and Function. *Perspectives in Psychological Science, 3*, 56-64. doi: 10.1111/j.1745-6916.2008.00062.x

17   The Berlin Wisdom Paradigm: An expert knowledge system. (2016, September 18). In evidence-based wisdom. [web log comment]. Retrieved from https://evidencebasedwisdom.com/2015/09/20/the-berlin-wisdom-paradigm-an-expert-knowledge-system/

18   Sternberg, R. (2004). Words to the Wise about Wisdom? A Commentary on Ardelt's Critique of Baltes. *Human Development, 47*, 286–289. doi: 10.1159/000079155. Quote taken from p. 286.

19   Ibid. Except quote.

20   Sternberg, R. (2004). What Is Wisdom and How Can We Develop It? *Annals of the American Academy of Political and Social Science, 591*, 164–174. doi: 10.1177/0002716203260097

21   Cassidy, C. (n.d.). Wisdom Profiles Series Dilip Jeste. In *Evidence-based Wisdom*. Retreived from https://evidencebasedwisdom.com/wisdom-profiles-dilip-jeste/#ComparingAncientandModernConceptionsofWisdom

22   Cassidy, C. (n.d.). Wisdom Profiles Series Monika Ardelt. In *Evidence-based Wisdom*. Retrieved from https://evidencebasedwisdom.com/wisdom-profiles-monika-ardelt/

23   Ardelt, M. (2003). Empirical assessment of a three-dimensional wisdom scale. *Research on Aging, 25*(3), 275-324. doi: 10.1177/0164027503025003004

24 Ardelt, M. (2004). Wisdom as Expert Knowledge System: A critical review of a contemporary operationalization of an ancient concept. *Human Development, 47*, 257-285. doi: 10.1159/000079154

25 Ardelt, M. (2004). Where Can Wisdom Be Found? A Reply to the Commentaries by Baltes and Kunzmann, Sternberg, and Achenbaum. *Human Development, 47*, 304–307.

26 Ardelt, M. (2003). Empirical assessment of a three-dimensional wisdom scale. *Research on Aging, 25*(3), 275-324. doi: 10.1177/0164027503025003004. Quote taken from p. 278.

27 Sternberg, R.J. (2009). *Cognitive Psychology* (5th ed.). Belmont, USA: Wadsworth.

28 Devaine, M., Hollard, G., & Daunizeau, J. (2014). Theory of Mind: Did Evolution Fool Us? *PLOS One, 9*(2), e87619. doi: 10.1371/journal.pone.0087619

29 Edelson, S.M. (2017). *Theory of the Mind*. Retrieved from https://www.autism.com/understanding_theoryofmind

30 Frith, U. (2001). Mind Blindness and the Brain in Autism. *Neuron, 32*, 969–979. doi: 10.1016/S0896-6273(01)00552-9

31 Batson, C.D. (2011). *Altruism in Humans*. Oxford: Oxford University Press.

32 Kanazawa, S. (2008, October 19). *Two logical fallacies that we must avoid*. Retrieved from https://www.psychologytoday.com/us/blog/the-scientific-fundamentalist/200810/two-logical-fallacies-we-must-avoid

33 Dwyer, C. (2017, August 25). *18 Common Logical Fallacies and Persuasion Techniques*. Retrieved from https://www.psychologytoday.com/us/blog/thoughts-thinking/201708/18-common-logical-fallacies-and-persuasion-techniques

34 Taylor, J. (2011, July 18). *Cognitive Biases v.s. Common Sense*. Retrieved from https://www.psychologytoday.com/us/blog/the-power-prime/201107/cognitive-biases-vs-common-sense

35 Storr, A. (1983). *The Essential Jung: Selected writings*. London: Harper Collins. Quote taken from Psychology and Religion (1938), p. 242.

36 Pulkkinen, L., & Pulkkinen, T. (2010). Temperance and strengths of personality: Evidence from a 35-year longitudinal study. In R. Schwarzer & P.A. Frensch (Eds.), *Personality, Human Development, and Culture*, vol. 2 (pp. 127–140). Hove, UK: Psychology Press.

37 An overview of the study. (2010). In *University of Jyväskylä*. Retrieved from the University of Jyväskylä website https://www.jyu.fi/ytk/laitokset/psykologia/en/old-research/programs-and-projects/jyls/overview

38 Anokhin, A.P., Golosheykin, S., Grant, J.D., & Heath A.C. (2011). Heritability of Delay Discounting in Adolescence: A Longitudinal Twin Study. *Behavior*

Genetics, 41(2), 175-183. doi: 10.1007/s10519-010-9384-7. Retrieved from https://link.springer.com/article/10.1007/s10519-010-9384-7 doi:10.1007/s10519-010-9384-7

39 Green, L., Fry, A.F., & Myerson, J. (1994). Discounting of Delayed Rewards: A Life-Span Comparison. *Psychological Science, 5*(1), 33-36. doi: 10.1111/j.1467-9280.1994.tb00610.x

40 Hirsh, J.B., Morisano, D., & Peterson, J.B. (2008). Delay discounting: Interactions between personality and cognitive ability. *Journal of Research in Personality, 42*(6), 1646-1650. doi: 10.1016/j.jrp.2008.07.005

41 McGuire, J.T., & Kable, J.W. (2013). Rational temporal predictions can underlie apparent failures to delay gratification. *Psychological Review, 120*(2), 395–410. doi: 10.1037/a0031910

42 Wittmann, M., & Paulus, M.P. (2008). Decision making, impulsivity and time perception. *Trends in Cognitive Sciences, 12*(1), 7–12. doi: 10.1016/j.tics.2007.10.004

43 Liu, L., Feng, T., Suo, T., Lee, K., & Li, H. (2012). Adapting to the Destitute Situations: Poverty Cues Lead to Short-Term Choice. *PLoS ONE 7*(4), e33950. doi: 10.1371/journal.pone.0033950

44 Michaelson, L., de la Vega, A., Chatham, C.H., & Munakata, Y. (2013). Delaying Gratification Depends on Social Trust. *Frontiers in Cognition, 4*, 355. doi: 10.3389/fpsyg.2013.0035541

45 Horney, K. (1945). *Our Inner Conflicts.* New York: W.W. Norton & Co. Quote taken from p. 137.

46 Nicolaides, A. (2015). Generative learning: Adults learning with ambiguity. *Adult Education Quarterly, 65*(3), 179–195. doi: 10.1177/0741713614568887

47 Ibid. Quote taken from p. 191.

48 Ibid. Quote taken from p. 192.

Chapter 5

1 Stewart, F. (2012, August 7) *An Anthropologist Looks at Honor (part 2)* [video file]. 36th Annual Midwest Philosophy Colloquium titled 'Honor and Ethics' mini-conference, University of Minnesota. Retrieved from https://www.youtube.com/watch?v=ExdWQxuxt2o

2 Stewart, F. (2012, August, 2). *An Anthropologist Looks at Honor (part 1)* [video file]. 36th Annual Midwest Philosophy Colloquium titled 'Honor and Ethics' mini-conference, University of Minnesota. Retrieved from https://www.youtube.com/watch?v=mTQPkoobEiI

3 Stewart, F. (1994). *Honor.* Chicago: University of Chicago Press.

4   Oprisko, R.L. (2011). *The Phenomenology of Honor* (doctoral dissertation). Purdue University, Indiana, USA). Retrieved from https://www.researchgate.net/publication/254640285
5   Peristiany, J.G. (1966). *Honour and Shame: The Values of Mediterranean Society.* Chicago: University of Chicago Press.
6   Peristiany, J.G., & Pitt-Rivers, J. (Eds.). (1992). *Honor and Grace in Anthropology.* Cambridge: Cambridge University Press.
7   Orwell, G. (1945). *Animal Farm.* Harmondsworth, UK: Penguin. Quote taken from p. 114.
8   Sessions, W.L. (2010). *Honor for Us: A Philosophical Analysis, Interpretation and Defense.* New York: Continuum. Quote taken from p. 189.
9   Ibid. Except quote.
10 Braudy, L. (2005). *From Chivalry to Terrorism: War and the Changing Nature of Masculinity.* New York, NY: Random House. In Oprisko, R.L. (2011). *The Phenomenology of Honor* (doctoral dissertation). Purdue University, Indiana, USA. Retrieved from https://www.researchgate.net/publication/254640285. Quote taken from p. 31.
11 Colmenares, F., Esteban, M.M., & Zaragoza, F. (2006). One-male units and clans in a colony of hamadryas baboons (*Papio hamadryas hamadryas*): effect of male number and clan cohesion on feeding success. *American Journal of Primatology, 68*(1), 21–37. doi: 10.1002/ajp.20204
12 Nowak, A., Gelfand, M.J., Borkowski, W., Cohen, D., & Hernandez, I. (2015). The Evolutionary Basis of Honor Cultures. *Psychological Science, 27*(1), 12–24. doi: 10.1177/0956797615602860
13 Breitenstein, D. (2014, May 25). U.S. Catholics face shortage of priests. In *USA Today.* Retrieved from https://www.usatoday.com/story/news/2014/05/25/us-catholics-face-shortage-of-priests/9548931/
14 Daniszewski, J. (2005, April 17). Catholicism losing ground in Ireland. In *Los Angeles Times.* Retrieved from http://www.latimes.com/news/la-fg-ireland17apr17-story.html
15 Gilmore, D.D. (Ed.). (1987). *Honor And Shame And The Unity Of The Mediterranean.* Washington DC: American Anthropological Association.
16 Principles & Culture. (n.d.). In *Bridgewater.* Retrieved from https://www.bridgewater.com
17 Bridgewater Associates. (n.d.). Retrieved from https://ipfs.io/ipfs/QmXoypizjW3WknFiJnKLwHCnL72vedxjQkDDP1mXWo6uco/wiki/Bridgewater_Associates.html#cite_note-BloombergTeitelbaum-10. A good introduction to unique corporate practices.

18 Trigg, S. (2006). 'Shamed be …': historicizing shame in medieval and early modern courtly ritual. *Exemplaria, 19*(1), 67-89. doi: 10.1179/175330707X203228. Quote taken from p. 80.

19 Logan, A., & King, F. (2016). Self-esteem: Defining, measuring and promoting an elusive concept. *REACH Journal of Special Needs Education in Ireland, 29*(2), 116–127.

20 Sachs, D. (1981). How to Distinguish Self-Respect from Self-Esteem. *Philosophy & Public Affairs, 10*(4), 346-360. Quote taken from pp. 346–347.

21 French, S. (2012, August 7). *Honor Through the Ages (part 1)* [video file]. 36th Annual Midwest Philosophy Colloquium titled 'Honor and Ethics' mini-conference, University of Minnesota. Retrieved from https://www.youtube.com/watch?v=m-xjegbGf2E

22 Excerpts from Remarks by General H. Norman Schwarzkopf. (2000, August 2). In *The New York Times*. Retrieved from https://partners.nytimes.com/library/politics/camp/080200norm-text.html

23 French Foreign Legion Traditions. (n.d.). In *Foreign Legion Info*. Retrieved from http://foreignlegion.info/traditions/

24 Battle of Camerone. (n.d.). In *Foreign Legion Info*. Retrieved from http://foreign-legion.info/battle-of-camerone/

25 Le Boudin. (n.d.). In *Wikipedia*. Retrieved from https://en.wikipedia.org/wiki/Le_Boudin

Chapter 6

1 Wallace, S. (2007). Last of the Amazon. *National Geographic*. (January), 44–71. Retrieved from www.scottwallace.com/PDF/Jan07.pdf. Quotes taken from pp. 44 and 49.

2 Plato. (1971). *The Republic* (A.D. Lindsay, Trans.). London: Heron Books. (Original work published 4th century BC).

3 Ibid. Quote taken from p. 5.

4 Campbell, T. (2010). *Justice*. Houndmills, Basingstoke, UK: Palgrave Macmillan.

5 Justinian. (n.d.). *The Institutes of Justinian*. (Original work published 6th century AD). Retrieved from the Syracuse University website http://classes.maxwell.syr.edu/his381/InstitutesofJustinian.htm

6 Kohlberg, L. (1971). *Stages of Moral Development*. Retrieved from Prince Sultan University website http://info.psu.edu.sa/psu/maths/Stages%20of%20Moral%20Development%20According%20to%20Kohlberg.pdf

7   Blasi, A. (1980). Bridging moral cognition and moral action: A critical review of the literature. *Psychological Bulletin, 88*(1), 1–45. doi: 10.1037/0033-2909.88.1.1

8   Snarey, J.R., & Samuelson, P.L. (2014). Lawrence Kohlberg's revolutionary ideas: Moral education in the Cognitive-developmental tradition. In L. Nucci, D. Narvaez, & T. Krettenauer (Eds.), *Handbook of Moral and Character Education* (pp. 61–83). New York: Routledge.

9   Gilligan, C. (1982). New maps of development: New visions of maturity. *American Journal of Orthopsychiatry, 52*(2), 199–212. doi: 10.1111/j.1939-0025.1982.tb02682.x

10 Ibid. Quote taken from p. 203.

11 Ibid. Quote taken from p. 204.

12 Snarey, J.R. (1985). Cross-Cultural Universality of Social-Moral Development: A Critical Review of Kohlbergian Research. *Psychological Bulletin, 97*(2), 202–232. doi: 10.1037//0033-2909.97.2.202

13 Skoe, E.E.A. (2014). Measuring care-based moral development: The ethic of care interview. *Behavioral Development Bulletin, 19*(3), 95–104. doi: 10.1037/h0100594

14 Anderson, J.L. (1997). *Che Guevara: A Revolutionary Life*. New York: Grove Press. Quote taken from p. 237.

15 Power, P.F. (1961). *Ghandi on World Affairs: A Survey of Ghandian Influence on International and Intercultural Relations*. Bombay: The Perennial Press. Quote taken from p. 65.

16 Jack, H.A. (Ed.) (1956). *The Ghandi Reader: A Sourcebook of his Life and Writings*. New York: Grove Press. Quote taken from p. 345.

17 Blyth, M.N. (2016). Introduction to the section on restorative justice (OJLR-Jan 2016). *Oxford Journal of Law and Religion, 5*(1), 49–53. doi: 10.1093/ojlr/rww003

18 Fiddes, P.S. (2016). Restorative justice and the theological dynamic of forgiveness. *Oxford Journal of Law and Religion, 5*(1), 54–65. doi: 10.1093/ojlr/rwv037

19 Lomax, E. (2010, March 29). Eric Lomax (Scotland). In *The Forgiveness Project*. Retrieved from http://theforgivenessproject.com/stories/eric-lomax-scotland/

20 Chapman, T., & Chapman, A. (2016). Forgiveness in restorative justice: Experienced but not heard?. *Oxford Journal of Law and Religion, 5*(1), 135–152.

21. Shapland, J. (2016). Forgiveness and restorative justice: Is it necessary? Is it helpful?. *Oxford Journal of Law and Religion, 5*(1), 94–112. doi: 10.1093/ojlr/rwv038

22. Blyth, M.N. (2016). Re-imagining restorative justice: The value of forgiveness. *Oxford Journal of Law and Religion, 5*(1), 66-78. doi: 10.1093/ojlr/rwv036

23. McCullough, M.E., Kurzban, R., & Tabak, B.A. (2011). Evolved mechanisms for revenge and forgiveness. In P.R. Shaver & M. Mikulincer (Eds.), *Human Aggression and Violence: Causes, Manifestations, and Consequences* (p. 221–238). Washington, DC: American Psychological Association.

24. Freedman, S., & Chang, W. (2010). An analysis of a sample of the general population's understanding of forgiveness: Implications for mental health counselors. *Journal of Mental Health Counseling, 32*(1), 5–34. doi: 10.17744/mehc.32.1.a0x246r8l6025053

25. Worthington, E. (Ed.). (2005). *Handbook of Forgiveness*. New York: Routledge Taylors & Francis Group.

26. Knutson, J., Enright, R., & Garbers, B. (2008). Validating the developmental pathway of forgiveness. *Journal of Counseling and Development, 86*(2), 193–199. doi: 10.1002/j.1556-6678.2008.tb00497.x

27. Worthington, E. (2003). *Forgiving and Reconciling: Bridges to Wholeness and Hope*. Downers Grove, Ill: InterVarsity Press.

28. Walker, D., & Gorsuch, R. (2004). Dimensions underlying sixteen models of forgiveness and Reconciliation. *Journal of Psychology and Theology, 32*(1), 12–25.

29. Freeman, S., & Zarifkar, T. (2016). The Psychology of Interpersonal Forgiveness and Guidelines for Forgiveness Therapy: What Therapists Need to Know to Help Their Clients Forgive. *Spirituality in Clinical Practice, 3*(1), 45–58. doi: 10.1037/scp0000087

30. Klatt, J., & Enright, R. (2011). Initial validation of the unfolding forgiveness process in a natural environment. *Counselling and Values, 56,* 25-42. doi: 10.1002/j.2161-007X.2011.tb01029.x

31. Enright, R., & Fitzgibbons, R. (2000). *Helping Clients Forgive: An Empirical Guide for Resolving Anger and Restoring Hope*. Washington DC: American Psychological Association.

32. Augustine, M. E., & Stifter, C.A. (2015). Temperament, Parenting, and Moral Development: Specificity of Behavior and Context. *Social Development 24*(2), 285–303. doi: 10.1111/sode.12092

33. Killen, M., & Smetana, J.G. (Eds.). (2006). *Handbook of Moral Development*. New York: Psychology Press.

34 Kochanska, G., & Murray, K.T. (2000). Mother-child mutually responsive orientation and conscience development: From toddler to early school age. *Child Development, 71*, 417–431. doi: 10.1111/1467-8624.00154

35 Polak-Toste, C.P., & Gunnar, M.R. (2006). Temperamental exuberance: Correlates and consequences. In P. J. Marshall, & N. A. Fox (Eds.), *The development of social engagement: Neurobiological perspectives* (pp. 19–45). New York: Oxford University Press.

36 Rothbart, M.K., & Bates, J.E. (2006). Temperament. In N. Eisenberg (Ed.), *Handbook of Child Psychology: Social, Emotional, and Personality Development* (pp. 99–166). New York: Wiley & Sons.

37 Snarey, J.R., & Samuelson, P.L. (2014). Lawrence Kohlberg's revolutionary ideas: Moral education in the Cognitive-developmental tradition. In L. Nucci, D. Narvaez, & T. Krettenauer (Eds.), *Handbook of Moral and Character Education* (pp. 61–83). New York: Routledge. Quote taken from p. 73.

38 Kohlberg, L., & Hersh R.H. (1977). Moral Development: A Review of the Theory. *Theory into Practice, 16*(2), 53–59. doi: 10.1080/00405847709542675. Quote taken from p. 57.

39 Blatt, M.M., & Kohlberg, L. (1975). The Effects of Classroom Moral Discussion upon Children's Level of Moral Judgment. *Journal of Moral Education, 4*(2), 129-161. doi: 10.1080/0305724750040207. Quote taken from p. 133.

40 Snarey, J.R., & Samuelson, P.L. (2014). Lawrence Kohlberg's revolutionary ideas: Moral education in the Cognitive-developmental tradition. In L. Nucci, D. Narvaez, & T. Krettenauer (Eds.), *Handbook of Moral and Character Education* (pp. 61–83). New York: Routledge. Quote taken from p. 77.

41 Kohlberg, L., & Hersh R.H. (1977). Moral Development: A Review of the Theory. *Theory into Practice, 16*(2), 53–59. doi: 10.1080/00405847709542675. Quote taken from p. 57.

42 Snarey, J.R., & Samuelson, P.L. (2014). Lawrence Kohlberg's revolutionary ideas: Moral education in the Cognitive-developmental tradition. In L. Nucci, D. Narvaez, & T. Krettenauer (Eds.), Handbook of Moral and Character Education (pp. 61–83). New York: Routledge. Quote taken from p. 78.

Chapter 7

1 DiSalvo, D. (2009). Forget Survival of the Fittest: It Is Kindness That Counts. In *Scientific American*. Retrieved from
https://www.scientificamerican.com/article/kindness-emotions-psychology/

2 Galante, J., Galante, I., Bekkers, M.-J., & Gallacher, J. (2014). Effect of Kindness-Based Meditation on Health and Well-Being: A Systematic Review and

Meta-Analysis. *Journal of Consulting and Clinical Psychology, 82*(6), 1101–1114. Advance online publication. doi:10.1037/a0037249

3   Krakovsky, M. (2013). *The Psychology of Kindness in the Workplace*. Retrieved from https://www.gsb.stanford.edu/insights/psychology-kindness-workplace

4   Ogunyemi, K. (2014). Justice, Care and Benevolence as Spurs to Employee Loyalty. *International Journal of Academic Research in Management 3*(2), 110–125. doi: 10.5840/pom201413315

5   Generosity of Spirit in World Folktales and Myths. (n.d.). In *Learning to Give*. Retrieved from http://www.learningtogive.org/resources/generosity-spirit-world-folktales-and-myths

6   *Luke*, 15:11–32, NIV.

7   Colson, C. (Producer), Boyle, D., & Tandan, L. (Directors). (2008). *Slumdog Millionaire* [Motion Picture]. United Kingdom: Fox Searchlight Pictures.

8   Konnikova, M. (2012, January 4). The Psychology Behind Gift-Giving and Generosity [web log comment]. In *Scientific American*. Retrieved from http://blogs.scientificamerican.com/literally-psyched/the-psychology-behind-gift-giving-and-generosity/

9   Stevens, J.R. (2004). The selfish nature of generosity: harassment and food sharing in primates. *Proceedings of the Royal Society London — B, 271,* 451–456. doi: 10.1098/rspb.2003.2625

10 Jaeggi, A.V., & Van Schaik, C.P. (2011). The evolution of food sharing in primates. *Behavioral Ecology and Sociobiology, 65,* 2125. doi: 10.1007/s00265-011-1221-3

11 Jaeggi, A.V., De Groot, E., Stevens, J.M., & Van Schaik, C.P. (2013) Mechanisms of reciprocity in primates: testing for short-term contingency of grooming and food sharing in bonobos and chimpanzees. *Evolution & Human Behavior, 34*(2), 69-77. doi: 10.1016/j.evolhumbehav.2012.09.005

12 Yirka, B. (2013). *Study suggests humans, apes and monkeys all expect something in return for generosity*. Retrieved from https://phys.org/news/2013-08-humans-apes-monkeys-generosity.html

13 Komter, A. (2010). The Evolutionary Origins of Human Generosity. *International Sociology, 25*(3), 443-464 doi: 10.1177/0268580909360301. Quote taken from p. 443.

14 Lazarus, R.S. (1991). *Emotion and adaptation*. Oxford: Oxford University Press.

15 Williams, C.R. (2008). Compassion, Suffering and the Self, A Moral Psychology of Social Justice. *Current Sociology, 56*(1), 5–24. doi: 10.1177/0011392107084376

16 Halifax, J. (2009). *Being with Dying: Cultivating Compassion and Fearlessness in the Presence of Death*. Boston: Shambhala. Quote taken from p. 25.
17 *Dhammapada*, Verse 5. Retrieved from http://www.tipitaka.net/tipitaka/dhp/verseload.php?verse=005
18 Makransky, J. (2012). Compassion in Buddhist Psychology. In C.K. Germer & R.D. Siegel (Eds.), *Compassion and Wisdom in Psychotherapy* (pp. 61–74). New York: Guilford Press.
19 Williams, C.R. (2008). Compassion, Suffering and the Self, A Moral Psychology of Social Justice. *Current Sociology, 56*(1), 5–24. doi: 10.1177/0011392107084376. Quote taken from p. 10.
20 Goetz, J.L., Keltner, D., & Simon-Thomas, E. (2010). Compassion: An Evolutionary Analysis and Empirical Review. *Psychological Bulletin, 136*(3), 351–374. doi: 10.1037/a0018807
21 Choi, H.J., Lee, S., & No, S.-R. (2016). Effects of Compassion on Employees' Self-Regulation. *Social Behavior and Personality, 44*(7), 1173–1190. doi: 10.2224/sbp.2016.44.7.1173
22 Neff, K.D., & Germer, C.K. (2013). A Pilot Study and Randomized Controlled Trial of the Mindful Self-Compassion Program. *Journal of Clinical Psychology, 69*(1), 28-44. doi:10.1002/jclp.21923. Quote taken from p. 29.
23 Neff, K.D., & Germer, C.K. (2013). A Pilot Study and Randomized Controlled Trial of the Mindful Self-Compassion Program. *Journal of Clinical Psychology, 69*(1), 28-44. doi: 10.1002/jclp.21923.
24 Ashton, M.C., Paunonen, S.V., Helmes, E., & Jackson, D.N. (1998). Kin Altruism, Reciprocal Altruism, and the Big Five Personality Factors. *Evolution and Human Behavior, 19*(4), 243-255. doi: 10.1016/S1090-5138(98)00009
25 Sommerfeld, E. (2010) The Subjective Experience of Generosity. In M. Mikulincer & P.R. Shaver (Eds.), *Prosocial Motives, Emotions, and Behavior* (pp. 303–324). Washington, DC: American Psychological Association.
26 Jazaieri, H., Jinpa, G.T., McGonigal, K., Rosenberg, E.L., Finkelstein, J., Simon-Thomas, E., … Goldin, P. R. (2013). Enhancing Compassion: A Randomized Controlled Trial of a Compassion Cultivation Training Program. *Journal of Happiness Studies, 14*(4), 1113–1126. doi: 10.1007/s10902-012-9373-z
27 Ibid. Quote taken from pp. 1117–1118.
28 Ibid. Quote taken from p. 1118.
29 Beaumont, E., & Hollins-Martin, C.J. (2015). A narrative review exploring the effectiveness of Compassion-Focused Therapy. *Counselling Psychology Review, 30*(1), 21–32.

30 Gale, C., Gilbert, P., Read, N., & Goss, K. (2014). An Evaluation of the Impact of Introducing Compassion Focused Therapy to a Standard Treatment Programme for People with Eating Disorders. *Clinical Psychology and Psychotherapy, 21*, 1-12. doi: 10.1002/cpp.1806

31 Welford, M., & Langmead, K. (2015). Compassion-based initiatives in educational settings. *Educational & Child Psychology, 32*(1), 71–80.

32 Kuyken, W., Watkins, E., Holden, E., White, K., Taylor, R.S., Byford, S., & Dalgleish, T. (2010). How does mindfulness-based cognitive therapy work? *Behavior Research and Therapy, 48*(11), 1105–1112. doi: 10.1016/j.brat.2010.08.003

33 Leppma, M., & Young, M.E. (2016). Loving-Kindness Meditation and Empathy: A Wellness Group Intervention for Counseling Students. *Journal of Counseling & Development, 94*(3), 297–305. doi: 10.1002/jcad.12086

34 Shapiro, S.L., Astin, J.A., Bishop, S.R., & Cordova, M. (2005). Mindfulness-based stress reduction for health care professionals: Results from a randomized trial. *International Journal of Stress Management, 12*(2), 164–176. doi: 10.1037/1072-5245.12.2.164

35 Dhammarakkhita, the Venerable. (2010). *Metta Bhavana: Loving-kindness Mediation.* Thailand: Dhammodaya meditation Centre. Mantras taken from pp. 2, 54–56.

36 Makransky, J. (2012). Compassion in Buddhist Psychology. In C.K. Germer & R.D. Siegel (Eds.), *Compassion and Wisdom in Psychotherapy* (pp. 61–74). New York: Guilford Press. Quote taken from p. 7.

37 Ciarrochi, J., Randle, M., Miller, L., & Dolnicar, S. (2012). Hope for the Future: Identifying the Individual Difference Characteristics of People Who Are Interested In and Intend To Foster-Care. *British Journal of Social Work, 42*(1), 7–25. doi: 10.1093/bjsw/bcr052

38 Luke, N., & Sebba, J. (2013). *How are foster carers selected?: An international literature review of instruments used within foster carer selection.* Oxford: Rees Centre, University of Oxford.

Chapter 8

1 Wilderness Years. (n.d.). In *Churchill.* Retrieved from the International Churchill Society website https://winstonchurchill.org/the-life-of-churchill/wilderness-years/

2 Churchill: Leader and Statesman. (n.d.) In *Churchill.* Retrieved from the International Churchill Society website https://www.winstonchurchill.org/the-life-of-churchill/life/churchill-leader-and-statesman

3 Biography of Nelson Mandela. (n.d.). In *Nelson Mandela Foundation*. Retrieved from the Nelson Mandela Foundation website https://www.nelsonmandela.org/content/page/biography/

4 Names. (n.d.). In *Nelson Mandela Foundation*. Retrieved from the Nelson Mandela Foundation website https://www.nelsonmandela.org/content/page/names

5 Shea, G. (2010). In I'm no saint, Mandela says in excerpt from new book. In *ABS-CBN News*. Retrieved from http://news.abs-cbn.com/global-filipino/world/10/11/10/im-no-saint-mandela-says-excerpt-new-book

6 Mandela, N. (2003, May 6). Nelson Mandela's tribute to Walter Sisulu. In *BBC News*. Retrieved from http://news.bbc.co.uk/2/hi/africa/3003849.stm

7 Linder, D.O. (2010). In *The Nelson Mandela (Rivonia) Trial: An Account*. Retrieved from the University of Missouri website http://law2.umkc.edu/faculty/projects/ftrials/mandela/mandelaaccount.html

8 Linder, D.O. (2010). In *Sentencing Statement of Justice Quartus de Wet in the Trial of Nelson Mandela (Rivonia Trial)*. Retrieved from the University of Missouri website http://law2.umkc.edu/faculty/projects/ftrials/mandela/mandelasentence.html

9 Mandela, N. (1994). *Long Walk to Freedom*. London: Little, Brown and Company. Quote taken from p. 403.

10 Ibid. Quote taken from p. 404.

11 Unit 6. The End of Apartheid and the Birth of Democracy. (n.d.). In *South Africa: Overcoming Apartheid Building Democracy*. Retrieved from Michigan State University website http://overcomingapartheid.msu.edu/unit.php?id=65-24E-6

12 Mandela, N. (1994). *Long Walk to Freedom*. London: Little, Brown and Company. Quote taken from pp. 376–377.

13 Kammer, R. (1978). *Zen and Confucius in the Art of Swordsmanship: The Tengu-geijutsu-ron of Chozan Shissai* (B.J. Fitzgerald, Trans.). Great Britain: Routledge. (Original work published 1969).

14 McGilloway, A., Ghosh, P., & Bhui K. (2015). A systematic review of pathways to and processes associated with radicalization and extremism amongst Muslims in Western societies. *International Review of Psychiatry, 27*(1), 39–50. doi: 10.3109/09540261.2014.992008

15 Roosevelt, F.D. (1933). *FDR Nothing to Fear But Fear Itself 1933 Inaugural Address* [video file]. Retrieved from https://www.youtube.com/watch?v=nHFTtz3uucY

The Freedom of Virtue: Navigating excellence in the art of living amongst a world of instant gratification

Index

A
accolades, 56, 138
addiction, 56
adventure-based education, 62
advertising, 176, 209
affective control, 96, 106-108, 110
affective domain (i.e., Wisdom), 95-96, 106-107, 110-111
afraid, 16, 42, 146, 179, 199, 212
agape, 172
agency, 209
Agreeableness (i.e., personality trait), 184-186
Ahimsa, 27-28, 158
altruism, 93, 174-176, 184
ambiguity, 90, 94, 95, 109-111, 193
ambition, 68
Analects, 32
Ancient Near East, 11, 12
Aparigraha, 27
Apology, The, 90, 123
Aquinas, Thomas, 5, 18, 19
Ard, 117, 118
Ardelt, Monika, 92
Aristotle, 5, 13, 14, 19, 20, 44-46, 90, 91, 93, 108, 206
arrogance, 17, 31, 203
Artificial Intelligence, 209
Asteya, 27
Athens, 10, 12-14, 19
athlete, 56, 66, 75, 116
attachment, 114, 120, 209
Aurelius, Marcus, 45
avoidance, 28, 31, 73

B

Babylon, 12, 198
bad courage, 55
Balance Theory, 93, 104
Baltes, Paul, 92
Bedouin, 117-119, 123
benevolence, 17, 32, 34, 172, 174, 175, 177
Beowulf, 26
Beyond Good & Evil, 5
bomb disposal, 49, 57
Boudica (Queen), 197
Brahmacharya, 27
brain, 13, 43, 48, 61, 158, 207
bravery, 37, 43, 46-48
Bridgewater Associates, 134
Buddha, Gautama, 32
Buddhism, 28, 29, 31, 34
Buffett, Warren, 3
bullying, 70, 71, 135
burn-out, 75-79, 81, 182
business, 2-4, 7, 26, 34, 66, 77, 87-89, 99-103, 114, 116, 122, 123, 131, 134, 140, 141, 160, 191

C

Cairo Declaration on Human Rights, 23
Calabria, 121
Campbell, Tom, 147
cardinal virtues, 9, 13, 20, 34
career success, 66-68, 196, 198
caritas, 172
catastrophisation, 49
ceremony of degradation, 135-136
challenge, 38, 42, 138, 139, 147, 150, 167
character, 3, 4, 8-10, 23, 47, 55, 124, 125, 127, 130, 151, 152, 181, 201
charity (i.e., financial), 16, 150, 174-177, 181

charity (i.e., love), 16, 17, 34
chesed, 172
chih, 33
Christ, 17-19, 21, 161, 162
Christianity, 15, 17-20
Churchill, Winston, 37, 198
classroom, 67, 165, 167, 183
Clinton, Hillary, 209
coach, 55, 56, 129, 165
cognitive bias, 102, 103
cognitive domain (i.e., Wisdom), 95, 96, 110
commitment honour, 125
communication, 7
compassion, 23, 25, 28, 30, 35, 55, 93, 106, 159, 160, 172, 174, 178-183, 186-191, 194
compassion-focused therapy, 187
conferred honour, 125
conflict resolution, 156
Confucianism, 31
Confucius, 32-34, 206
Conscientiousness (i.e., personality trait), 50, 57, 67-72, 75-78, 83, 84, 184-186
conventional level of moral development, 154
coping, 51, 61, 73, 159, 163, 187
Corrigan, Mairead, 198
cortisol, 48
counsellor, 11, 47, 50, 51, 75, 78, 81, 91, 96, 139, 163, 167, 184, 187, 201, 208
Courage, 2, 9, 10, 12-14, 16-18, 20, 25-27, 34-38, 40, 42-48, 50-63, 68, 77, 107, 111, 113, 139-142, 156, 169, 180, 193, 194, 196-200, 206, 207, 209, 212, 213
cowardice, 44, 140
creativity, 92, 104
culture of continuous improvement, 84, 185
Curie, Marie, 66
curriculum, 104, 167, 186, 208

D
Damien (Father), 197
Dark Ages, 24

deductive reasoning, 99
Default Mode Network (DMN), 207
depression, 20, 88, 171, 182, 200
deradicalisation, 210
Developmental Psychology, 138
dharma, 28
difference principle, 148-151, 174
dignity, 23, 25, 116, 124, 125, 148, 154, 155, 168, 169, 203, 213
Diligence, 18, 26-28, 30, 34-36, 50, 65-72, 75-78, 80-84, 111, 113, 134, 193, 196-199, 206, 207, 209, 211, 213
Diogenes, 13
dishonour, 127, 134, 135
dissent, 52-54, 131,
diversity, 9, 21, 94
Djokovic, Novak, 65

E
economic justice, 27, 151
education, 3, 4, 6, 9, 53, 66, 82, 97, 98, 138, 151, 167
Egypt, 11, 12, 15
emotional regulation, 12, 13, 19, 25, 28, 35, 50, 51, 84, 93, 94, 96, 106-110, 164, 187, 190, 191
empathy, 54, 55, 93, 97, 147, 162, 163, 166, 179-181, 190, 194
employment, 131
evolution, 8, 35, 53, 121, 122, 126, 163, 174, 176, 181, 183, 207
expert knowledge, 97
extraordinary kindness, 178-183, 190, 213

F
face, 35, 40, 43, 44, 63, 97, 123, 131, 132, 136
Factorum ac Dictorum Memorabilium Libri IX, 24
faith, 16, 20, 22, 24, 42, 131, 204
false beliefs, 100, 103
family, 2, 4, 16, 20, 23, 32, 33, 60, 69-71, 73, 75, 77, 79, 81, 82, 87, 97, 101, 102, 107, 113-115, 118-122, 130, 132, 135, 138, 139, 142, 151, 154, 158-161, 168, 169, 174, 182-186, 190, 199, 201, 211

fear, 3, 10, 16, 38, 43, 44, 46, 48-52, 55, 57, 59, 61, 62, 80, 94, 104, 121, 132, 138, 141, 142, 145, 159, 169, 176, 180, 182, 184, 186-188, 193, 196, 202, 211, 212

fear (i.e., appraisal), 43, 44, 48-50, 61, 80, 179, 180, 212

Findlay, Hazel, 38-40, 42-44, 51

Five Precepts, 28, 30, 31

folly, 85-88, 105, 132

foolhardiness, 46

foolishness, 85, 86, 88, 89, 111

forgiveness, 22, 28, 34, 158-163, 188, 189, 194

Forgiveness Process Model, 162, 163

forgiveness-focused therapy, 162, 163

foster carers, 178, 190, 191

foundational virtues, 1, 6-8, 34-36, 78, 113-115, 150, 179, 193-198, 200, 201, 203, 205-211

Four Noble Truths, 29

French Foreign Legion, 142, 143

French Revolution, 26

G

generosity, 14, 17, 25, 28, 32, 34, 172-178, 183-186, 194

Ghandi, Mohandas, 4, 6, 157, 158, 197

Global Financial Crisis (GFC), 88

glory, 116, 121-123, 127-129, 138, 139, 209, 210

God, 15-23, 41, 42, 111

golden mean, 14, 93, 108

good life, the, 10, 90, 91

gospel, 17, 18

grace, 35, 124, 172

Greece, 4, 14, 45, 88, 89

grief and loss, 190, 191

grit, 2, 50

group honour, 126, 127, 137, 139-143, 168, 194, 206, 208

Guevara, Ernesto 'Che', 157, 158

H

Hammurabi, 12, 198

happiness, 2, 5, 9-12, 91, 147, 148, 152, 171, 180, 182, 205, 212

Harrington, Emily, 38-40, 51

hedonism, 8-10

hero, 12, 44, 46, 47, 87, 121

heroic rescue fantasy, 46, 47

heroism, 46, 47, 62

heuristics, 100, 103

hierarchy, 26, 115, 120, 127, 129, 130, 132, 154, 155

Hinduism, 27, 31

homework, 67, 68, 82

Honour, 4, 19, 23, 25-27, 33-36, 111, 113-137, 139-145, 157, 168, 169, 185, 186, 194, 196-198, 201, 203, 206-213

honour code, 141-143

honour culture, 25, 115, 117-120, 122, 123, 127-129, 131, 133-136, 140, 141, 143, 168, 169

honour group, 126, 127, 137, 139, 140, 168, 194, 206, 208

hope, 4, 7, 16, 19, 20, 24, 25, 32, 42, 51, 53, 63, 67, 71, 74, 80, 83, 87, 94, 96, 97, 101, 107, 138, 174, 177, 190, 191, 194, 199, 203-205, 212, 213

horizontal honour, 124

Horney, Karen, 109

Human Resources (HR), 47, 58, 83, 84, 105, 115, 131, 133, 134, 143, 182, 185

I

identity, 21, 135, 141, 142, 200, 209, 210

inductive reasoning, 99

industry, 114, 134, 209

insight, 13, 50, 93-95, 104, 109, 158, 193, 205

instinct, 179, 209

insult, 123

integrity, 23, 33, 34, 48, 116, 137, 185, 212, 213

intelligence (i.e., emotional), 35, 50, 51, 67, 76, 79, 83, 84, 89, 93, 96, 182, 183, 187, 190, 191

intelligence (i.e., government/military), 106

intelligence (i.e., psychological), 2, 3, 14, 18, 20, 29, 32, 39, 43, 48, 53, 58, 59, 67, 68, 76, 78, 80, 85, 86, 89-104, 108-111, 153-155, 157, 158, 162, 165, 166, 186, 190, 191, 201, 211

IQ, 57, 68

Ishvarapranidhana, 28
Islam, 15, 20-23

J
Jeste, Dilip, 92-94
Jesus, 17-19, 21, 161, 162
job, 16, 58, 77, 98, 105, 135, 166, 182, 210, 213
Judaism, 15, 16, 20
judge, 7, 22, 118, 144
Jung, Carl, 36, 105
Justice, 2, 9, 12-14, 16-18, 20-23, 25-28, 30, 31, 33-36, 54, 107, 111, 113, 114, 117, 118, 145-159, 162-165, 167-169, 180, 181, 188, 194, 196-198, 201-203, 206-213
Justinian (Emperor), 151
Jyväskylä Longitudinal Study of Personality and Social Development (JYLS), 107

K
Kindness, 17, 19, 22, 23, 25, 32, 34-36, 55, 78, 111, 113, 114, 131, 171-179, 181-184, 194, 196-198, 201, 203, 206, 207, 209, 211-213
King, Martin Luther (Jr), 6, 37, 145,
Kohlberg, Lawrence, 153-157, 165-169

L
Laches, 44
leadership, 119, 199
li, 32
lifesaving, 138
literature, 12, 16, 31, 34, 36, 43, 44, 51, 67, 81, 91, 137, 142, 159, 161, 180, 209
longevity, 20, 66, 68
love, 8, 12, 15, 18-20, 25, 32, 34, 63, 65, 70, 74, 85, 95, 120, 152, 174, 175, 181, 189, 210

M
Ma'at, 12, 34
management, 9, 77, 131, 133, 134, 140
Mandela, Nelson, 178, 194, 198, 201-204
marketing (i.e., advertising), 176, 209
Marshall, George, 197

mastery experiences, 61, 62
Mawson, Douglas, 40-42, 51
Maximus, Valerius, 24
Meares, Anna, 197
Medieval world, 24
meditation, 27, 28, 49, 65, 80, 83, 186, 188-190
Meditations (i.e., Aurelius, Marcus), 45
membership (i.e., group), 4, 23-26, 30, 32-35, 59, 60, 71, 81, 82, 113-115, 117-136, 139-144, 154, 158, 167-169, 183-186, 194, 206, 208,
mental health, 14, 45, 78, 198, 200, 201
mentor, 5, 60, 106, 178
mercy, 15, 17, 22, 25, 34, 45, 55, 159, 172
meritocracy, 129, 130, 134
metaphor, 109-111, 113
metta, 172, 188-190
metta meditation, 188-190
military, 14, 25, 36, 44, 46, 47, 53, 63, 93, 114, 129, 136, 141, 142, 144
mindfulness practices, 4, 29-30, 49, 80, 188
Mirror Neuron System (MNS), 207
misadventure, 85-87, 89, 118
mitzvot, 15-17
model, the, 206-208
Modern Period, 26
moral courage, 37, 51-57, 62, 139, 212
moral development, 154, 157, 165, 167
morality, 3, 4, 8, 33, 85, 150, 153, 154, 165
Moses, 15, 21
Mother Theresa, 178, 191
Muhammad, 20, 21, 23, 197
Muslim, 20-23, 190, 210
myth, 46, 199

N
Nelson (i.e., Lord), 197
neurology, 207
Neuroticism (i.e., personality trait), 57, 77-78, 184-186

New Testament, 18
Nicomachean Ethics, 44, 90
Nietzsche, Friedrich, 5
niyama, 28
Nobel Prize, 66, 103, 198
Noble Eightfold Path, 29-31
Nozick, Robert, 148-150, 152

O
Old Testament, 15, 16, 19
Openness to experience (i.e., personality trait), 57, 77
operator (e.g., temperance & hope), 107
Oprisko, Robert, 124, 127, 135
ordinary kindness, 174-178
outdoor education, 55, 62, 127, 138, 139

P
parable of the prodigal son, 172, 173
paratrooper, 50
parent, 12, 16, 26, 53, 66, 69-72, 78, 81, 82, 107, 108, 128, 129, 139, 154, 164, 165, 167, 168, 188, 208
parenting, 54, 55, 69-71, 78, 152, 164, 183
Paul, St., 18-20
perfectionism, 75, 78, 80, 81, 182
Peristiany, J.G., 124
perseverance, 12, 48, 50, 51, 57
persistence, 31, 48
personal honour, 23, 36, 125-127, 137-139, 194, 198, 201, 203, 206, 208
personality, 50, 57, 67, 68, 76-78, 107, 184, 185
phronesis, 33, 90, 91
Pitt-Rivers, Julian, 124
Plato, 5, 10, 13, 14, 44, 90, 146, 147
political justice, 27
politics, 2, 31, 100, 101, 105, 106, 130, 146, 147, 149, 199, 201, 209
positional honour, 125, 126, 130, 131, 141
Positive Psychology, 9-11

post-conventional level of moral development, 154, 157-158
practice, 5, 17, 19, 27, 29-31, 34, 44, 51, 53, 61, 81, 82, 91, 105, 106, 186-190, 200
precision, 66, 75
pre-conventional level of moral development, 154
pride, 114, 209
Pride and Prejudice, 209
prisoner of war, 199
problem solving, 42, 57, 62, 95-100, 103, 196
procrastination, 72-75
projection, 105, 106
pro-social behaviour, 54, 174, 184
prudence, 2, 13, 14, 20
psychologist, 11, 47, 50, 51, 75, 78, 81, 91, 92, 109, 139, 153, 163, 182, 184, 187, 201, 208
Ptah-hotep, 12, 14
purpose (i.e., group), 35, 115, 120-122, 124-126, 129-136, 139-144, 181, 182, 185, 186, 209
purpose in life, 6, 205
Pury, Cynthia, 48

Q
quid pro quo, 154, 177
Qur'an, 21-22

R
radicalisation, 210
rashness, 14
Rawls, John, 148, 149, 153
recognition honour, 125
recruitment (i.e., staff), 47, 58, 105
reflective domain (i.e., Wisdom), 95, 96, 106
rehabilitation, 132, 161
rei, 208
relationships (i.e., inter-personal), 3, 6, 12-16, 19, 22, 23, 27, 29-35, 60, 61, 77, 114, 115, 119, 129, 140, 141, 156, 158, 162, 168, 174, 176, 178, 183, 208
ren, 32, 34, 172
Republic, The, 24, 146

reputation, 3, 23, 25, 116, 119, 121-123, 132, 148

resilience, 50, 51, 57, 127, 136, 190

respect, 6, 16, 25, 31, 32, 43, 66, 69, 80, 116, 118, 120, 122, 124, 125, 127, 140, 142, 154, 155, 162, 164, 168, 169, 182, 196, 198, 205, 213

restorative justice, 163, 180, 188

revenge, 22, 25, 162

righteousness, 17, 19, 21, 33

rights, 18, 23, 37, 148-152, 168, 197

risk-taking, 56, 60, 196

Roman Empire, 24-26

rumination, 182

S

Sacks, Jonathan (former Chief Rabbi), 16

sagas, 26, 209

Samma, 30

Santosa, 27

SAS, 139, 142

Satya, 27, 28

satyagraha, 158

Sauca, 27

school, 2, 4, 9, 15, 26, 32, 58, 66, 72, 82, 101, 107, 135, 138, 140, 149, 163, 165, 167-169, 183, 184

school teacher, 4, 11, 16, 53, 55, 69, 70, 81-83, 99, 104, 107, 108, 129, 139, 154, 165-168, 179, 187, 188, 208, 209

Scouts, 55, 127, 129

self-compassion, 182, 183, 186-188

self-concept, 51, 71, 137, 138

self-control, 12, 13, 19, 25, 28, 109, 164

self-efficacy, 75, 137-139

self-esteem, 9, 55, 75, 137-139

self-image, 137, 138

selfishness, 35, 161, 177

self-kindness, 78, 79, 81

self-narrative, 209, 210

self-respect, 125, 127, 137-139, 194

Selfridge, Harry, 87, 88, 105

self-worth, 159
Seligman, Martin, 9
shame, 114, 124, 132-135, 141, 147, 162
shari'ah, 22, 23
Siena, 1, 2
situational virtues, 6, 8, 9, 150, 154, 200, 208
Snyder Hope Theory, 51
social contract, 149
social justice, 18, 27, 151
social supports, 59
social work, 47, 139, 182
socio-economic status (SES), 70
Socrates, 5, 44, 90, 146, 147, 150, 204
Socratic dialogue, 44, 90, 146, 147, 165-167
sophia, 85, 90, 91
sport, 69, 82, 89, 121, 128, 184, 202
staff, 12, 47, 53, 83, 84, 99, 100, 107, 115, 131, 134, 182, 185, 187, 199, 203
Sternberg, Robert, 92
Stewart, Frank, 117
Stockdale, James, 45
Stoicism, 45
strategic decision making, 99-101
stress, 59, 77
suffering, 29, 77, 132, 162, 179, 180, 186, 188, 189, 200, 203, 213
Summa Theologica, 20
survival (e.g., strategy), 8, 34-36, 108, 114, 124, 177
Svadhyaya, 28
Sympathetic Nervous System, 48, 50

T
taboos, 135, 140, 141
Tao, 4, 5
Tapas, 28
teacher, 5, 10, 11, 13-21, 27, 32, 44-46, 53, 55, 81, 83, 90, 91, 93, 99, 104, 108, 129, 146, 147, 165-168, 179, 188, 206

team building, 83, 84, 114, 123, 126-136, 139, 140-143, 167-169, 177, 178, 182, 185, 186

temperance, 2, 9, 13, 14, 16, 20, 30, 31, 34, 35, 107-110

Ten Commandments (or Statements), 15, 16

Terman Sample, 68

terrorism, 55, 201, 210

Tertia Aemilia, 25

theological virtues, 20

therapist, 11, 47, 50, 51, 75, 78, 81, 91, 92, 96, 109, 139, 153, 163, 167, 179, 182, 184, 187, 201, 208

therapy, 105, 162, 163, 187, 209

Torah, 15-17

trauma, 159-161

Trump, Donald, 130, 209

trust, 23, 25, 33, 34, 48, 63, 110, 115, 116, 118, 121, 125, 126, 137, 139, 159, 185, 212, 213

trust honour, 125

truthfulness, 12, 27, 28, 30, 208

U

Universal Declaration of Human Rights, 18, 23, 150

US Presidential Election, 105, 130, 209

utilitarianism, 147, 148

V

values (i.e., group), 3, 4, 12, 16, 17, 19, 23, 24-26, 31, 59, 60, 114, 115, 124, 135, 138, 139-143, 154, 158, 166, 168, 169, 185, 186

values (i.e., personal), 60, 62, 137-139, 155, 166, 211

vengefulness, 22, 25, 162

vertical honour, 125

vice, 8, 22, 75, 86

violence, 23, 55, 109, 161, 198, 201, 203, 210

virtue checklist, 195, 196

virtue strengths, 58, 59, 195, 196, 198, 207

virtue sub-system, 207, 208

virtue weaknesses, 58, 59, 195, 196, 207

W

Watson, Jessica, 86

welfare, 4, 18, 47, 66, 88, 107, 114, 115, 148, 187

wellbeing, 20, 79, 91, 171

Williams, Betty, 198

Wisdom, 2, 3, 9, 10, 12-14, 16, 19, 25, 28-31, 33-36, 76, 85, 86, 88-97, 104, 105, 107, 109-111, 113, 130, 132, 166, 174, 180, 182, 189, 193, 194, 196-199, 201, 203, 206, 207, 209-213

wisdom literature, 12, 16

X

xin, 33

Y

yama, 28

yi, 4, 33, 34

Z

Zaleucus, 25

zhi, 33

Lightning Source UK Ltd.
Milton Keynes UK
UKHW022017201119
353927UK00003B/177/P